Socialism in Theory and Practice

SOCIALISM IN THEORY AND PRACTICE

BY

MORRIS HILLQUIT

AUTHOR OF "HISTORY OF SOCIALISM IN THE UNITED STATES"

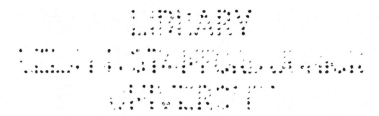
New York
THE MACMILLAN COMPANY
1909

Norwood Press
J. S. Cushing Co. — Berwick & Smith Co.
Norwood, Mass., U.S.A.

PREFACE

THE socialist movement has grown immensely within the last decade, and its growth still continues unabated in all civilized countries of the world. What is the secret of that growth; what are the aims and methods of the movement; and what does it portend for the future of the human race? These are questions which persons of intellect can ignore no longer, and they are questions which cannot be answered without much thought and study.

In this book I have endeavored to present to the public a brief summary of the socialist philosophy in its bearing on the most important social institutions and problems of our time, and a condensed account of the history, methods, and achievements of the socialist movement of the world.

Socialism is a criticism of modern social conditions, a theory of social progress, an ideal of social organization, and a practical movement of the masses. To be fully understood it must be studied in all of these phases, and the fact that this book is probably the first attempt to accomplish that task, inadequate as that attempt may be, is sufficient justification for its publication.

Grateful acknowledgment is hereby made for many valuable suggestions which I have received from Mr. W. J. Ghent, who has carefully read the proofs, and from Mr. Rufus W. Weeks, who has read the manuscript.

MORRIS HILLQUIT.

NEW YORK, January 10, 1909.

CONTENTS

PART I

THE SOCIALIST PHILOSOPHY AND MOVEMENT

CHAPTER I

CHAPTER II

SOCIALISM AND INDIVIDUALISM

CHAPTER III

SOCIALISM AND ETHICS

CHAPTER IV

SOCIALISM AND LAW

CHAPTER V

SOCIALISM AND THE STATE

CHAPTER VI

SOCIALISM AND POLITICS

PART II

SOCIALISM AND REFORM

CHAPTER I

CHAPTER II

THE INDUSTRIAL REFORM MOVEMENTS

CHAPTER III

CHAPTER IV

THE POLITICAL REFORM MOVEMENTS

CHAPTER V

ADMINISTRATIVE REFORMS

CHAPTER VI

SOCIAL REFORM

APPENDIX

HISTORICAL SKETCH OF THE SOCIALIST MOVEMENT

PART I

THE SOCIALIST PHILOSOPHY AND MOVEMENT

CHAPTER I

THE history of our civilization presents one unbroken chain of social changes. The interval between the primitive tribe of cave-dwellers and modern industrial society is filled with a variety of intermediate social types.

Each of these types constitutes a separate phase of civilization. Within the same civilization each type is superior to the one preceding it, and inferior to the one succeeding it. Each phase of civilization is evolved from the preceding phase and gives birth to the succeeding phase. Each phase of civilization passes through the stages of formation, bloom, and decay.

The present phase of our civilization forms no exception to this immutable rule of social development. We have reached a state vastly superior to all conditions of the past. Men in modern society on the whole enjoy more individual freedom and security, more physical comforts and intellectual and æsthetic pleasures than did the savages and members of societies based on slavery or serfdom.

But we have not reached perfection. We never shall reach perfection. A state of perfection in society would imply the arrest of all human endeavors and progress, the

3

death of civilization. It is improvement, not perfection, for which we are striving, and our contemporary social organization is capable of improvement just as all societies of the past were.

Our social order of to-day did not spring into existence suddenly and full-fledged. It developed gradually from preceding social conditions, and it is still in process of evolution. It has had its period of formation, and the socialists contend that it has passed its period of bloom. It has entered on the stage of decay and must be followed by a new phase of civilization of a more advanced type.

The all-important factor in modern society is industry. In former ages industry — that is, production of goods for exchange — played a rather subordinate part in the lives of the nations. Agriculture was the basis of the community.

But recent times, and particularly the last century, have witnessed a stupendous industrial growth. The modest workshop of former ages has been superseded by the huge modern factory; the simple, almost primitive tool of the old-time mechanic has developed into the gigantic machine of to-day; and the power of steam and electricity has increased the productivity of labor a hundred fold. New objects of use have been invented, new needs have been created, while the railroads, steamships and other improved means of communication and distribution have united the entire civilized world into one international market.

This industrial revolution has brought in its wake a radical change of social institutions. It has created new classes of society. The privileged type of former ages, the landowning and titled nobleman, the courtier and warrior, has been relegated to the background, and in his place has arisen the captain of industry — the modern capitalist.

With the ancient aristocracy have also disappeared the ancient types of the dependent class, the slave and the serf, and their place has been taken by the modern wage worker.

In the earlier stages of its career the capitalist class was revolutionary and useful. It abolished absolute monarchies and introduced modern representative government, it rooted out old prejudices and beliefs, it tore down the artificial barriers between nations, it gave to the world the most marvelous inventions, and ushered in a distinctly superior system of society.

But these achievements belong largely to the pioneer days of capitalism, to the period when the modern industries were in process of formation. To-day our principal industries are fully organized. They have largely been reduced to mere routine and their progress depends but little on individual initiative.

The typical capitalist of to-day has long ceased to be the manager of the industries. He is "engaged" in whatever industry the vicissitudes of the stock market and the tricks of stock jobbery may thrust upon him. It may happen to be a railway system or a gas plant, a mine or a steel foundry, a rubber factory or water works, or all of them in turn. He need not know, and as a rule he does not know, the intimate workings of the industry he controls. The actual work of management and operation is done by hired labor, whether such labor be that of the high-priced superintendent or that of a common laborer employed at starvation wages. There is hardly a capitalist to-day whose existence is necessary to the continuance of any essential industry. The days of the actual usefulness of the capitalist class in the social economy of the nation are rapidly passing. And like so many other classes in history under similar conditions, the capitalists have become reactionary, and the régime developed by them has become irrational, unjust and oppressive.

In the merciless war of competition the big capitalist enterprises are gradually extinguishing the smaller independent concerns. Our "national" wealth and principal industries concentrate in the hands of ever fewer combines. Trusts and monopolies are becoming the modern form of industrial organization. A new capitalist type is thus developed, the type of the trust magnate and multi-millionaire.

But the large masses of the people share but little in the benefits of this unprecedented growth of wealth. While a certain portion of the working class, the trained or skilled laborers, probably enjoy to-day larger material comforts than did their ancestors in the past, the increase of their comforts does not keep pace with the increase of the general productivity and wealth. The condition of this favored class of the working population is one of absolute improvement but of relative deterioration. And side by side with the more fortunate strata of the working class there are the large masses of laborers whose conditions of life have greatly deteriorated, absolutely as well as relatively. Millions of workingmen maintain themselves with difficulty above the bare margin of starvation, while large masses of the population, rendered "superfluous" by the invention of improved machinery, are driven to vagabondage and forced into the paths of vice and crime.

The boundless luxuries of the few find their logical counterpart in the dire misery of the many.

In the mad capitalist race for profits, morals are useless and cumbersome ballast. The earlier merchant and manufacturer had some sense of commercial probity. The modern trust magnate has none. To him all means are fair so long as they satisfy his greed. His ideal is to increase his power, to get possession of all the sources of wealth of his country, to own his fellow-men, body and soul.

To reach this aim he corrupts legislatures, buys courts of justice, bribes public officials and pollutes the public press.

The "interests of industry" — his interests — shape the entire life of modern nations. They influence our laws, dominate our politics, direct our public opinion, determine our internal and external policy, and decide upon war and peace between nations. The trust magnate is a more dangerous potentate than any political despot.

And these conditions are not mere accidental abuses; they are the necessary results of our industrial institutions. Even the beneficiaries of these institutions are without power to change them. The capitalists are driven into the fatal course by the inexorable laws of industrial development. We may well foresee a time, if the present order lasts long enough, when practically all of our most important industries will have become trusts, when the entire wealth of the nations and all the powers of government will be in the hands of a small number of monopolists, and when the people will depend upon them absolutely for their physical, intellectual and moral existence.

Such conditions are not unparalleled in history. The

Roman Empire found itself in such a situation in the fourth and fifth centuries of our era, and Roman civilization succumbed. France faced a similar crisis thirteen hundred years later, but the French nation suppressed the dangerous order and built a better and more vigorous society on its ruins.

Will the modern nation share the fate of Rome, or follow the example of France?

The answer to this momentous question is contained in the question itself.

Rome perished for the lack of a class to save it. The slaves were beyond the pale of Roman society, and the proletarians of the capital and the provinces were too ignorant, demoralized and feeble to combat the greedy and profligate patricians. The degenerate Roman population fell an easy prey to the advancing barbarian hordes.

In France, on the other hand, the haughty and parasitic nobility was confronted by the men of science, industry, commerce and labor, the vigorous and intelligent "third estate." The "third estate" saved France, even though the salvation was accomplished at the cost of a revolution.

Modern society has developed a new "third estate," — the industrial working class. The working class to-day is the principal social power operating against the formation of a capitalist oligarchy. And it is a power to be reckoned with. The modern workingmen are not the helots of ancient Greece, nor the proletarians of ancient Rome, nor the serfs of mediæval ages. They are more intelligent and better organized than any dependent class in the past: their conditions of existence and instinct of self-preservation naturally array them against the present system of exploitation of labor, and force them into active resistance against it. As capitalism grows more acute and menacing, the cohorts of labor become more unified, powerful and aggressive, and more fully able and determined to carry their struggles to victory.

Only half a century ago the labor movement was barely in its inception, weak in numbers, inefficient in organization and uncertain in its aims. To-day the working-men are organized in legions of powerful trade unions, trained and drilled in the everyday battles for the advancement of their conditions of life. In a large number of countries they have created immense coöperative establishments successfully competing with the capitalist enterprises in the same industries. In all civilized countries of the world they have developed a socialist movement, so uniform in its aims and methods, so persistent in its struggles, so inspiring in its propaganda and so irresistible in its spread, that with perhaps the single exception of early Christianity the movement stands unparalleled in the annals of written history.

The trade unions fight the immediate and particular battles of the workers in the factories, mills, mines and shops, and educate their members to a sense of their economic rights. The coöperative labor enterprises train their members in the collective operation and democratic management of industries. The socialist parties emphasize the general and ultimate interests of the entire working class, and train their members in political action and in the administration of the affairs of government and state.

Marching over different routes, operating with different methods and conscious or unconscious of the effects of their own activity, all these forms of the labor movement

make for one inevitable goal: the building up of a new
and regenerated society.

And the workingmen are not alone in this movement.
They receive large and ever larger accretions from all
other classes — from the small business men displaced
by the trust, the professionals reduced to the state of
"intellectual proletarians"; the farmers, exploited less
directly but not less effectively by trustified capital, and
even from the ranks of the capitalist class itself. The
number of men of the "better classes" who embrace the
cause of the people from motives of enlightened self-
interest or from purely ethical motives grows as the evils
of the decaying capitalist system become more apparent.
These "desertions" from the ranks of the dominant classes
into the camp of the subjugated class, are an infallible sign
of the approaching collapse of the rule of the former.

The economic development which has thus furnished
the conditions for a radical transformation of society and
produced the forces to accomplish it, is also building up
the basis of that transformation.

The great modern trust organizes industry on a national
scale; it regulates the production and distribution of
commodities, and brings all workers of the country under
one administration. A trustified industry is in its essence
a nationalized industry. It would be just as easy to-day
for a governmental agency to run such an industry as it is
for the individual trust magnates or their agents.

And it would be much more just. Our highly effective
system of industry is the achievement of many generations,
the heritage of all mankind; our marvelous tools of production and distribution are the fruit of the collective
industry and intellect of the laboring population; they are

operated collectively by the whole working class, and they are indispensable to the life of the entire nation. In equity and justice the capitalist has no better title to the modern social tools than the slaveholder had to his chattel slaves.

Socialism advocates the transfer of ownership in the social tools of production — the land, factories, machinery, railroads, mines, etc. — from the individual capitalists to the people, to be operated for the benefit of all.

This program has been denounced as confiscatory and revolutionary, but it is no more so than was the abolition of chattel slavery. It has been ridiculed as utopian and fantastic, but it is no more so than the demands of the eighteenth century capitalist for the abolition of the privileges of birth were to his contemporaries.

Our social progress is a movement towards perfect democracy. The successive stages of our civilization mark the disappearance of one class privilege after another. Why should mankind halt in reverence and awe before the privilege of wealth? When an heir to millions is born to-day, he has the same exceptional position in society and the same power over thousands of his fellow-men that the newborn duke or marquis had in times past; and the justice and logic of the situation are the same in both cases. A true democracy is one in which all babes are born alike, and all human beings enjoy the same rights and opportunities.

CHAPTER II

The System of Individualism

SOCIALISM and individualism are the two main contending principles underlying all modern social theories and movements. Both ideas are, comparatively speaking, new in the history of human thought, and the social philosophy based on individualism is the older of the two. Some writers discern the origin of the idea of individualism in the movement of the Reformation, and its first practical application in the demand for liberty of the conscience, *i.e.*, the religious self-determination of the individual. The idea of religious liberty according to the noted Russian scholar, Peter Struve, led to the broader conception of the liberty of the individual, and the latter to the theory of political self-government of the nations.

"In connection with the idea of the self-determination of the individual," he observes, "the idea of the self-government of society originates in the same surroundings and under the same conditions and becomes a moving force. In the study of the events and ideas of the English revolution of the seventeenth century, nothing is more striking than the fact that that wonderful period produced, as with one blow and in quite finished form, the idea of individual liberty, liberalism, as well as the idea of political self-government, democracy." [1]

The theory is no doubt historically true, but it utterly

[1] "Individualism i Socialism," *Polyarnaya Zvesda*, No. 11.

fails to account for the causes of the phenomenon. The religious movement of the Reformation was one of the manifestations of the struggle for individualism, but not its cause. The Reformation and the nascent idea of individualism involved in it were but the symptoms and results of a deeper and more material process — the birth of the modern social and industrial system.

The modern philosophy of individualism came into life as a reaction against the excessive centralization of the feudal state and church, and as a protest against the unchecked powers of the crown, nobility and clergy over the population, and especially over the growing class of industrials. "Individual Liberty" was the battle cry with which the young bourgeoisie (the industrial and trading class) entered the arena of political struggle. That battle cry meant for it freedom of competition — Industrial Liberty; the right to use the powers of the state for the advancement of manufacture and commerce — Political Liberty; the freedom from interference by the church with the political and industrial management of the people — Religious Liberty; and above all it meant the freedom and sacredness of private property. "What they (the liberal bourgeois) meant by the freedom of the individual," says Mr. E. Belfort Bax, "was, first and foremost, the liberty of private property as such, to be controlled in its operation by naught else than the will of the individual possessing it. What was cared for was not so much the liberty of the individual as the liberty of private property. The liberty of the individual as such was secondary. It was as the possessor and controller of property that it was specially desired to assure his liberty." [1]

[1] "Socialism and Individualism," London, Personal Rights Series, p. 10.

The idea of individual liberty thus conceived animates all phases of the struggle of the bourgeoisie against feudal society. It is at the bottom of Rousseau's "Social Contract" and the social philosophy of the Encyclopedists; it asserts itself in the principle of non-interference proclaimed by Adam Smith and the founders of classical political economy; and it is the true meaning of the rationalistic criticisms of Voltaire and his followers.

Individual liberty with or without other verbal adornments was the motto that inspired the battles of the English middle classes under Cromwell towards the end of the seventeenth century, and those of the French "third estate" and the American colonists a century later.

"All men are born and continue free," [1] and "All men are endowed by their Creator with the 'inalienable right' of liberty," [2] were the maxims adopted as the foundation of all political constitutions by the victorious bourgeoisie of all countries.

The battles fought by the pre-Revolutionary bourgeoisie in the name of Individual Liberty have given to civilization a few great acquisitions. They have to a large extent emancipated man in the purely individual sphere of his life, and rendered into his own keeping his beliefs, views and tastes, his individual mind and soul. The freedom of press, speech, conscience and person are such acquisitions, and they are of everlasting benefit to mankind.

But the historical watchword had an altogether different fate in the field of politics and industry.

In the revolutionary period of the career of our ruling classes "Individual Liberty" in those fields stood princi-

---

[1] French Declaration of the Rights of Man.
[2] American Declaration of Independence.

pally for freedom from arbitrary political, industrial and social restraint, but with the fall of feudalism and the removal of feudal restraints, the phrase lost its original significance. The manufacturing and trading classes, as the struggling and subjected bourgeois of the seventeenth and eighteenth centuries, appealed to the sacred right of individual freedom as a means to deliver them from the oppression of the ruling classes of their time; but the possessing classes of the nineteenth and twentieth centuries, themselves in power and confronting a new dependent class, the class of wage workers, invoke the old god of their fathers only in order to strengthen their own rule. The "Individual Liberty" of the modern capitalist has come very largely to stand for the right to deal with his employees as he pleases, the unrestricted right to exploit men, women and children of the working class, and to be free from the interference of the state in his process of exploitation. An economic order based entirely on the principles of "laissez-faire," and a political organization of the type characterized by Huxley as "Administrative Nihilism" are the ideals of the modern priests of the god "Individual Liberty." In the hands of the capitalist individual liberty has degenerated into individual license, its philosophy is that of shortsighted egoism. The most consistent and logical representative of that philosophy is probably Max Stirner, whose work, "The Ego and His Own," has only recently, more than sixty years after its first appearance, been placed before the English-reading bourgeois to be acclaimed by them with unbounded delight. The views of that philosopher of individualism may be summed up in the following two brief quotations from the work mentioned: —

"Away then with every concern that is not altogether

my concern! You think at least 'the good cause' must be my concern. What's good and what's bad! Why, I myself am my concern, and I am neither good nor bad. Neither has meaning for me.

"The divine is God's concern; the human man's. My concern is neither the divine nor the human, not the true, good, just, free, etc., but solely what is mine, and it is not a general one, but is unique, as I am unique.

"Nothing is more to me than myself." [1]

And again :—

"Every state is a despotism, be the despot one or (as one is likely to imagine about a republic), if all be the lords, i.e., despotize one over the other." [2]

And in this extreme view of individual freedom the liberal capitalists find themselves entirely in accord with the radical anarchists. Both would rob society of all its social functions. Both base their philosophy on individual competition and the brutal struggle for existence rather than on the principle of human coöperation, both make an idol of individual liberty, both suffer from a morbid exaggeration of the Ego, and both sanction all means to attain the end of individual happiness.

The only difference between the conservative and patriotic capitalist and the violent anarchist is that the former represents the "individualism" of the rich, and the latter that of the poor.

The philosophy of individualism supplies a moral and pseudo-scientific sanction for the economic struggle between man and man, and appeals to the different classes of the population favorably or unfavorably according to their

[1] Max Stirner, "The Ego and His Own," New York, 1907, p. 6.
[2] Ibid., p. 256.

chances and position in that struggle. The ruling classes with their overwhelming economic powers are best equipped for the uneven struggle of existence; they are bound to prevail in it and to reap all the advantages of the victory if not interfered with — they are, therefore, naturally inclined to individualism.

The dependent and non-possessing classes, on the other hand, are powerless in the individual struggle for existence under prevailing conditions. They stand in need of social protection against the abuses of the dominant class, and thus their strength lies in concerted action and coöperation. To the intelligent workingmen, individualism is as repellent as it is hostile to their interests—they naturally lean towards the opposite philosophy. Socialism is the manifestation of the working class revolt against the excessive individualism of the capitalists, just as individualism appeared originally as the expression of the revolt of the bourgeoisie against the excessive centralization of the ancient régime.

The frequent and heated modern discussions on the merits and demerits of the "systems" of individualism and socialism are, therefore, at bottom only the theoretical and somewhat veiled expression of the practical struggles between the ruling and dependent classes of our times.

In the words of Sidney Ball, "Socialism and Individualism, when contrasted, have an economic connotation,"[1] but in ordinary discussion they assume, as a rule, the guise of purely abstract political or philosophical issues.

These issues between the "individualists" and the socialists are many in number and multiform in character,

[1] "Socialism and Individualism," in *Economic Review*, Vol. VII, p. 490.

c

but for the convenience of treatment they may all be grouped under the following three main heads: —

1. The Relations of the Individual to Society.
2. The Mutual Relations of Individuals in Production.
3. The Fate of Individual Liberty under a System of Socialism.

We shall consider the points presented by each of these three subjects separately.

The Individual and Society

At the bottom of the individualist philosophy in politics lies the conception that organized society is a mere aggregation of individuals freely and deliberately associating for certain common purposes — a sort of business partnership which may be formed, shaped and dissolved by the contracting parties at will. In this view of our social organization every member of modern society is an independent party to the "social contract" who has entered into contractual relations with society in order to gain some individual advantages and who may cancel these relations if the sacrifices imposed on him should exceed such advantages. The logical result of these views is an attitude of jealousy and suspicion towards organized society or the "state," [1] an apprehension that the latter may strive to exact from the individual more than he has bargained to give, that it may "exceed the sphere of its legitimate functions." [2]

[1] For the purposes of the present discussion the terms are here employed interchangeably.

[2] M. Yves Guyot, the leading apostle of individualism in France, would limit the activities of the state to the following functions: —

"1. To guarantee exterior and interior security.

This somewhat crude social philosophy found its clearest expression in the French pre-Revolutionary "literature of enlightenment"; it was the key to the social theories of the English Utilitarian school of Locke, Bentham and Mill, and it held practically undisputed sway of the human mind until about the middle of the last century. The doctrine is most naïvely asserted in the Massachusetts Bill of Rights, in the following language: "The body politic is formed by a voluntary association of individuals; it is a social compact by which the whole people covenants with each citizen and each citizen with the whole people, that all shall be governed by certain laws for the common good."

But the discoveries in the domain of organic evolution and the growing recognition of the laws which are operating to shape individual life everywhere, finally caused the students of social life and phenomena to subject their views to a critical examination. Conditions of social existence, past and present, were carefully investigated and collated, and laws of social development were gradually established.

In the light of the newly acquired knowledge the *à priori* social theories of the early thinkers had to be abandoned one by one, and to-day it is quite generally accepted that organized society is not an arbitrary invention, but the result of a definite and logical process of historical development.

It is probable that men never were purely individual

"2. To secure to each individual the freedom to dispose of his person and the freedom of the environment in which he must act.

"3. Not to intervene in contracts except to enforce their performance."

"Le Socialisme et L'Individualisme," *Journal des Economistes*, June, 1898.

beings, but that they evolved from gregarious or social ancestors in the kingdom of animal life. "As far as we can go back in the palæo-ethnology of mankind," observes Kropotkin, "we find men living in societies — in tribes similar to those of the higher mammals." And further: "The earliest traces of man, dating from the glacial or the early post-glacial period, afford unmistakable proofs of man having lived even then in societies. Isolated finds of stone implements, even from the old stone age, are very rare; on the contrary, wherever one flint implement is discovered, others are sure to be found, in most cases in very large quantities. At a time when men were dwelling in caves, or under occasionally protruding rocks, in company with mammals now extinct, and hardly succeeded in making the roughest sorts of flint hatchets, they already knew the advantages of life in societies."[1]

The entire history of man's progress has been one of increasing growth and importance of his social organization. According to Lewis H. Morgan,[2] whose studies of social development are among the most complete and reliable contributions to modern sociology, the first definite form of social organization is the primitive family or *Gens*, which still prevails among certain savages. This is a rather loose form of organization, consisting of a body of human beings descended from a common ancestor. The next step in social development is the *Association of Several Gentes* or *Phratry*, which is followed by the closer and more complex organization of the *Tribe*, a union of many *gentes* speaking a common dialect and occupying a common territory. From the *Tribe* to the

[1] P. Kropotkin, "Mutual Aid a Factor of Evolution," London, 1902, pp. 79, 80.   [2] "Ancient Society."

Confederacy of Tribes, which is formed for mutual defense, and gradually and naturally develops into the *Nation*, there is but one step.

This in brief is the history of social growth in ancient society. With the development of property in goods and land, the social organization gradually transformed itself into a political society based on territorial relations. The Township, the County and the National Domain or State, are the successive steps of that development.

Thus mankind has imperceptibly evolved from an aggregation of loosely connected social units to the present state of society, in which the entire globe is divided politically into a very small number of governments compactly and closely organized.

The process took countless ages for its accomplishment and was in all its phases determined by the instinctive needs of mankind. The successive types of social organization, ever stronger and more compact, were evolved in the incessant struggle for existence as efficient weapons in that struggle. "The state," says Professor Ward, "is a natural product, as much as an animal or plant, or as man himself." [1] Whatever progress has been made by mankind in its long career has been made through its social organizations. There is no civilization and there is no liberty outside of organized society, and in this sense the individual man is the child and creature of the state and tied to it with every fiber of his existence. [2]

---

[1] Lester F. Ward, "Pure Sociology," New York, 1903, p. 549.

[2] "There never was and there never can be any liberty upon this earth among human beings outside of state organization. . . . Liberty is as truly a creation of the state as is government." — PROFESSOR J. W. BURGESS, "Political Science and Constitutional Law," Boston, 1890, p. 88.

The historical and uniform course of the evolution of the state and its overwhelming importance as a factor in human civilization have led the school of thinkers of which Auguste Comte, Saint-Simon and Hegel are the typical representatives, to the opposite extreme—the conception of the state as an organism. The "historical" or "organic" school sees in the abstract phenomenon of the state a concrete and independent being with a life, interests and natural history of its own. To these thinkers human society is a social organism very much like the biological organism. The social institutions are so many of its organs performing certain vital functions required for the life and well-being of the organism itself, while the individual members of society are but its cells. Mr. M. J. Novicov,[1] probably the most ingenious exponent of the "organic" school of sociology, carries the parallelism between the social organism and the biological organism to the point of practical identity, and Mr. Benjamin Kidd, criticising the utilitarian motto, "The greatest happiness of the greatest number," says: "The greatest good which the evolutionary forces operating in society are working out, is the good of the social organism as a whole. The greatest number in this sense is comprised of the members of generations yet unborn or unthought of, to whose interests the existing individuals are absolutely indifferent. And, in the process of social evolution which the race is undergoing, it is these latter interests which are always in the ascendant."[2]

In short, the state is the end, the citizen is only the

---

[1] "Conscience et Volonté Sociales," Paris, 1897; "La Théorie Organique des Sociétés," in *Annales de L'Institut International de Sociologie*, Vol. V.   [2] "Social Evolution," p. 312.

means. It is the old parable of the shrewd Mucius Sce-vola presenting itself before us in the fashionable garb of modern science.

And here again the two extremes meet. The extreme individualist deprecates all attempts on the part of the state to regulate the affairs of the citizens, on the plea that the state *should* not interfere with the liberty of the individual; the extreme sociocrat discountenances all attempts on the part of the citizens to model the state in their interests on the ground that the individual *cannot* shape the life of the social organism. One bases his objections on the ground of expediency, the other on scientific necessity; but the practical results are the same in both cases — the separation of the state and the individual.

Although the ultra "organic" theory of the state has found some adherents among socialist writers,[1] contemporary socialism has, on the whole, as little sympathy with the extreme sociocratic view as it has with that of the extreme individualist.

It is always dangerous to engraft a ready-made principle of any branch of scientific research on an entirely different branch, notwithstanding apparent analogies between the two, and the fallacy of that method is probably best illustrated by the introduction of purely biological laws into the domain of sociology. The social organization of men is a phenomenon vastly different from the biological organism. In the case of the latter it is the organism as such which is endowed with sensation, reflection and life — the individual cell has no conscious life of its own, and serves only to support the existence of the organism. In

[1] For example, the well-known Marxian scholar, F. v. d. Goes, in "Organische Ontwikkeling der Maatschappij," Amsterdam, 1894.

the case of the "social organism," on the other hand, it is the individual members of it who are endowed with conscious life, and it is the so-called organism that serves to support their individual existences.

The state is not the voluntary and arbitrary creation of man, but it is just as little a factor imposed on man by some power outside of him. The state is a product of logical historical development, but that only as an accompaniment of the logical historical development of man. The individual cannot dissociate himself from society, nor can society have any existence outside of the individuals composing it. The state represents the collective mind and attainments of all past generations, but also the collective intellect, will and powers of its present living, feeling and thinking members. The state has the power to regulate the conduct of its individual citizens, but its citizens have the power to determine the scope and nature of such regulations, and the higher mankind ascends in the scale of intellectual development, the more effective is its direction of the functions of the state. Man to-day is in a position to employ the state not merely for the good of the abstract "social organism as a whole," nor yet merely for the good of remote generations to come, but for his own present concrete good.

This is the view from which all socialist political activity proceeds, and this view is steadily gaining practical recognition in all spheres of society, as is eloquently attested by the ever greater extensions of the social functions of the modern state.

Individualism in Industry

If the tendency of political development of mankind has, on the whole, been in the direction of socialization, the same tendency asserts itself even more strongly in the process of industrial development.

Individualism in production is a mark of economic immaturity.

The primitive man, without experience, tools, weapons or arts, living in trees or in caves, and subsisting on the wild fruit of the tropical forest, may to a large extent be economically independent of his fellow-man in the neighboring tree. But the succeeding fishing, hunting, agricultural and pastoral occupations already presuppose the existence of certain uniform tools, a certain common experience, common methods of work, and even the possibility of occasional exchanges of products.

But these early institutions are, on the whole, too uncertain and unexplored to enable us to build any sober conclusions upon them. To ascertain the real tendency of industrial development, we must take a more recent and better-known period, — a period, besides, which has uncovered the laws of industrial evolution more clearly than the entire history before it, — the period of the last century. And if there is any doubt in our minds as to the tendency of our industrial life, the examination of this period will rapidly dispel it.

In the beginning of the nineteenth century, the production and distribution of goods was in the main operated on an individualist basis. The artisan worked as an individual either at his home or in his shop, generally alone and sometimes with the aid of a helper or apprentice. His simple tool was owned and operated by him individually. His product was in most cases due entirely to his individual labor and skill, and was rightly and properly his individual possession.

But with the development of the simple tool into a variety of huge, steam-propelled machines, specialized for the mass production of minute parts of commodities, the little workshop grew into the enormous modern factory in which hundreds and thousands of men are brought together from all parts of the country, organized into a complex hierarchy of labor, each one doing one small thing, each working into the hands of the other, all of them collectively producing one article which may have to go through numerous similar operations in other immense and complex factories before it turns into a commodity for direct consumption. The modern machine is a social tool, the modern factory is a social workshop, the modern workingman is a social servant, and the modern goods are social products.

Let us take the most simple articles of use: the coat we wear, the chair we sit on, the bed we sleep in, and ask ourselves, Who produced these articles? To answer that question we shall have to consider the unknown thousands who contributed to the work of their immediate design and manufacture, to the production and transportation of the material contained in them, to the work of constructing the wonderful machinery employed at the countless steps of the process, and to the work of operating the machinery of transportation, etc. In modern production the individual laborer is practically obliterated; what is before us is a world-wide community of socially organized labor of all gradations, from the highest and most skillful to the lowest and most common, working together collectively for the needs of our race..

And it is this collective labor of our times that sustains modern comforts and modern civilization. Were it pos-

sible for us to return to the régime of absolute individualism in production, to prepare our own food, make our
own clothing, build our own dwellings, without taking
advantage of the material prepared by others, without
accepting the coöperation of our fellow-men, we should
relapse into a state of savagery in less than a generation.

While the feature of individualism has been almost
eliminated from the field of production by the last century,
it has, during that period, shown much greater vitality in
the sphere of management of our industries.

The management of our industries by individual capitalists for their own private benefit and in rivalry with
each other — *industrial competition* — has for decades
been the favorite topic of controversy between the adherents of the individualist philosophy and the partisans
of the socialist school of political economy. To the
sturdy individualist the competitive system of industry is
the source of all blessings of civilization : he never tires of
extolling the merits of that system as an incentive to industrial enterprise, inventiveness and efficiency, as a character builder and lever of all social and individual progress.
The socialist, on the other hand, points a warning finger
to the evils of competition : the anarchy in management
and waste in production which the system entails, and the
tremendous social, economic and ethical losses which it
imposes on the producers, the consumers and the community at large.[1]

But while the discussion on the merits and demerits of
competition is assuming ever more intense forms, the mute

[1] A most notable contribution to that phase of the discussion is the
recent work of Mr. Sidney A. Reeve, "The Cost of Competition,"
McClure, Phillips & Co., 1906.

forces of economic evolution, unconcerned by theories and abstractions, are rapidly working towards a practical solution of the problem. The individual capitalist steadily yields his place in the industrial world to the corporation and the trust, and the latter combine and consolidate the independent managements of numerous individual concerns under one corporate direction, and reorganize the management of industries, frequently on a national and even international scale. The irresistible growth of trusts and monopolies is the central fact of all recent economic development, and it sounds the death knell of individual competition.

The only sphere of our industrial life in which the principle of individualism has survived in all its pristine vigor, is that of the appropriation or distribution of the products.

Although the instruments of production have become social in their character and use, and indispensable to the entire working community, they are still owned and controlled by the individual capitalists. Although the production of goods is a collective process, and its management and direction are fast becoming so, it is still conducted principally for the benefit of the individual captains of industry. Although all useful members of the community collectively contribute to the so-called national wealth, only a comparatively small number of individuals share in it. In short, although the production of wealth is practically socialistic, its distribution is entirely individualistic.

And this contradiction between the modern methods of production and distribution is the only real issue between the individualist and the socialist in the domain of economic discussion.

The beneficiaries of the present system of wealth distribution have a very obvious material interest in maintaining it, and there never was a ruling class that did not have the abundant support of scientific and ethical theories to justify it in the continued enjoyment of its privileges. In the present case this function is being performed by the school of "individualistic" philosophers and moralizers.

The socialists, on the other hand, consider the present system of individual appropriation of social wealth as an anachronism, a survival of a past economic order, and a disturbing factor in the process of social, economic and ethical progress.

The main object of socialism is to adjust the principles of wealth distribution to those of production — to make the one as social and general in function and effect as the other already is.

The Individual under Socialism

The commonest of all objections to the socialist ideal is that a state of socialism would endanger individual liberty. From such unimaginative novelists as Eugen Richter [1] and David M. Parry,[2] whose conceptions of the socialist commonwealth are those of the modern factory regulations extended to the scope of a national order, up to the thinker of the keenness of mind and universality of knowledge of Herbert Spencer who asserts that "all socialism implies slavery," [3] all bourgeois philosophers seem to take it for granted that mankind is to-day enjoying a large measure of individual freedom and that socialism would greatly curtail if not entirely suppress it.

[1] "Sozialdemokratische Zukunftsbilder."
[2] "The Scarlet Empire," Indianapolis, 1906.
[3] "The Coming Slavery."

The socialists deny both assertions with equal emphasis.

Under our present system of economic dependence and struggles, individual liberty is but a fiction. The very small "leisure class," *i.e.*, the class of persons enjoying a workless and ample income and entirely removed from active participation in the industrial, professional, commercial and financial strife, no doubt enjoy considerable individual liberty, but for all other strata of modern society that liberty does not exist.

The workingmen, the largest class of the population, are anything but free: their work and their pleasures, their dress and their dwellings, their mode of life and their habits, are forced on them by their economic condition.

"Not as an exception, but universally," says Mr. H. D. Lloyd,[1] "labor is doing what it does not want to do, and not getting what it wants or needs. Laborers want to work eight hours a day; they must work ten, fourteen, eighteen. . . . They want to send their children to school; they must send them to the factory. They want their wives to keep house for them; but they too must throw some shuttle or guide some wheel. They must work when they are sick; they must stop work at another's will; they must work life out to keep life in. The people have to ask for work, and then do not get it. They have to take less than a fair share of the product; they have to risk life, limb or health — their own, their wives', their children's — for others' selfishness or whim."

Nor is the workingman alone deprived of individual liberty under present conditions. The toiling farmer burdened by mortgages and oppressed by the railroad com-

[1] Quoted in Richard T. Ely's "Socialism and Social Reform," pp. 209, 210.

panies, the professional man dependent on private and
unregulated calls for his services, and the small business
man struggling against odds to maintain his "independence," they are all tied to a routine of life and action not
voluntarily chosen, but inexorably imposed on them by
the economic exigencies of their business pursuits and
callings.

And even the "powerful" and wealthy, the heads of
the modern industrial structure, are anything but free:
their wealth as live, active, investment-seeking capital,
dominates them and suppresses their individual volition;
they are the slaves of their wealth rather than its masters.

All these purely economic checks on individual liberty
must of necessity be greatly palliated, if not entirely removed, in a socialist community, for the system of socialism
implies primarily a state of greater economic security and
industrial equality.

"But," it is asked, "assuming that socialism would
remove some of the elements operating to-day against the
full exercise of the freedom of the individual, would it not
create new and more formidable restraints upon liberty?
Under the present régime the individual has some say in
the choice of his occupation and the mode of exercising
his trade or calling; under socialism, on the other hand,
the state would be the sole employer, and would determine
for every citizen what, where and how he should work;
would not the citizen thus become the slave of the
state?"

This argument, so frequently urged against socialism,
contains two fundamental errors: it assumes that a socialist state may be a power independent of and opposed
to the body of individuals composing it, and that in a sys-

tem of socialism, all industries must be concentrated in and controlled by the national government or "state."

The basic principle of every socialist community must be its democratic administration: the socialist state will assume such concrete form, powers and functions as the majority of citizens, unbiased by conflicting class interests, will freely choose to confer on it, and it is not at all reasonable to suppose that these citizens will deliberately encase themselves in an iron cage of rigid laws and rules of their own making.

Much more likely the men who will have the framing of the political and industrial system of a socialist commonwealth, will take ample care of their own individual freedom.

Nor is there any reason to suppose that under socialism "the state" would be the sole employer. Socialism implies the *collective* ownership of the social tools of production, and the *collective* management of industries based upon the use of social tools. Does that necessarily imply state ownership and management? By no means. Certain industries are even to-day organized on a national scale, and may be best managed or controlled as state functions; others come more appropriately within the scope of the municipal administration, others still may be most efficiently managed by voluntary coöperative associations with or without state control, while a variety of industries of an individual nature, such as the various arts and crafts, must of necessity remain purely individual pursuits. The phantom of the "despotic state" has taken such a strong hold of the minds of our social philosophers trained in the individualistic school of thought, that even writers like Professor Richard T. Ely, of whose candor

and analytical powers there can be no doubt, and who is by
no means unsympathetic to socialism, is not quite free from
the fear of it. "Even," says Professor Ely, "if the functions of government should be reduced to the lowest forms
compatible with socialism, those in whose hands were
centered political and economic control would have tremendous power, however they might be selected or appointed. Nor can we forget the possibilities of combinations between different parties for certain purposes. It
would, under socialism, be quite possible for two or three
parties to act together as sometimes they do now. The
frequent assertion that the Democratic and Republican
parties have acted together in New York City to control
the civil service, seems to be well founded; and it is quite
conceivable that two or three parties might act together
to promote the interests favorable to a few leaders, and to
keep down, if not persecute, obnoxious persons." [1]

In voicing these apprehensions Professor Ely unconsciously transfers present conditions into an order of things
in which the very causes of such conditions are altogether
lacking. Political parties are the creatures and tools of
class interests, and "the interests favorable to a few
leaders" which he mentions, are the economic interests of
the class or group of men represented in politics by those
leaders. Modern party politics is, as we shall attempt
to show in a later chapter, a manifestation of the capitalist mode of production and of the economic struggle of the
classes, and must disappear with the abolition of the present
economic order.

Under socialism there can be no party politics, in the
present sense, and whatever abuses may develop in the

[1] Richard T. Ely, "Socialism and Social Reform," pp. 212, 213.

D

administration of the state or the industries, can be only casual, based on inexperience or error of judgment of the community or on personal incompetence, malice or ambition of the responsible officers, and in either case they can be more readily remedied than in a state in which such abuses have their roots in the very foundation of the industrial organization of society.

On a par with the assertion that socialism would be fatal to individual liberty is the kindred claim that socialism would destroy the individuality of man. The "dead level of intellectual equality and homogeneity" under socialism is a specter almost as terrifying to the good "individualist" as the phantom of socialist slavery. And it is fully as unreal. For if any industrial system tends to destroy the individuality of men, it is not the proposed system of socialism, but our present economic order. The aggregation of millions of workingmen in the modern industrial centers, employed under similar conditions, tied everlastingly to the same monotonous machine work, dwelling in the same uniform tenements and leading the same stereotyped bleak existence, tends to turn them into one undistinguishable, homogeneous mass, dressing, talking, looking and thinking substantially alike. The men of our active upper classes, all engaged in the same all-absorbing pursuit of wealth by the same methods and under the same conditions, and our leisure classes sorely tried by the rigid rules of conventional etiquette, and tied to a blasé life of uniform and tiring social functions, fashionable sports and prescribed recreations, develop a different but not less homogeneous nor more attractive type. This natural uniformity of type within the different social classes is accompanied by a sort of artificial uniformity produced by the present economic conditions operating in a more indirect manner. "One has only to look on whilst the sons of the *nouveaux riches* spend their money," remarks Mr. Macdonald, "or whilst the crowds which our industrial quarters have disgorged enjoy themselves, to appreciate the meaningless monotony of our pleasure. From our furniture, made by the thousand pieces by machine, to our religion, stereotyped in set formulæ and pursued by clockwork methods, individuality is an exceptional characteristic." [1]

"Our standard of decency in expenditure," observes Professor Veblen, "as in other ends of emulation, is set by the usage of those next above us in reputability; until, in this way, especially in any community where class distinctions are somewhat vague, all canons of respectability and decency, and all standards of consumption, are traced back by insensible gradations to the usages and habits of thought of the highest social and pecuniary class — the wealthy leisure class." [2]

And Mr. Vail expresses the same idea when he says: "The tendency toward uniformity is due to the lack of equality in economic conditions. The inferior classes strive to imitate the superior classes in order to avoid an apparent social inferiority. The result is, society is continually run in the same groove. On the other hand, any system which would tend to decrease economic inequality would tend to kill imitation. Just in proportion as men become equal, they cease to gain by imitating each other. It is always among equals that we find true independence." [3]

[1] J. Ramsay Macdonald, "Socialism and Society," London, 1905, p. 7.

[2] Thorstein Veblen, "The Theory of the Leisure Class," New York, 1905, p. 104.

[3] Charles H. Vail, "Principles of Scientific Socialism," p. 227.

CHAPTER III

The Essence and Scope of Ethics

THE branch of social philosophy known as Ethics presents itself to us in a dual aspect. Theoretical or scientific ethics aims to ascertain the principles and true meaning of "right and wrong" in human conduct. Practical or applied ethics seeks to draw concrete conclusions from the knowledge so gained, and to base on it a code of "right" conduct for the practical guidance of mankind. Scientific ethics takes cognizance of actions and relations as they are, while practical ethics considers them as they ought to be. And it is largely on account of this dual character of ethics that the standard definitions of the term present such a striking divergence. Some of the writers on the subject have attempted to cover both aspects of ethics in one definition, while others either give separate definitions for each, or emphasize only one side, entirely ignoring the other.[1]

But whether ethics be considered as a science or as an

---

[1] The following are among the better-known definitions of ethics, both as a science and an art: —

Professor John Dewey in the *Encyclopedia Americana:* "Ethics is that branch of human conduct which is concerned with the *formation* and *use* of judgments of right and wrong, and with the intellectual, emotional, and executive or overt phenomena which are associated with such judgments, either as antecedents or consequents."

Francis L. Patton in *Syllabus of Ethics:* "Ethics is the science that offers a rational explanation of *Rightness* and *Oughtness;* and that deals art, all authorities agree that in either case it is concerned with "right" or "good" human conduct. That is, however, as far as the agreement goes. The more fundamental problems of the kind of human conduct properly coming within the sphere of ethics, and of the adoption of a universally valid standard of "right and wrong" or "good and bad" in such conduct, is still the subject of much discussion.

It is pretty generally agreed that the conduct of which ethics takes cognizance is not the conduct of associated human beings acting as such (for that properly belongs to

with the Life of free personal beings under these conceptions, considering it as related to an Ideal or norm of Excellence, conformity to which is obligatory."

Harald Höffding in *Ethik:* "A scientific system of Ethics endeavors to discover in accordance with what principles we direct our life, and to secure for these, when ascertained, greater clearness and inner harmony."

Ethics is considered as a critical science only, in the following definitions: —

Herbert Spencer in *Data of Ethics:* "Morality is the science of right conduct, and has for its object to determine how and why certain modes of conduct are detrimental, and certain other modes beneficial."

New International Encyclopedia: "Ethics is the voluntary conduct of a self-conscious person, in so far as that action is amenable to a standard of obligation imposed on him by social influence or by a supreme plan of life that draws its material from society."

The following definitions deal with ethics as a constructive art: —

Henry Sidgwick in *The Methods of Ethics:* "By 'methods of ethics' is meant any rational procedure by which we determine what individual human beings 'ought' or what it is 'right' for them to do, or to seek to realize by voluntary action."

Jeremy Bentham: "Ethics is the art of directing men's action to the production of the greatest possible quantity of happiness."

American Encyclopedia: "Ethics is the principle which prescribes what ought to take place in human conduct."

Webster's Dictionary: "Ethics is a system of rules for regulating the actions and manners of men in society."

the domain of politics), but the conduct of the individual. At the same time, however, it is not all individual human conduct that falls within the sphere of ethics. "Conduct" has been aptly defined by Herbert Spencer as "acts adjusted to ends,"[1] and it is very obvious that within the scope of his biological functions and even in his intellectual life and social relations man performs daily numerous acts fully adjusted to ends which have no ethical implications. To be ethical or unethical, human actions must have some bearing on beings other than the actor himself; they must be tested by their social effects. A number of authorities extend the operation of ethics to conduct towards one's self and one's fellow-men; philosophers of the theological school include conduct towards God within the purview of ethics, while the thinkers of the evolutionary biological school, with Spencer at the head, classify ethical conduct as conduct towards self, offspring and race. But on closer examination, it will be found that the addition of all factors other than the purely social factor, is meaningless or confusing. Ethics remains indifferent to the conduct of the individual towards himself, so long as that conduct does not directly or indirectly affect the well-being of his fellow-men or of the human race. When an individual wastes his physical or mental resources in a manner calculated to cripple his own life without, however, involving the well-being of other individuals, we call his conduct improvident or unwise, and only when he abuses his own body in a manner likely to injure his offspring or to enfeeble or degenerate the race, do we call him immoral. Similarly, we consider an individual immoral if he is in the habit of transgressing those religious precepts which happen to be

[1] "Data of Ethics," New York, 1893. p. 5.

in accord with the generally accepted secular notions of "right" or "good" in social conduct, but if he neglects to comply with certain prescribed religious observances which have no bearing on the well-being of his fellow-men, we merely call him irreligious. And finally the conduct of the individual towards his offspring is no more than a special phase of his conduct towards his fellow-men or his race.

Without fear of serious contradiction we may, therefore, define ethics as the science or art of "right" individual conduct of men towards their fellow-men.

A much greater uncertainty and divergence of views confront us when we attempt to discover the meaning of the term "right" as applied to human conduct in the various philosophical systems of ethics. As a matter of fact, there is no code of morality universally recognized and conformed to by all mankind at all times. Human actions which are condemned as atrocious by some races under some circumstances, are sanctioned and even praised by other races and under other circumstances. Under normal conditions civilized men consider the act of deliberate murder as the most revolting and heinous of crimes, but in war the same act is glorified by them as one of greatest virtue, while among the food-lacking tribes of cannibals, it is considered as an indifferent act of commonplace household economy. Other offenses against the person, and still more so offenses against property, have received even more varying estimates at different periods of human history and from different portions of the human race, while the astounding changes of the social standards of sex morality with time and place, are familiar to every student of sociology and reader of descriptive travel.

And still the fundamental precepts of morality are by no means an arbitrary figment of the human brain. For the epoch and place in which they prevail they have universal validity, and even their modifications from time to time and variations from place to place will always be found to have legitimate reasons and realistic roots in the conditions of such times and places. If there are no absolute standards of right and wrong, there certainly must be relative standards of right and wrong at every given time and place, and these relative standards, furthermore, must have some common principle determining their formation. What are those standards, and what is that principle? These are the main questions which exercised the minds of the early founders of the science of ethics and which still constitute the brunt of discussions of the modern moral philosophers. And it is largely the difference in the answers to these questions which separates the numerous existing ethical systems from each other.

The theological school of thinkers, of which St. Augustine, the mediæval monk Ambrose and especially Thomas Aquinas are the classical exponents, and which still has numerous and vigorous adherents, assumes that there is a universal and supreme standard of right and wrong. That standard is the divine command which has been given to all mankind and is expressed in the holy scriptures. In particular instances that command is to be ascertained by revelation or by interpretation and application of the general rules obtained from texts of scripture and by analogical inferences from scriptural examples. Any departure from that command as so interpreted by individuals or whole races is merely evidence of apostasy.

In this theory ethics is practically synonymous with theology.

Closely cognate with the theological system of ethics, but considerably secularized, is the doctrine of Natural Laws first developed into a comprehensive system by Hugo Grotius and followed by many modern writers, principally in England. That school, like the theological school, recognizes an absolute and universal standard of right and wrong in human conduct, but in distinction to the theological school it bases that standard not on a divine command but on "the essential nature of man." According to Grotius and his followers there are implanted in the human being certain notions of right and wrong which form a part of his very existence and which are as unalterable and true as the truths of mathematics. The test and the proof of such truths is their universal acceptance by human societies. In conformity with this conception the writers of that school have evolved a code of ethics based entirely on the fundamental notions of morality prevailing among the civilized nations of their times.

Barely distinguishable from the juridical school of Natural Laws is the philosophical school of Intuitionalism. This school, which may claim Socrates and Plato for its founders, has in more recent times had many brilliant exponents and defenders in the field of philosophic thought, chief among them being Kant and Whewell. According to the intuitional doctrine the sense of duty is innate in every normal human being and its commands and principles are known to them by intuition and without the aid of any process of reasoning or demonstration. This doctrine is developed with the greatest elaborateness by Kant, who distinguishes between the world of "phenomena," or objects as they appear to us through our limited senses and powers of perception, and the world of "noümena," the real world of objects as they exist regardless of our perception of them (Die Dinge an sich). The sense of duty is one of such "noümena." It manifests itself to us in a greater or smaller degree according to the development of our powers of perception, but it has an absolute and real existence outside of our perceptions.

To all these systems of ethics which may be collectively designated as Idealistic, are opposed the so-called Rationalistic systems, which seek to evolve standards of right and wrong from reason and experience rather than from revelation or intuition.

The earliest of such schools is the Hedonistic or Epicurean, which considers individual happiness as the end of life and all conduct conducive to that end as good and right. This theory is not grossly materialistic, since it recognizes the intellectual and æsthetic pleasures as the ones conducive to greater and more lasting happiness. Like the school of Intuitionalism the school of Hedonism dates back to Greek antiquity. The philosophers Aristippus and Epicurus were among its first exponents. The theory was revived by Hobbes and considerably modified and extended by him and his followers. The more recent writers of this school frequently substitute the more definite standard of pleasure and pain for the old hedonistic test of happiness and unhappiness, and several of them see the true application of the principle of hedonism not in the happiness of the individual, but in universal or social happiness. Hedonism in one form or another was the favorite doctrine of the rationalistic philosophers of pre-Revolutionary France — Lamettrie, Helvetius and others.

The notion of the "social contract," which appeared together with the victory of the European industrials and the establishment of constitutional government, logically led to the formation of the Utilitarian school of ethics. The adherents of the "social contract" theory, as stated in a previous chapter, assume that organized society was formed by its individual members for their mutual benefit and protection, and that it is deliberately maintained by them for that purpose. Since, however, the rules or acts of organized society cannot always benefit all of its members alike, each individual member must occasionally sacrifice some right to his fellow-men, upon the theory that in the long run the advantages derived by him from society would outweigh the disadvantages suffered. This is the "rational" sanction for the majority rule in all popular government, and Bentham only translated the political doctrine into ethical terms, when he asserted that "right" conduct is such as results in the greatest good to the greatest number.

The Utilitarian school, in the language of Sidgwick, "holds that all rules of conduct which men prescribe to one another as moral rules, are really — though in part unconsciously — prescribed as means to the general happiness of mankind."[1] The chief exponents of this school are Paley, Bentham and the Mills, father and son, although Kant's ethical injunction, "Act only on such a maxim as may also be a universal law," may also be considered essentially utilitarian, inconsistent as it is with the intuitional theory of the famous philosopher.

Finally, the school of social thought which goes to

[1] Henry Sidgwick, "The Methods of Ethics," 5th Edition, London, 1893, p. 8.

biology for the discovery of rules of human conduct, has introduced another and more realistic standard of right and wrong in human conduct. According to Darwinian conceptions the strongest motives in all organic life are the instincts of self-preservation and preservation of the species. Applied to men in a social state that theory means that the main concern of human beings is the preservation of life, and that such conduct of the individual will be regarded as good or right as tends to preserve and enhance the life of his fellow-men, while conduct which tends to curtail or impair such life will be considered bad or wrong.

"Goodness," says Herbert Spencer, "standing by itself, suggests, above all other things, the conduct of one who aids the sick in re-acquiring normal vitality, assists the unfortunate to recover the means of maintaining themselves, defends those who are threatened with harm in person, property, or reputation, and aids whatever promises to improve the living of all his fellows. Contrariwise, badness brings to mind, as its leading correlative, the conduct of the one who, in caring for his own life, damages the lives of others by injuring their bodies, destroying their possessions, defrauding them, calumniating them."[1] And Lester F. Ward tersely expresses the same thought in the following language: "'Duty' is simply conduct favorable to race safety. Virtue is an attribute of life and character consistent with the preservation and continuance of man on earth. Vice is the reverse of this, and is felt as an attack upon the race."[2]

These, then, are the main theories of right and wrong, as conceived by the contending systems of ethical thought.

[1] "Data of Ethics," pp. 24, 25.   [2] "Pure Sociology," p. 420.

But this branch of the subject does not by any means exhaust the field of ethical inquiry. For assuming that a true standard of right conduct is discovered, there still remains the more important question as to the motives which impel or ought to impel human beings to conform to that standard. The mere fact that we recognize a certain mode of action as right and another as wrong does not imply that we will in all cases follow the one and shun the other. What, then, is the factor that makes or ought to make us choose good conduct in preference to bad conduct?

To that question the different schools make different replies according to their conceptions of the nature of the moral obligation. The theological school holds out the promise of reward in a life beyond the grave. The intuitional school declares that no reward is required, since the individual is impelled to obey the moral impulse innate in him, the irresistible command of nature, or, as Kant terms it, the Categorical Imperative. "Thou must always fulfill thy destiny," decrees the celebrated German philosopher Fichte, and the biological school of ethics practically makes the same reply except that it substitutes the instinct of preservation of the species for the intuitive moral sense.

The most contradictory and, therefore, the least satisfactory explanations of the ethical motives of men are those offered by the schools which pride themselves with being founded on pure reason, — those of hedonism and utilitarianism.

Recognizing that mere individual self-interest is entirely inadequate to account for the acts of altruism which chiefly constitute high moral conduct, the hedonists early resorted to the theory of "intelligent egoism" as distinct from that of shortsighted selfishness. The well-developed human being, they argue, is so constituted that he experiences greater pleasure in serving his fellow-men than in gratifying his own narrow desires.   In promoting the well-being of his fellows he, therefore, primarily procures a pleasurable emotion for himself and only incidentally renders a service to his neighbor.   But this argument carries its own destruction, for it makes the basis of right human conduct not the self-interest of the actor, but his inner consciousness or instinct of duty to his fellow-men, the performance of which causes him pleasure.   Neither the hedonistic theory nor the utilitarian conception, which represents man in organized society as engaged in constant cold-blooded bargaining with his fellow-men for advantages, can account for such acts as the voluntary sacrifice of one's life in the service of society.   And on the other hand the idealistic theories of ethics do not even attempt to explain motives of human conduct, but virtually abandon the subject as beyond their ken.

Within this charmed circle of contradictions the philosophy of ethics oscillated during almost the entire intellectual period of the human race, and little, if any, substantial progress was made in twenty-five centuries of the career of that important branch of thought.   It was only when the discussion was removed from the domain of metaphysical speculation to the field of positive science, that ethics acquired a realistic basis.   This great work was primarily accomplished by Charles Darwin and his disciples.

The Evolution of the Moral Sense

The main features of the Darwinian theory of organic evolution are, as is generally known, the doctrine of the struggle for existence and the resulting natural selection through the survival of the fittest, the development of useful organs and hereditary transmission.

In a state of nature each individual is engaged in constant struggle with individuals of its own or different species and with surrounding nature. In this universal struggle the individuals least equipped for the fight and least adapted to their surroundings, perish, while those who happen to possess organs or features of particular advantage in the struggle, survive, and by the frequent application of such useful organs and features, develop them ever more and transmit them to their offspring in a higher degree of development. Thus results a constant process of increasing adaptation to surroundings and a breed of more highly and efficiently organized individuals. The struggle for existence is a purely individual struggle in the lowest forms of life, and the struggle between individuals of the same species predominates in those forms. But in the ascending scale of organic existence the struggle between individuals of the same species gradually abates and is superseded by the collective struggles of such individuals against hostile kinds and the adverse forces of nature around them. Social organizations thus arise among animals, including the progenitors of primitive men, and these organizations prove a powerful weapon in the struggle for existence against hostile groups or species. The more compact and harmonious the organization, the greater its efficiency as a weapon in the struggle for existence. Henceforward the process of evolution is one of growing solidarity and cohesion among the individuals of the same group or species as against their common enemies, and this instinct of solidarity and cohesion is the first germ of the sense of social duty or moral consciousness.

"The feeling of pleasure from society," says Darwin, "is probably an extension of the parental or filial affections, since the social instinct seems to be developed by the young remaining for a long time with their parents; and this extension may be attributed in part to habit, but chiefly to natural selection. With those animals which were benefited by living in close association, the individuals which took the greatest pleasure in society would best escape various dangers, whilst those that cared least for their comrades, and lived solitary, would perish in greater numbers. With respect to the origin of the paternal and filial affections, which apparently lie at the base of the social instincts, we know not the steps by which they have been gained; but we may infer that it has been to a large extent through natural selection." [1]

And again : "When two tribes of primeval men, living in the same country, came into competition (other circumstances being equal) if the one tribe included a greater number of courageous, sympathetic and faithful members, who were always ready to warn each other of danger, to aid and defend each other, this tribe would succeed better and conquer the other. . . . Selfish and contentious people will not cohere, and without coherence nothing can be effected. A tribe rich in the above qualities would spread and be victorious over other tribes; but in the course of time it would, judging from all past history, be in its turn overcome by some other tribe still more highly endowed. Thus the social and moral qualities would tend to slowly advance and be diffused throughout the world." [2]

[1] "The Descent of Man," Collier Edition, New York, 1901, pp. 144, 145.

[2] *Ibid.*, pp. 175, 176.

These mental and moral qualities once generated will on the whole grow in the course of evolution. The higher a tribe of men stands in the scale of civilization, the less will its members depend on their purely physical powers and the greater will be the importance of their mental and moral qualities.

"In proportion as physical characteristics become less important," says Alfred Russel Wallace, who shares with Darwin the merit of the discovery of the theory of natural selection, "mental and moral qualities will have an increasing influence on the well-being of the race."[1]

Thus the moral sense is a product of the process of evolution of man, gained in his early struggle for existence, precisely in the same manner as his intellectual qualities. It is a property of man in a state of society just as much as any of his physical organs, or as Mr. Bax puts it, "the ethical sentiment is the correlate in the ideal sphere, of the fact of social existence itself in the material sphere. The one is as necessarily implied in the other as the man is implied in his shadow."[2]

This conception of the nature of morality and its origin and development in the human being overthrows all earlier theories of ethics, but at the same time it reconciles all elements of truth that are contained in them.

The primitive men did not deliberately form their first social organizations on the strength of such considerations as are contained in Rousseau's "Social Contract." They did not bargain for advantages or pleasures to be bestowed on them by society. They were forced into organization by the superior powers of struggle. They probably first

[1] In "Contributions to Natural Selection."
[2] E. Belfort Bax, "The Ethics of Socialism," p. 4.

E

herded themselves together blindly, unreasoningly. But the instinct which impelled them to form such organizations was the instinct of self-preservation, the inarticulate and unexpressed conviction that in organization lay their greater safety and protection, and that by their own devotion to the social aggregation they would help to strengthen the weapon upon the efficiency of which their lives largely depended. The primitive men or their progenitors were in that sense unconscious hedonistic and utilitarian philosophers.

But the moral sense once evolved, in the course of time became a permanent trait of the human being, an innate or intuitive feeling, and in this sense the Idealistic theories of ethics have a certain degree of reason and justification. "The social instinct," says Ernst Haeckel, "is always a physical habit, which was originally acquired, but which, becoming in the course of time hereditary, appears at last innate."[1]

The conclusion of the foremost Darwinian scholar in Germany thus largely coincides with those of the foremost German philosopher of Intuitionalism, Immanuel Kant.

The moral sense once acquired is, like all other properties of the human being, subject to growth. The rudimentary moral instinct of the primitive man must have undergone countless phases of development before it evolved into the lofty conceptions of the contemporary moral philosopher.

But it would be a mistake to consider that growth as a continuous, automatic and regular process. The moral sentiment in mankind does not grow in the same sense as a plant or other physical organism grows, i.e., by steadily

[1] Quoted by C. M. Williams, "A Review of the Systems of Ethics," etc., New York, 1893.

increasing in dimension with the lapse of time. Different races, though perhaps of the same age, exhibit different moral perceptions in kind and degree, and even within the same society and age different individuals present the most divergent degrees of the moral sentiment.

The growth of the moral sense, like the growth of the intellect, depends upon a multiplicity of external conditions which shape its contents and further or arrest its progress. What is the nature of these conditions? The theory of natural selection traces the origin and reveals the quality of the moral sense in man, but it fails to account for the mode and laws of its further development. In fact the founders of the modern school of biological evolution distinctly disclaim the effectiveness of that factor as applied to a more advanced state of human society.

"With civilized nations," declares Darwin, "as far as an advanced standard of morality and an increased number of fairly good men are concerned, natural selection apparently effects but little; though the fundamental social instincts were originally thus gained," [1] and Mr. Wallace is still more emphatic in this view of the limited scope of operation of the principle of natural selection.

What, then, are the factors determining the degree and direction of moral development?

The answer to that momentous question will be found in the philosophy of the school of Karl Marx, who alone consistently introduced the spirit of Darwinism into the study of social phenomena by substituting the economic interpretation of history and the resulting doctrine of the class struggle in the more modern stages of social develop-

[1] "The Descent of Man," p. 185.

ment for the instinct of self-preservation and the resulting doctrine of the struggle for existence in its lower stages.

Class Ethics

The prime concern of men in a state of society is the production of the means for the sustenance of the members of that society. A community engaged chiefly in hunting, pastoral, agricultural or manufacturing pursuits and largely depending on the success of such pursuits for its existence, will in all cases arrange its organization and regulate its functions primarily with a view of enhancing the efficiency of that particular mode of securing the material life of its members. This object determines all economic and political forms of society, and in the last analysis it also dominates all social motives and notions.

"In the social production which men carry on," says Marx, "they enter into definite relations that are indispensable and independent of their will; these relations of production correspond to a definite stage of development of their material powers of production. The sum total of these relations of production constitute the economic structure of society — the real foundation, on which rise legal and political superstructures and to which correspond definite forms of social consciousness. The mode of production in material life determines the general character of the social, political and spiritual processes of life. It is not the consciousness of men that determines their existence, but, on the contrary, their social existence determines their consciousness." [1]

Morality, which has been defined by Professor Ward as

[1] Karl Marx, "A Contribution to the Critique of Political Economy," English Translation, New York, 1904, p. 11.

conduct conducive to "race safety," and by Mr. Stephen as conduct conducive to the "health of society,"[1] and which in the earlier stages of social evolution stands principally for courage and loyalty in combat, in a more advanced society comes to a large extent to signify conduct favoring the economic efficiency and prosperity of the nation.

The glaring differences which confront us in the codes of ethics of different communities, or within the same communities at different times, mostly reflect the differences or changes of the economic conditions of such communities, the manner of maintaining the lives of their members. A savage tribe suffering from a scarcity of food may have its own rudimentary code of ethics, but such a code will not extend its ban to the practices of devouring its captives in war or slaying its aged and feeble members. When, however, the same tribe develops to the point of using tools and implements and learns to produce food in greater abundance, the practices of man-eating and of killing its own members become immoral. A nation like the ancient Spartans, whose subsistence largely depends on success in war, may have a very definite and strict code of ethics, but the virtues recognized by that code will be principally those of military worth, physical strength, courage and quick-wittedness, whereas honesty will be considered a matter of moral indifference, and the practice of killing feeble children, even a moral duty. Conversely, peaceful, pastoral and agricultural communities will rate honesty and industry as the highest virtues, and show but little regard for courage and daring.

[1] Leslie Stephen, "The Science of Ethics," 2d Edition, New York, 1907.

Thus each community primarily formulates in its code of ethics the material or economic welfare of its members, while within each community the standard of individual morality is the degree to which each member advances or impairs the material interests of his fellow-members. In the earlier types of social organization in which the material interests of all members were practically identical and in which the individual member necessarily benefited from every advantage accruing to the totality of members, and *vice versa*, there could be no conflict between the interests of the individual and those of society. The material welfare of the community was easily, we may say instinctively, ascertainable and readily conformed to. The system of morality, such as it was, was perfect.

But in modern communities the relations of the individuals to society and to each other are by no means so simple and harmonious. The division of labor or specialization of functions which has marked the social progress of man, together with the accumulation of property made possible by the ever growing productivity of human labor, have split up all more modern societies into different groups of members, with distinct economic interests. Society or "the nation" no longer represents a homogeneous aggregation of individuals with uniform and harmonious material interests, and the standard of individual morality as conduct favoring the safety, health or economic interests of the "nation" loses much of its force. For in the modern class state conduct which is beneficial to certain groups or classes of society is very often detrimental to other groups or classes, and especially within the most vital sphere of economic activity it is almost impossible to conceive of any action which would be beneficial to all society alike.

The individual who invents a labor-saving device may be said in the abstract to be benefiting mankind at large, but as society is constituted to-day, his invention also results in depriving large numbers of workingmen of a chance to earn their living. The legislator who forces the introduction of safety appliances in dangerous works benefits a certain class of workers but at the same time he injures the material interests of a number of employers.

What, then, is the true standard of morality applicable to modern society?

We have mentioned that modern society consists of various interest groups or classes. These classes are formed by the economic relations of men and are friendly, indifferent or hostile to each other according to the nature of such relations. But between all these divergent social classes we may draw one sharp line of demarcation, the line that separates the possessing from the non-possessing, the dominant from the dependent classes. And while the material interests of the several possessing classes between themselves may be conflicting at different points of contact, they are as a rule fairly harmonious as regards their common relations to the dependent classes. And whenever the interests of these dominant classes come in conflict with those of the dependent classes, the former have always understood it to represent their special interests as the interests of society. This attitude is made all the easier for the ruling classes because their interests always coincide with the maintenance of the existing order and relations, and are, therefore, conservative, while the interests of the dependent classes lie in the direction of a change of such conditions and are, therefore, revolutionary.

Moral conduct, as ordinarily interpreted, is conduct

tending to conserve the existing order. In the modern class state such conduct is, therefore, conduct conducive to the perpetuation of the advantages of the ruling classes.

"Ethics," says Mr. La Monte rather forcibly, "simply registers the decrees by which the ruling class stamps with approval or brands with censure human conduct solely with reference to the effect of that conduct on the welfare of their class. This does not mean that any ruling class has ever had the wit to devise *ab initio* a code of ethics perfectly adapted to further their interests. Far from it. The process has seldom, if ever, been a conscious one. By a process akin to natural selection in the organic world, the ruling class learns by experience what conduct is helpful and what hurtful to it, and blesses in the one case and damns in the other. And as the ruling class has always controlled all the avenues by which ideas reach the so-called lower classes, they have heretofore been able to impose upon the subject classes just those morals which were best adapted to prolong their subjection." [1]

It is only on the theory of the class character of modern ethics that the curious inconsistencies in our moral conceptions can be accounted for. The strong man who should deliberately injure a weak child outside of his business pursuits, would be considered by his fellow-men as an individual of a low moral character, but the powerful and wealthy mill owner who daily undermines the health and saps the life of hundreds of inoffensive children of tender age in the "legitimate" pursuit of his business, *i.e.*, in the process of profit making, is regarded by us as a perfectly moral being. He may be the superintendent of a Sunday

[1] Robert Rives La Monte, "Socialism: Positive and Negative," Chicago, 1907, pp. 60, 61.

school, an honored member of an Ethical Culture Society, or may be sincerely interested in the missionary task of improving the moral conditions of some South African tribe of savages.

Similarly the owners of the factories, mines and railroads, who suffer or cause large numbers of their fellow-men to lose their lives on account of insufficient safety appliances in their works, and the dealers in food stuffs, who poison their fellow-men by adulterated food, meet with no particular opprobrium on the part of society, while they would have been condemned as immoral wretches if they had been guilty of similar conduct outside of their business pursuits, and not for the sake of profits.

The socialists of the Marxian school do not agree with thinkers of the type of Mandeville,[1] who considers morality purely artificial and a device of the "politicians" to strengthen their rule on their fellow-men. They fully recognize that the moral sentiment is implanted in the normal human being and capable of very high development even under adverse conditions. Instances of men and women rising above their class interests and sacrificing their material welfare, sometimes even their lives, in the service of their fellow-men, are of frequent, almost daily occurrence, and cannot be accounted for on any economic or materialistic theory. The socialists also recognize that outside of the economic sphere of human activity, there is a large field of human interest, in which the individuals of all classes meet on common ground, and in which the moral conceptions correspond to the actual welfare of all mankind. But they maintain that as a rule

[1] The author of a book entitled "The Fable of the Bees, or Private Vices Public Benefits," published in 1724.

the ethical conceptions dominating the "business" interests of modern nations, and the various social activities and organs subservient to these interests, such as politics, the agencies molding public opinion, etc., are conceptions favoring the interests of the dominant classes only. They are the ethics of the ruling classes falsely parading as general social ethics.

The Ethical Ideal and Socialist Morality

When we speak of a certain degree of development of the moral faculty and when we distinguish a rudimentary form of morality from a highly evolved form, we must necessarily have in mind a standard of comparison. Such a standard of comparison is the ethical ideal, which to us represents the limit of all moral conduct and by the approach to which we judge a concrete code of morals to be high or low.

An ethical ideal — Absolute Ethics, Spencer terms it — does not imply a belief in a code of morality good for all times and places and independent of all existing physical conditions. It merely represents our view of the last phase of moral evolution in civilized society, based upon our observation of the course of such evolution in the past. Such an ideal is as useful for the purposes of practical ethics as general and abstract laws of pure science are useful for the study of concrete phenomena.

Most of the modern writers on the subject have, therefore, outlined ideal standards of ethics, and most of these outlines agree in their fundamental characteristics.

According to Spencer's definition ethical conduct is such as is conducive to the welfare of self, offspring and race, and the best, *i.e.*, most normal conduct is that which fulfills all the three conditions simultaneously and most efficiently. Such conduct, however, can only be attained in a state of society in which the interests of the individual and those of society are entirely identical, and in which "general happiness is to be achieved mainly through the adequate pursuit of their own happiness by individuals, while reciprocally, the happiness of the individual is to be achieved in part by the pursuit of the general happiness." [1]

Whether we agree in all parts with this definition or whether we confine the scope of ethics to conduct towards society or one's fellow-men, does not alter the validity of the conclusion. The relations of the individual and society are those of mutual service, and the progress of morality consists in the growth of these relations, or in the words of Huxley, "in the gradual strengthening of the social bond." [2]

The limit of moral evolution can thus be reached only in a state of society free from material and other antagonisms between the individuals among themselves and between the individual and society. In such society the question of right and wrong is entirely obviated, since no normal conduct of the individual can hurt society, and all acts of society must benefit the individual. Organic morality takes the place of ethics.

Such an ideal state of organic morality may be unattainable in its absolute purity, but the trend of evolution is in its general direction. All factors which impede the path to its approximate realization are anti-ethical or immoral;

[1] Herbert Spencer, "Social Statics."
[2] Thomas H. Huxley, "Evolution and Ethics," New York, 1896, p. 35.

contrariwise, all factors or movements which tend in its direction are ethical.

In modern society the checks to the realization of ideal morality are numerous. As indicated in the previous chapter, the existence of social classes and the resulting class struggles are the chief impediments to a true social morality. But the direct action of the struggle between antagonistic classes in the same society does not by any means exhaust the evil. Some of the indirect effects of the class state based on individual production are even more disastrous to the progress of true morality than its direct operations. And chief among such effects are the two most anti-social institutions — competition and war.

"The competitive struggle," says Kautsky, "affects the social instincts of the individuals in the same society most distinctively. For in this struggle each individual maintains himself best the less he permits himself to be influenced by social considerations and the more he is guided by his own interests. For the member of the capitalist society based on individual competitive production, it is, therefore, quite natural to consider egoism as the only legitimate instinct in man, and to regard the social instincts as refined forms of egoism or as an invention of the priests to fasten their rule on men or as a supernatural mystery." [1]

Wars are regarded by Herbert Spencer as the chief obstacle to the progress of moral development, and in his "Data of Ethics," as well as in his later work, "The Deductions of Ethics," the theory occurs again and again that a "state of war" is incompatible with an ideal morality, and

[1] Karl Kautsky, "Ethik und Materialistische Geschichtsauffassung," Stuttgart, 1906, pp. 105, 106.

that the latter is only attainable in perfectly peaceful societies. Spencer does not take cognizance of the class struggle and of the economic interpretation of history. To him "a state of war" and "a state of peace" are merely phases of moral development in human society. But as a matter of fact wars depend but little on the degree of civilization attained by the community. The most advanced states are frequently also the most warlike states. Wars in modern times are most often caused by economic motives. They are usually the results of the competitive struggles of the capitalist classes of the belligerent nations for the markets of the world, the logical counterparts of competition in the national markets.

To the industrial individualism which is the leading feature of modern society corresponds a gross egoism in all spheres of our material existence which sets individual against individual and throttles all nobler social instincts in man. Employer and employee, producer and consumer, buyer and seller, landlord and tenant, lender and borrower, are always arrayed against each other, constantly and necessarily meeting in a spirit of antagonism of interests, incessantly engaged in conscious or unconscious economic struggle with each other. And all these forms of economic struggle are but single phases of the broader and deeper class struggle which is the dominant factor in modern industrial life and largely determines all current moral conceptions.

But the class struggle is not an unmitigated evil. Just as the struggle for existence among individuals in the lower forms of human existence led to the improvement of the race and eventually matured the conditions of its own destruction, just so the class struggles in advanced societies have often been the instruments for the improvement of the social type and will eventually lead to the abolition of all classes and class struggles.

The struggles between the bourgeoisie, the progenitors of the modern capitalist class, and the ruling class of land-owners, have yielded many valuable acquisitions to modern civilization, and have resulted in the establishment of modern society, which with all its faults and imperfections is vastly superior to the feudal order which it displaced. The struggles of the dependent classes against the ruling classes in modern society have already produced the rudiments of a nobler social morality, and are rapidly preparing the ground for a still higher order of civilization.

The modern working class is gradually but rapidly emancipating itself from the special morality of the ruling classes. In their common struggles against the oppression of the capitalist class the workers are naturally led to the recognition of the value of compact organization and solidary, harmonious action. Within their own ranks they have no motive for struggle or competition; their interests are in the opposite direction. And as the struggles of their class against the rule of capitalism become more general and concrete, more conscious and effective, there grows in them a sentiment of class loyalty, class solidarity and class consciousness which is the basis of a new and distinct code of ethics. The modern labor movement is maturing its own standards of right and wrong conduct, its own social ideals and morality. Good or bad conduct has largely come to mean to them conduct conducive to the welfare and success of their class in its struggles for emancipation. They admire the true, militant and devoted "labor leader," the hero in their struggles against the employing class. They detest the "scab," the deserter from their ranks in these struggles.

The two historical slogans given to the modern socialist and labor movement by Karl Marx and Frederick Engels, "The emancipation of the workingmen can only be accomplished by the workingmen themselves," and "Workingmen of all countries unite, you have nothing to lose but your chains, you have a world to gain!" — may truly be said to be the main precepts of the new morality of the working class. They inspire the "lower" classes with the consciousness of a great social mission to be performed by them in modern society; they foster the virtues of comradeship and self-reliance in their ranks, and develop the qualities of fidelity and devotion to their common cause.

This new morality is by no means ideal social morality. It is the ethics of struggle, class ethics as yet. But just because it is the ethics of a subjugated class engaged in the struggle for its emancipation, it is superior to the prevailing ethics of the class bent upon maintaining acquired privileges. The workingmen cannot abolish the capitalist class rule without abolishing all class rule; they cannot emancipate themselves without emancipating all mankind. Behind the socialist theory of the existing class struggle lies the conception of a classless, harmonious society; behind the conception of the international solidarity of the working class lies the ideal of the world-wide solidarity of the human race. The ideals of the modern socialist and labor movement thus generally coincide with the scientific conceptions of absolute morality.

Of course, in both cases we are dealing with ideals, and ideals only. We must recognize that the realities of life always fall short of social ideals. Socialism does not imply a state of absolute and universal harmony. The human mind cannot conceive to-day a state of society free from all antagonism and frictions caused by differences in temperament, views and even temporary material interests. There will probably always be some individual infractions of the accepted canons of social morality, but there will be no universal economic motive for such infractions, and they will necessarily become less flagrant in character and less frequent in number, they will cease to be the rule in human conduct, and will become the exception.

"The conflict of the individual with society," says Charles Kendall Franklin, "is of two kinds. On the one hand, it is carried on by specialized individuals whose function is to develop and perfect society by developing the moral and social senses; on the other, the conflict is between society and the rank individualist who will not be subdued by society, who persists in expending his energies in as wasteful a manner as he sees fit so it benefits himself. Civilization is full of such people to-day. They are powerful individuals, they head corporations, they compose the professions, they constitute the classes. They believe in society for their own benefit and hoot at the socialization of the race as the rankest nonsense. . . . Their worst representative is the degenerate and criminal; individuals who cannot adapt themselves at all to the development of society to-day." [1]

Of the two kinds of anti-social individuals so characterized by Franklin, the "specialized" individual and the pathological criminal, the men physically and morally constituted above or below their fellow-men, may survive forever in larger or smaller numbers, but the "rank indi-

[1] "The Socialization of Humanity," Chicago, 1904, p. 210.

vidualist" who preys upon his fellow-men and tramples on social solidarity, mainly from motives of material gain, can find but little room in a society based on coöperative production and common social enjoyment. With the change of his economic interests and motives man will necessarily change his conduct.

"The ethics of socialism," observes Bax on this point, "seeks not the ideal society through the ideal individual, but conversely the ideal individual through the ideal society. It finds in an adequate, a free and harmonious social life, at once the primary condition and the end and completion of individuality." [1]

[1] "The Ethics of Socialism," p. 19.

CHAPTER IV

SOCIALISM AND LAW

The Law

IN our occasional contact with the law we are but too apt to concentrate our attention on the concrete legal enactments and rules of procedure, and to lose sight of the body of the law as a dynamic system.

Here we will not concern ourselves with the anatomy of the law, but rather with its physiology, and will consider the law as a social force in its relation to the general process of social development.

Under the designation "Law" in the broadest sense of the term, we understand the entire body of legislative enactments, rules and regulations which prescribe the relations of man to man, man to state, state to man and state to state.

The law thus defined is not fixed or universal: it varies with the different types of civilization past and present. There is a radical difference between the laws of the ancient Greek communities, mediæval European society, and the modern civilized states, and there is as radical a difference between the systems of law prevalent in the semi-barbaric countries of South Africa, the empire of China and the democracy of the United States.

Nor are the laws of any given country immutable. In

fact, nothing is more changeable than the system of national laws in the modern countries. Every year volumes of new laws and ordinances are issued from the halls of Congress or parliaments, the inferior legislative chambers and the councils of thousands of municipalities; every year innumerable old laws are repealed or amended, and innumerable new laws are enacted. The thing that is legal to-day may be branded as a crime to-morrow, new rights may be conferred on or taken from us, and new duties may be imposed on us by every legislative session, and especially in the Anglo-Saxon countries new laws may grow out overnight by the process of judicial "construction."

But these changes in the law are by no means arbitrary. Individual measures may at times be needless and illogical, but in the long run all changes in a given system of law mark a development in a certain definite direction. A system of jurisprudence is just as much subject to the laws of evolution as any other social institution.

The primitive man has but little use or occasion for laws. But the higher the plane of human civilization, the closer the interrelation of men, the greater becomes the need of definite rules of conduct of the members of such organization in all matters pertaining to the common welfare. Those of such rules that are more vital to the maintenance of the social fabric are as a rule enacted into formal laws, while those of less direct and important bearing are left within the domain of ethics. "Normally," says Mr. Sidgwick, "in a well-organized society the most important and indispensable rules of social behavior will be legally enforced, and the less important left to be maintained by Positive Morality. . . . Law will constitute, as it were, the skeleton of social order, clothed by the flesh and blood of Morality." [1]   Law and ethics have thus a common origin, and while by no means identical in all respects, they present a great similarity in many aspects.

Law, like ethics, springs from the economic and social conditions of the nations, and from its very origin it must be adapted to and change with those conditions.   A tribe, race or nation will in each period establish such rules or laws as will be most conducive to the successful pursuit of its mode of subsistence, and as each of the succeeding economic and social orders gradually grow out of the preceding systems, new laws are created to meet the changed situation.   The feudal system gave us the Law of Real Property, the development of national and international commerce led to the Law of Negotiable Instruments, the rise of the factory inscribed the Labor Laws in our statute book, and practically in our own times the introduction of railroads, telegraphs and telephones added new and important branches to our body of law, while the more recent economic categories of corporations and trusts still keep our legislative mills busy.   "The evolution which led men to an orderly social life did not consist in the dialectic self-development of juridic ideas," says Arnold Lindwurm, "but in the economic development brought about by social necessity." [2]

The law of each civilization, again like its ethics, not only reflects the economic and social conditions of the times, but is primarily designed to safeguard and maintain those conditions.   That is why we find such a variance

[1] "The Methods of Ethics," p. 19.
[2] "Das Eigenthumsrecht und die Menschheits — Idee im Staate," Leipsic, 1878, p. 139.

in the criminal law of different states in its estimate of the gravity of certain crimes. "Every state," says Dr. Rudolph von Ihering, "punishes those crimes most severely which threaten its own peculiar condition of existence, while it allows a moderation to prevail in regard to other crimes which, not unfrequently, presents a very striking contrast to its severity as against the former. A theocracy brands blasphemy and idolatry as crimes deserving of death, while it looks on a boundary violation as a mere misdemeanor (Mosaic Law). The agricultural state, on the other hand, visits the latter with the severest punishment, while it lets the blasphemer go with the lightest punishment (Old Roman Law). The commercial state punishes most severely the uttering of false coin; the military state, insubordination and breach of official duty; the absolute state, high treason; the republic, the striving after regal power; and they all manifest a severity in these points which contrasts greatly with the manner in which they punish other crimes. In short, the reaction of the feeling of legal right, both of states and individuals, is most violent when they feel themselves threatened in the conditions of existence peculiar to them." [1]

The statement that the law is always designed to safeguard the existing economic conditions of society must, however, again as in the case of ethics, be qualified by the further statement that the law of each period is primarily designed to safeguard and protect the interests of the dominant classes within such society.

The legal systems of antiquity, the Greek and Roman Law, made no attempt to disguise that fact. The subject class, the class of slaves, frequently the overwhelming

[1] "Struggle for Law," English Translation, Chicago, 1879, pp. 45, 46.

majority of the population, was placed beyond the pale of the law. The slave was excluded from the protection of the law and left to the arbitrary treatment of his master. The institution of serfdom, which lasted throughout the Middle Ages and in some instances survived into the nineteenth century, presents a similar state of affairs.

Prior to the great French Revolution, the nobility and clergy openly enjoyed special legal privileges from which the common people were excluded, and while the form of legal class favoritism has been abolished in most of the enlightened contemporary states, our laws on the whole still favor the ruling classes.

Since the law is the expression of social and economic conditions in motion, every improvement in those conditions leads to a corresponding improvement in the system of law. The course of political and economic improvement which on the whole marks our social progress, reflects itself in the ever-growing tendency towards equity and justice in law. Compared with the iniquitous laws of mediæval ages, our laws to-day are exceedingly humane, and generally speaking, every succeeding phase of a legal system is superior to the preceding phase. This applies to all domains of the law — private, public and international.

But legal progress does not run parallel with social and economic advance. As a rule the law lags somewhat behind existing conditions. New factors in our industrial life from time to time create new social conditions, and produce new conceptions of social rights and obligations. These remain abstract and debatable theories until such time as they have been incorporated in the statute books, and a penalty has been attached to their violation. Then, and then only, they are transferred from the domain of ethics to that of law.

But the recognition of these rights, as a rule, does not occur automatically. Moral rights do not ripen into laws by a process of natural growth, nor are acquired laws self-executing. Reforms in law and legal redress are conquered in struggle, and, in most cases, in hard, obstinate struggle. The effort to effect equitable legal reform or secure such redress, the "struggle for law," as Dr. von Ihering terms it, assumes different forms in the different provinces of the law. In the domain of private law such efforts find daily application in litigation; in the domain of public law, these efforts are expressed in politics, and their realization is sometimes effected by revolutions; in international law the struggle is expressed in the diplomatic dealings of the nations, and sometimes culminates in war. "All social classes," says the eminent Italian jurist Alfredo Tortori, "are impelled to make such laws, to establish such institutions and to sanction such customs and beliefs as accord with their direct or indirect interests. Hence the perpetual movement which drives men and groups to change existing laws and to adapt them to new social interests." [1]

And this struggle for right and law is the key to all social progress. The man who suffers personal wrong without protest or opposition, the "peaceful" member of the community, is a demoralizing factor in our social fabric; the class that does not struggle for civic and industrial rights will eventually lapse into slavery; and the nation that passively countenances encroachments upon its rights and territory is doomed to dismemberment and national bankruptcy.

[1] "Socialisme et droit privé," in *Le Devenir Social*, 1896, p. 251.

It is the man who defends his rights, the class that battles for political and industrial advancement, and the nation that holds its own against the entire world; it is the "litigious" person, the "revolutionary" class and the "vigilant" nation that keep the world from stagnation and force it onward on the path of progress.

Conservatism and meekness and the pietistic veneration for the laws and customs of our forefathers, are not civic virtues, but vicious manifestations of mental indolence and political reaction. The progress of mankind lies in the future, not in the past.

Let us test the truth of these general observations by a comparison of three systems of law corresponding to three phases of human civilization; the feudal system, immediately preceding our own, the modern or capitalistic system and the proposed system of socialism.

The Feudal System of Law

The system of feudalism was evolved in the period of turbulence into which Europe was thrown by the migration of nations, and represented the first attempt to reduce the general social chaos and confusion of that period to some social order.

The system was based on landownership and agriculture, both of which were rendered highly precarious by incessant wars and pillage, and naturally produced all the complex features of the social, political and legal organization of feudal society.

The tiller of the soil in the early stages of feudal civilization was in constant danger of having his fields devastated and crops destroyed by the incursion of hostile hordes of marauders, and the protection from this ever present danger was a necessary part of his agricultural pursuits. The man with the sword was as indispensable to the cultivation of the land as the man with the plow, and the first division of labor in feudal society is formed on these lines. The warrior is a public functionary in the early feudal community; he protects the tillers of the soil from molestation in the pursuit of their daily occupations, and in return he receives from them his necessary means of subsistence in the shape of a portion of their crops. The warrior lives among the other members of the community; he is part of them, but his dwelling house is the largest in the settlement, and is fortified, so as to offer a refuge to the villagers and their property and cattle in case of attack.

In the further progress of feudal civilization the social relations become more permanent and fixed. The division of social functions develops into class differences. The warrior through long years of use and a process of hereditary transmission of social functions arrogates to himself the power over his fellow-men which the monopoly of arms places in his hands: the settlement becomes the feudal *Manor*, and the fortified manor house, the *Castle;* the warrior turns into the *Noble*, the worker into the *Villein*, and the voluntary compensation for military services grows into a fixed annual tribute — the *Tithe* and compulsory military service.

Land was now the principal wealth and source of power in feudal society, and pillage and robbery the accepted means of its acquisition. War became the industrial pursuit of the noble.

Conquering a strange community, the victorious leader frequently reduced its inhabitants to the state of serfdom, appropriated their land, and endowed his retainers with portions of it. But just as frequently the noble "protector" would rob his own subjects of large parcels of the communal land. The class of the nobles thus became a landowning class, and brute force was the origin of its title.

The greed for land and the necessity of defending their possessions engendered an ever increasing strife among the nobles and led to military offensive and defensive alliances between them which made up the graduated and complex political structure of mediæval society.

At this stage of development, which we may consider the period of bloom of feudal civilization, the social relations, notwithstanding their rough appearances, are still not altogether based on force. The social order, strange as it may seem, still rests very largely on the principle of mutual service between the classes.

"The feudal lord," says Lafargue, "only holds his land and possesses a claim on the labor and harvests of his tenants and vassals on condition of doing suit and service to his superiors and lending aid to his dependants. On accepting the oath of fealty and homage the lord engaged to protect his vassal against all and sundry by all the means at his command; in return for which support the vassal was bound to render military and personal service and make certain payments to his lord. The latter in his turn, for the sake of protection, commended himself to a more puissant feudal lord, who himself stood in the relation of vassalage to a suzerain, to the king or emperor.

All the members of the feudal hierarchy, from the serf upwards to the king or emperor, were bound by the ties of reciprocal duties." [1]

[1] Paul Lafargue, "The Evolution of Property," English Translation, London, 1894, p. 79.

Under the existing conditions of the times the class of nobility was, therefore, on the whole a socially useful class.

But in the succeeding centuries, the onward march of civilization gradually but radically changed the social conditions of Europe. The logical trend of feudal development led to ever vaster and more powerful alliances based on a hierarchy of power and duties, to political concentration and ultimately to the formation of monarchical states. The natural effect of this course of development was to limit strife and warfare, and a number of other causes served to accelerate that process. The introduction of gunpowder was a death blow to knight errantry, and the humanizing influences of a more enlightened civilization, ushered in by the period of the Renaissance as well as the rise of commerce and industry, destroyed the very foundation upon which the feudal order was built.

Feudal society was broken up, and the dominant class which it had produced was deprived of all its useful social functions. But not of its power. The nobility ceased to render service to the community, but it did not discard the habit of levying tribute upon it. As landowners, courtiers, magistrates and high dignitaries of church and state, the noblemen retained themselves in power for centuries after the passing of feudal society.

But in the course of those centuries, a new and formidable rival for power was slowly developing in the bosom of society — the class of commercial and industrial burghers — the bourgeoisie.

Manufacture, which in the earlier stages of feudalism was a very subordinate occupation confined to the village, and exercised by its followers as a sort of public service in

return for a scant living, received an ever larger extension
as society became more settled. The development of
village markets and the rise of towns encouraged independent production of commodities and stimulated trade,
which, with the discovery of the sea route to India and the
discovery of America, received a new and larger impulse.
The merchants' and manufacturers' guilds soon became
a power in the state, and the town, a growing factor in
the political life of the nation.

¬ Henceforward, the history of Europe is the history of
the struggle between these two classes for political supremacy. The titled descendants of the robber barons
of every country unite in the effort to maintain their inherited social, political and economic ascendency, and to
stem the threatening tide of the rising power of the churl-
ish newcomers, and in these efforts they are as a rule
supported by the Catholic clergy, whose social and economic position is very similar to their own. On the other
hand, the rising bourgeoisie strives everywhere for freedom from the fetters of the feudal order, which impede
its movement for the establishment of a free competitive
international market of commerce and manufacture.

The struggle results uniformly in the victory of the
young and vigorous bourgeoisie over the enfeebled nobility.
The last act in this historical drama is the general European Revolution which formally establishes the rule of the
industrial bourgeoisie in all countries of Europe, whether
such revolution is accomplished with little bloodshed, as in
Great Britain in the seventeenth century, or by spectacular
acts and carnage, as in France at the end of the eighteenth
century, or by a slow and almost imperceptible process, as
in Germany towards the middle of the last century.

Such, in brief, is the career of the feudal system, and that career with all its phases of development and struggles is faithfully portrayed in the laws of the period.

The formative stages of the feudal order are not conducive to the development of any general system of jurisprudence. Society is split into innumerable separate and very loosely connected communities, in each of which the arbitrary will of the feudal lord is the supreme law. The system of law of that period has been aptly described by Stubbs as "a graduated system of jurisprudence based on land tenure, in which every lord taxed and commanded the class next below him; in which abject slavery formed the lowest and irresponsible tyranny the highest grade; in which private war, private coinage, private prisons, took the place of the imperial institutions of the government." [1] The legal doctrine that the sovereign can do no wrong and the more modern doctrine of the immunity of the state from legal process, are directly traceable to that period of jurisprudence.

The succeeding phase of feudalism, with its hierarchic order of vassalage and the graduated system of reciprocal rights and duties, finds its expression in the law of property and inheritance. Land, practically the sole means of existence and the source of all social power, is not considered private property. The feudal lord holds his land and enjoys the right to its income as a sort of trustee for his dependants; his title to the land is not one in fee simple, or absolute ownership, but is subject to the superior rights of his immediate lord as well as to the numerous rights and easements of his subjects. The absolute legal title to all the land vests in the king as the representative

[1] "Constitutional History," pp. 255, 256.

of the nation, a theory which has left very distinct traces in the present-day legal doctrine of the right of Eminent Domain.

The feudal lord is the military officer in command of the fief or manor, and that office upon his death descends to his oldest son, together with the duties of protection which it entails. His landownership is merely an incident of office and, therefore, descends to his oldest son. as his successor in office. The entailed estates, the law of intestacy and primogeniture are the juridical expression of the social order of that epoch of feudal bloom.

The period of dissolution of feudal society with its accompanying struggles between the landowning noble class and the industrial class are written in large letters in the legal evolution of that period of social transition. The downfall of feudalism and the triumph of the bourgeoisie are signalized by the removal of restrictions upon the alienation of land and freedom of trading, the introduction of the testament, the abolition of guilds and guild laws, and the eradication of all legal privileges of nobility and clergy.

The Modern System of Law

The basis of modern society differs from that of the feudal system in every essential. Under feudalism, as we have seen, the principal pursuit is agriculture and the principal form of wealth is landownership. The ownership of land is the basis of all social relations and political rights. It creates the hierarchy of rank, the feeling of territorial solidarity, the sense of communal interest, and the spirit of conservatism which are characteristic of that phase of civilization.

Contemporary society, on the other hand, rests mainly on manufacture and trading. The wealth of modern nations is represented principally by movable objects and commodities, or personal property, and all our social relations are based on the ownership of such property.

The right to produce, consume and dispose of all commodities at will, is a necessary incident of their full enjoyment, hence the absolute ownership of all property, the freedom of its production and its unrestricted use, are the pillars upon which all modern law rests.

Private Property and its logical corollaries, Competitive Industry and Individual Liberty, are the new Trinity which the rule of the bourgeoisie has established in modern civilization. These three guiding principles find their most eloquent and finished expression in the American Declaration of Independence and the French Declaration of Human Rights, the two instruments framed spontaneously and in their entirety as the expression of violent political revolutions; they animate the unwritten constitution of England and the written constitutions of all other parliamentary countries.

Private property is also the foundation of all modern legislation, for all modern systems of law are principally designed for its protection.

"In a general way," says the well-known criminologist, Zerboglio, "it may be considered as an established fact that the foundation and objects of criminal law are the preservation and the defense of that class which has constituted the modern system of jurisprudence for the purpose of safeguarding its economic power." [1]

[1] A. Zerboglio, "Lutte de classe dans la legislation," in *Le Devenir Social*, 1896, p. 142.

"Offenses against property" are acts committed in an endeavor to acquire property by means not sanctioned by law,— crimes committed for gain. But the direct offenses against property are not the only crimes committed from motives of gain. The overwhelming majority of crimes against the person, from murder in the first degree to simple assault, are most frequently committed with the object of material advantages: if they are not crimes against property they may be fitly designated as crimes for property.

And what our criminal laws conceal and disguise to some extent, our civil laws reveal with the utmost frankness; the civil codes of every modern nation are chiefly a compilation of rules governing the regulation of disputes over property rights and regulating relations of property owners between themselves.

"If we examine any ground of civil action," remarks Mr. Bax, "we shall find it almost always turns directly or indirectly on a question of property; that is, on what individual shall possess certain wealth — the chances being invariably on the side of the wealthy litigant."[1]

Except for its protection of private property and the principle of free competition as instanced by the anti-trust and anti-monopoly legislation, the general policy of our modern law is one of non-interference. The famous watchword, "Laissez-faire," applies to bourgeois laws as well as to bourgeois economics.

This policy is based on the assumption of equality of all citizens and their ability to adjust their own relations without the interference of the state. And in the period

[1] Ernest Belfort Bax, "The Religion of Socialism," London, 1901, p. 147.

of inception of the present social order this assumption was not entirely unwarranted. When manufacture was in its infancy, and was carried on by primitive methods and with the aid of simple and inexpensive tools, the industrial field was practically free to all artisans. There were no fixed lines between "capitalists" and "wage workers" as distinct and permanent classes: employer and employee met on terms of some equality; their relations were largely created by voluntary and reciprocal contract. But with the development of the complex and expensive modern instruments of production, these instruments passed into the hands of the possessing classes, who thus acquired a monopoly of the modern industrial process, while the non-possessing classes were reduced to the status of wage workers.

The assumed equality of all men thus became a mere fiction, at least as far as the economic relations of the citizens are concerned, and all social legislation based on that assumption henceforward had the effect of sanctioning the power of the strong to exploit the weak. In a society of economic equals the law might properly abstain from interfering with the industrial relations of the citizens, but in a society in which economic supremacy places one class of citizens in an artificial position of advantage over their fellow-citizens, the office of just legislation should be to protect the weak against the abuses of the strong. The failure of modern law to afford such protection to the workingmen in itself shows partiality in the interests of the ruling classes.

"Upon this point," observes Loria, "a comparison between modern and mediæval law is enlightening. During the Middle Ages, when capital was weak and

G

labor acquired its strength from the existence of free land, the law came to the assistance of capital by regulating the labor contract in a manner hostile to the laborer's interest. In our times, on the contrary, when capital is strong and labor is deprived of its liberty of action, the law amply fulfills its office of guardian of property by abstaining from regulating the wage contract at all, and leaving it to the dictation of capital." [1]

A striking instance of this rule is to be found in the enactment and repeal of the famous English "Statute of Laborers." The epidemic of the "black death" in the middle of the fourteenth century had vastly decreased the supply of labor, and wages were going up rapidly. Parliament passed a law making work compulsory on all propertyless persons below the age of sixty years at wages that had been customary in the year 1347, *i.e.*, before the plague, and this law with a number of successive amendments and variations remained in force until the beginning of the nineteenth century, when the development of machinery and the modern processes of production had created a superfluity of labor and a ruinous competition among the workers themselves. The laws fixing the rate of wages then became useless and embarrassing to the employing classes, and were speedily repealed.

But the wage contract is not the only instance of the disadvantage of the workingmen under the law arising from the principle of non-interference. Another and perhaps more conspicuous illustration of the iniquitous effect of that principle is to be found in the employers' liability laws of modern nations, particularly the nations whose

[1] Achille Loria, "The Economic Foundations of Society," English Translation, p. 104.

systems of jurisprudence are based on the Anglo-Saxon common law. The doctrine of the assumption by the workingman of the "obvious risks of employment," and his inability to recover damages for injuries where such injuries were caused in whole or in part by his "contributory negligence" or by the negligence of a "fellow-servant," have for their theoretical basis the fiction that the modern workingman of his own free choice determines how, where and with whom he shall work. The practical effect of these doctrines is that in most cases the workingman remains without remedy against his employer.

The fictitious "equality of all citizens before the law" furthermore favors the possessing classes as against the classes of non-possessors in matters of modern legal procedure at least as much as in matters of substantial law. The fact that the practice of law is a business pursuit of the private practitioner coupled with the complicated, technical and expensive nature of litigation, frequently puts justice beyond the reach of the poor. "The law," exclaims the eminent Italian jurist already quoted, "is a monopoly of wealth, and in the temple of Themis there is no place reserved for the laborer." [1]

Nor is the character of modern law as the guardian of the possessing classes and the whip of the poor, evidenced by its passive attitude alone. The rigid prohibitions against labor combinations in the various modern countries, the strict penalties for all labor interferences with the "rights" of the employing class, and the severe treatment by the courts of all "transgressions" of workingmen in their struggles against their employers, furnish eloquent proof of the law's positive partiality for the ruling classes.

[1] Loria, "Economic Foundations of Society," p. 114.

Social Legislation and Socialist Jurisprudence

As the feudal régime at a certain stage of its development became burdensome on the class of the "bourgeoisie" and caused them to revolt against that régime, so has the modern industrial order become burdensome upon the working classes, and the latter already show symptoms of revolt against it. The more advanced workingmen of all countries begin to regard the economic dependence of their class and the privileged position of the employing classes as a social injustice. They feel that the part of the toilers in the process of production entitles them to a larger share of the national product, and that they are despoiled and deprived of their just due by the classes in power. They demand an ever greater consideration and protection for labor, and an ever larger curtailment of the privileges of wealth.

These demands of the workingmen assume for them the form of social or ethical rights, and their struggles are struggles to realize their rights as laws. The character of the legislation which the working class thus advocates and strives for, is diametrically opposed to all the fundamental principles of modern or bourgeois law. It is based on the right of persons instead of property rights, and on social regulation, control and protection, instead of the principles of free competition and non-interference. And as the working-class movement grows in strength, intelligence and determination, the ruling classes are forced to make concessions to it, either by way of granting or forestalling its demands.

This is the secret of the recent reaction against the sacred "laissez-faire" principle of modern law, and the

source of all "social legislation" of the last few decades.
In Germany, social legislation was inaugurated at a time
when the socialist movement had demonstrated that it
was strong enough to withstand the assault of the anti-
socialist laws. The motive of the government in introducing such legislation was revealed by the Iron Chancellor with his characteristic frankness in the following
speech, delivered in the Imperial Diet in 1881:—

"That the state should take better care of its needy
members than heretofore is not only a dictate of humaneness and Christianity, but also a necessity of conservative
politics which should aim to cultivate in the non-possessing
classes of the population, who are at the same time the
most numerous and least instructed, the view that the state
is not only a necessary but also a beneficent institution.
To this end they must be led by means of direct advantages,
derived through legislative enactment, to consider the
state not as an institution created solely for the protection
of the possessing classes, but as one serving their own
needs and interests. The objection that such legislation
would introduce a socialistic element must not deter us
from our course."

In France the first social legislation was introduced by
Napoleon III as a measure intended to combat the growing influence of the International Workingmen's Association. In England, in the United States and in all other
modern countries, the beginnings of systematic "factory
legislation" coincide, broadly speaking, with the beginnings of the organized labor movement, and its extension
keeps pace with the growth of the labor movement.

The current of social legislation takes two distinct
directions, one being designed to protect the workmen, and

the other to regulate and limit the power of industrial capitalism. To the former class belong the laws providing for workingmen's insurance in case of sickness and disability, the old-age pension laws, and the large body of laws popularly known as Factory Legislation, *i. e.*, laws limiting the hours of labor of women and children, and of men in certain lines of employment, establishing rules for the health and safety of the operatives in mines, mills, factories and other works, extending the liability of employers for injuries sustained by their workmen, regulating the payment of wages, and similar measures affecting the duties of employer to employed.

In the second class of legislation must be counted all laws which attempt to check the excessive accumulation of wealth in the hands of private individuals, such as the income and inheritance tax laws, and laws having for their object the control and regulation of certain industries, such as railroading, banking, insurance, etc.

The net result of all such social legislation is as yet insignificant. On the whole it has had no great effect in improving the condition of the poor or limiting the power of the wealthy. But the importance of this line of legislation lies not in its positive achievements as much as in its symptomatic significance. The "social" laws of the last few decades mark a growing change in the popular conception of the office of legislation — the approach of a new legal system expressive of a new social era. For the forces that gave birth to the weak rudiments of social legislation are still at work, steadily gaining in extent and intensity. The struggles of the organized workingmen of all countries for a fair distribution of the national wealth and for equitable social relations among all men are finding ever stronger support among all classes of the population, and are bound to continue. The logical end of all legal reforms accompanying these struggles is the substitution of a system of law based on the principle of socialism for the present individualistic system.

And while it would be folly to attempt at this time a comprehensive outline of a socialist system of law, we have sufficient concrete data in the present tendencies of social development to enable us to indicate the fundamental principles and general aspect of that proposed system of jurisprudence.

A socialist society is one based on the system of public or collective ownership of the material instruments of production, democratic administration of the industries, and coöperative labor; and the guiding principle of such society must be the recognition of the right of existence and enjoyment inherent in every human being.

The function of law under socialism will of necessity be to insure the stability of these principles and institutions, just as it has been its function at all earlier periods of human civilization to insure the stability of the institutions of such periods. But in a socialist society the function of law will be largely simplified by the disappearance of class distinctions. In a society of industrial equals, in which the material interests of all citizens are identical, and the interests of every citizen accord with those of the state, the motives for all crimes against property and for many crimes against the person are removed, and with their removal disappears the necessity of legislating against such crimes, while the abolition of private competitive industry and trading must have the effect of eradicating from our statute books the major part of all our civil and commercial laws.

In direct opposition to the modern system of law, which deals largely with the reciprocal relations and private conduct of individual citizens, and pays but scant attention to the industrial life of the nation, a socialist system of jurisprudence must of necessity occupy itself primarily with the regulation of the social processes of wealth production and distribution, and limit its interference with the private life and conduct of the citizen to a minimum.

CHAPTER V

SOCIALISM AND THE STATE

Nature and Evolution of the State

ONE of the most interesting theoretical discussions that ever occupied a modern political parliament was that conducted in the German Diet on the occasion of its deliberations on the proposed budget of 1893. It was towards the close of the session; the dissolution of the Diet was imminent, and the Social Democracy, which in the previous elections had polled close to one and a half million votes, loomed up large as a menacing factor in the coming elections. By common accord the subject under immediate consideration was suspended, the debate of the Diet was made the pretext for an electoral campaign and the sole topic of discussion was the proposed Socialist State. It was a battle royal which lasted three consecutive days. The most eloquent speakers of all anti-socialist parliamentary parties in Germany took part in the debate, mercilessly criticising the socialist aims and ideals, and demolishing the structure of the proposed socialist state as they conceived it.

When the turn came to the brilliant socialist leader, August Bebel, he rather nonplussed his colleagues in the Diet by the somewhat startling declaration that the phrase "Socialist State" was in itself an absurdity, and that a "state" could not possibly exist under a socialist order.

The same idea is expressed by Bebel more explicitly in his "Woman," where, in discussing the effects of the proposed economic ‿reforms of socialism on the political organization of society, he says: —

"The state organization as such gradually loses its foundation. The state is the organization of force for the maintenance of existing relations of property and social rule. But as the relations of master and servant disappear with the abolition of the present system of property, the political expression of the relationship ceases to have any meaning. The state expires with the expiration of the ruling class, just as religion expires when the belief in supernatural beings or supernatural reasoning ceases to exist. Words must represent ideas; if they lose their substance, they no longer correspond to anything." [1]

This conception of the state is by no means peculiar to Bebel. It has been expressed by many socialist thinkers of prominence before and after him, and its source is to be found in the following passage from the writings of Frederick Engels, one of the theoretical founders of modern socialism: —

"By reducing the ever greater majority of the population to the rank of proletarians, the capitalist mode of production creates the power which is compelled to bring about this social transformation under penalty of its own destruction. By forcing the conversion of the large socialized means of production into state ownership, it points itself the way towards the accomplishment of that transformation. The wage workers seize the powers of

[1] August Bebel, "Woman in the Past, Present and Future," San Francisco, 1897, p. 128.

the state and provisionally turn the means of production over to the state. But with this act they abolish their own existence as proletarians, and with this act they also abolish all class differences and class antagonisms and the state as a state. Heretofore society was based on class antagonisms and needed a 'state,' i.e., an organization of the exploiting classes for the preservation of the existing methods of production, and more particularly for the purpose of forcibly maintaining the exploited classes in the condition of dependence inherent in such methods of production (slavery, serfdom, wage labor). The state was the official representative of the whole society; it was its union in a visible body, but only inasmuch as it was the state of that class which represented to it the entire society: in antiquity, the state of the slave-owning citizens; in the Middle Ages, that of the feudal nobility; in our times, that of the bourgeoisie. By actually becoming the representative of the whole society, the state becomes superfluous. As soon as there is no longer any class in society to be held in subjection, as soon as the class rule and the struggle for existence based on the modern anarchy in production are removed, and with them also the resultant struggles and excesses, there is nothing more to repress, nothing requiring a special repressing power, a state. The first act in which the state appears as the representative of entire society — the seizure of the instruments of production in the name of society — is at the same time its last independent act as a state. The interference of the state with social relations becomes superfluous in one field after the other, and the state, as it were, falls asleep. The government of persons is replaced by the administration of things and the regulation of the process of production.   The state is not 'abolished,' it dies off.   The phrase of the 'socialist state' may thus be judged for its value as a slogan in the temporary propaganda of socialism, and for its scientific inefficiency." [1]

It will be noticed that the socialist writers quoted see in the state a social institution different and apart from organized society as such.   This is by no means the prevalent conception, and in fact there seems to be no fixed and generally accepted definition of the term in the popular or scientific literature of the subject.   Few expressions are used so vaguely and loosely as the term "state."   A large number of authoritative sociological writers and lexicographers by implication consider the state as a term synonymous with organized society, and expressly define it in that sense.[2]

The fault of all such definitions is, that they do not

[1] Frederick Engels, "Herrn Eugen Dühring's Umwälzung der Wissenschaften," 3d Edition, Stuttgart, 1894.

[2] "The whole body of the people united under one government, whatever may be the form of the government." — WEBSTER'S DICTIONARY.

"The state (πόλις) is an association of human beings — and the highest form of human association." — ARISTOTLE.

"The state (respublica) is the creature of the people, the people united by a common sense of right and by a community of interest." — CICERO.

"The state is organized mankind." — JOHANN K. BLUNTSCHLI in "Lehre vom modernen Staat."

"The state is an assemblage of persons united under the same government." — TURGOT.

"The state is the people living within certain geographical limits. It represents a body of people having, in general, like sentiments, feelings and aims, to carry out which they originate some organic law which provides for ministers or officers, and they constitute the government, which is but the agent of the people in executing the laws they have ordained." — CARROLL D. WRIGHT in "Outline of Practical Sociology," New York, 1899, pp. 88, 89.

define. All human society in a state of civilization is organized, and the term "organized society" applies with equal force to the collectivity of contemporary mankind as to each separate nation or community. The "state" has a more limited and definite significance, and is more properly defined as a body of people united under one political government.[1] That the distinction is not a mere scholastic quibble, but a very material and weighty differentiation, becomes apparent as soon as we attempt to analyze it. Every political government is not only well defined territorially, but it also has certain other fixed and essential attributes: it must be based on a constitution or on the will of an individual sovereign; it must be supported by laws that can be enforced; it must have the machinery to enforce such laws and the power to raise revenue for the maintenance of such machinery; it must also be represented by a person or class of persons invested

[1] "A political community organized under a distinct government, recognized and *conformed to by the people as supreme.*" — STANDARD DICTIONARY.

"When a number of persons are supposed to be in the habit of *paying obedience* to a person, or an assemblage of persons of a known and certain description, such persons altogether are said to be in a state of political society." — J. BENTHAM in "A Fragment of Government."

"The supreme will of a state, in whatever mode of sovereignty manifested, expresses itself and achieves its ends in various ways, but chiefly through Government, which may be defined as the requisition, direction and organization of obedience." — FRANKLIN H. GIDDINGS in "Readings in Descriptive and Historical Sociology."

"The state is an aggregation of individuals living in the same territory under the government of one supreme power." — ANTON MENGER in "Neue Staatslehre."

"The state is sovereign, *i.e.*, it has the original, absolute, unlimited power over the individual subject and over all associations of subjects." — J. W. BURGESS in "Political Science and Constitutional Law," New York, 1900, p. 4.

with the powers of government. In short, the element of repression and coercion is essential to the existence of every state.

"When the political community is regarded as 'society,'" says Mr. Ball, "it is looked at as a number of individuals or classes or professions — as an aggregate of units. When we speak of the 'state,' we understand a single personality, as it were, representing all these interests and endowed with force which it can exercise against any one of them. In other words 'the state' cannot be reduced to 'society' or to 'government,' which is only one of its functions, but is society organized and having force."[1]

The keen French economist Leroy-Beaulieu observes: "The concrete state, as we see it at work in all countries, manifests, as an organism, two essential characteristics, which it always possesses, and which, moreover, it is alone in possessing; the power of imposing by methods of constraint upon all the inhabitants of a territory the observance of certain injunctions known by the name of laws or administrative regulations, and the power of raising, also by methods of constraint, from the inhabitants of that territory large sums of money of which it has the free disposal. The organism of the state is, therefore, essentially coercive; the constraint it exercises takes two forms, the one of laws, the other of taxes."[2]

Charles Benoist in his "Politique"[3] states the same proposition more tersely in affirming that the state may be recognized by two signs; it makes laws and levies taxes.

[1] Sidney Ball, "The Moral Aspect of Socialism" in "Socialism and Individualism," Fabian Socialist Series, No. 3, London, 1908, pp. 75, 76.
[2] Paul Leroy-Beaulieu, "The Modern State," English Translation, London, 1891, p. 67.
[3] Quoted by Gabriel Deville, "The State and Socialism."

If we enlarge the definition somewhat, and say, The state makes and *enforces* laws and levies taxes, we have mentioned the most uniform and indispensable functions of every state.

But the enumeration of these functions alone is quite sufficient to convict the state as a product of class struggles. Law as distinguished from mere custom, law in the sense of a positive command of the state enforceable by a penalty, has its inception in an order of things in which it is already in the interest of one part of the population to act in a manner prejudicial to their fellow-men, and in which it becomes necessary for the latter to restrain the former by force. Such an order of things, however, is only possible in a class society. Primitive society is a society of economic equals. The community produces principally articles of immediate consumption, and that in quantities barely sufficient for the needs of its members. There is no opportunity for the accumulation of private wealth, there are no rich and no poor, and no social classes of any kind. There is neither motive nor chance for any man to covet the property or to trespass upon the "rights" of his neighbor, and there is no occasion to repress such desires by force. The primitive social organizations, the gentes and phratries, have no laws and no instruments to enforce laws. Courts, judges, constables, prisons and police are entirely unknown to them; they levy no taxes or compulsory tribute on their members; they are entirely free from the element of coercion — they are not states.

It is only when the productivity of human labor has increased to a degree beyond that required for the satisfaction of his indispensable personal needs, when man has become a possible object of exploitation, and when the first form of such exploitation has been introduced in the institution of slavery, it is only then that repressive laws and organized social force become necessary.

The state thus appears in the social development of mankind simultaneously with the institutions of private property and slavery and as their necessary concomitant. In its original form, it was frankly and without disguise the organization of the slave-owning class for the purpose of maintaining their authority over their slaves. The slaves themselves, as stated in the preceding chapter, were not members of the state, and there was no pretense that the state was "the body of the whole people." "The ancient state," says David G. Ritchie, "existed for the citizen and not for the unenfranchised multitudes, who were mere means to the state's existence and no part of the state itself. The Greek state existed for the few; the modern state professes to exist for all — and may do so some day in reality." [1]

With the gradual change of economic conditions and social relations, the state has steadily modified its outward garb, but its true functions and inner mechanism have largely remained unchanged. The state has at all times been the instrument of the possessing classes; its chief function has always been to maintain the existing order, i.e., the supremacy of the ruling classes and the dependence of the non-possessing classes, and even to-day it is the privilege of the classes in power "to make laws and to levy taxes," while it is the duty of the poor to obey the laws and to pay the taxes.

The socialist definition of the state as an organization of the ruling classes for the maintenance of the exploited

[1] "The Principle of State Interference," London, 1902, p. 101.

classes in a condition of dependence, is thus entirely correct in substance.

But in connection with this definition another factor must be considered. The ruling classes of every period are created by the prevalent economic conditions of that period and they change with the change in these conditions. The slave-owning class was superseded in history by the class of feudal landlords, and the latter by the modern bourgeoisie, and with the accession of every new class of rulers the character and constitution of the state assumed a different aspect. These changes are rarely distinguishable by definite lines of demarcation. As a rule they take place gradually and are accompanied by protracted and obstinate struggles between the declining and rising classes, and it is not always easy to determine which of the two contending classes is the ruling class. In such periods of transition the state reflects the indefinite character of the social and economic conditions, and while in the main it always serves the interests of the class temporarily in power, it frequently makes important concessions to the rebellious classes. Thus the state of the fourteenth century was a feudal state, pure and simple, without any admixture of foreign elements; but the state of the seventeenth century, while still feudal in its main characteristics, already presented many elements of bourgeois power. And similarly, the state of a century and even half a century ago was an unalloyed bourgeois state, while the present-day state already shows deep inroads made in its substance and functions by the rising class of wage workers.

Under the pressure of the socialist and labor movement in all civilized countries, the state has acquired a new significance as an instrument of social and economic reform.

H

Such reforms have already demonstrated the ability of the state to curb the industrial autocracy of the ruling classes and to protect the workers from excessive exploitation by their employers.

The modern state, originally the tool in the hands of the capitalist class for the exploitation of the workers, is gradually coming to be recognized by the latter as a most potent instrument for the modification and ultimate abolition of the capitalist class rule.   In the general scheme of socialism, the state has, therefore, the very important mission of paving the way for the transition from present conditions to socialism.   The state in that rôle is generally styled in the literature of socialism the "period of transition," or the "transitional state." Beyond it lies the pure socialist order.

Does that order still admit of the existence of a state, or must the state, as the product of class divisions in society, fall with the disappearance of those class divisions as asserted by Engels and his followers?

At the first glance the proposition seems almost axiomatic — with the removal of the cause, the effect must fail. But on closer analysis the question seems by no means free from doubt. A social institution may be called into life by certain conditions and for certain purposes, but may gradually adapt itself to new and entirely different conditions and purposes. In fact, the history of our civilization is replete with instances of social, political, religious and legal institutions which have long survived their original creating causes, and in an altered form have shown great vitality under new conditions. The modern state exhibits many features that seem to indicate just such adaptability and vitality. The state, which came into being solely as an instrument of class repression, has gradually, and especially within the last centuries, assumed other important social functions, functions in which it largely represents society as a whole, and not any particular class of it. Instances of such functions of the modern state may be found in the system of public education, sanitary and health regulations, and in the institutions of police and criminal justice to the extent to which they secure the personal safety and security of all citizens.

It is true, as Menger [1] observes, that these functions constitute but a very small part of the activity of the state, and are as a rule relegated to its subordinate organs, such as municipalities, etc.; but it is equally true that these generally useful functions are claiming and receiving ever greater attention from the state, and that under a system of socialism they are certain to receive an immense extension.

If we realize that the socialist commonwealth must of necessity be charged with the direction, regulation or control of at least its principal industries, and with the care of its old and decrepit, sick, invalid and orphaned members, we shall readily see that the socialist organization will have to be something more than a mere "administration of things," — it will in all likelihood be a quite definitely organized society.

But, it may be objected, a socialist society will be free from the element of coercion; hence it will not be a state in the true sense of the term.

Let us consider this objection.

For the purposes of public works, health, safety and relief, the socialist commonwealth will need vast material

[1] Anton Menger, "Neue Staatslehre," 2d Edition, Jena, 1904, p. 20.

resources, probably more than the modern state, and these resources, in whatever form and under whatever designation, can come only from the wealth-producing members of the commonwealth — thus there must be a direct or indirect tax on the labor or income of the citizen. The collection of this tax, the direction of the industries and the regulation of the relations between the citizens, will require some laws and some rules or instruments for their enforcement; hence even the element of coercion cannot be entirely absent in a socialist society, at least not as far as the human mind can at present conceive. The socialist society as conceived by modern socialists differs, of course, very radically from the modern state in form and substance. It is not a class state, it does not serve any part of the population and does not rule any other part of the population; it represents the interests of the entire community, and it is for the benefit of the entire community that it levies taxes and makes and enforces laws. It is not the slaveholding state, nor the feudal state, nor the state of the bourgeoisie, — it is a socialist state, but a state nevertheless, and since little or nothing can be gained by inventing a new term, we shall hereafter designate the proposed organized socialist society as the Socialist State.

The Transitional State

Modern socialists recognize that social institutions are not the results of arbitrary choice, but of historical growth. When the ever working forces of industrial evolution have created new economic interests and social relations, the political forms of society must be modified to meet these changes, and when these new interests and relations become incompatible with the very basis of the existing social system, that system is bound to give way to a more adequate order. The socialists contend that the present system of individual ownership in the large and social means of production, and the system of industrial competition based on such individual ownership, have become or are fast becoming incompatible with the interests of an ever growing majority of the population and with the progress of industry itself. They perceive a tendency in the modern industrial development towards the collective ownership of these means of production and the socialization of industries; they see the public necessity of such transformation, and advocate and demand its accomplishment.

That is the whole of the socialist program, and it is certainly wide enough. The transformation of the means of production from private to public ownership is by no means a simple task. It is not reasonable to suppose that the possessing classes, the owners of the land, the mines, railroads and factories, the financiers and capitalists of all descriptions, will some fine day voluntarily surrender all their privileges and possessions to the people, nor is it likely that the transformation will be accomplished by one single and simple decree of the victorious proletariat all over the civilized world. More likely the process of transformation will be complicated and diversified, and will be marked by a series of economic and social reforms and legislative measures tending to divest the ruling classes of their monopolies, privileges and advantages, step by step, until they are practically shorn of the power to exploit their fellow-men; i.e., until all the important means of production have passed into collective ownership and all the principal industries are reorganized on the basis of socialist coöperation. The proposed measures that are expected to effect this eventual transformation constitute the "immediate" or "transitional" demands of socialism, and are part of the general socialist program, each socialist party emphasizing those points which are of more immediate importance in view of the social and political conditions of its own country at any given time. The measures thus most generally advocated by the socialists are: universal suffrage and equal political rights for men and women; the initiative, referendum, proportional representation in legislative bodies, and the right of recall of representatives by their constituents; greater autonomy for the municipalities and limitation of the powers and functions of the central government; the abolition of standing armies; progressive reduction of the hours of labor and increase of wages; state employment of the unemployed; state insurance of workingmen in case of accidents and sickness; old age pensions for workingmen; state provisions for all orphans and invalids; abolition of all indirect taxes; a progressive tax on property, income and inheritance; municipal ownership of all municipal utilities; state or national ownership of all mines, means of transportation and communication, and of all industries controlled by monopolies, trusts and combines, and the gradual assumption by the municipality or state of all other industries as soon as they reach a stage where they become susceptible of socialization.

The socialists, of course, do not anticipate that these measures will in all cases be adopted in their logical order and in the pristine purity of their original conception according to program, nor that they will be realized in all

countries with absolute uniformity. More likely the
course of the social transformation will be different in the
different countries, slow and methodic in some, rapid and
tempestuous in others, according to the historic conditions, the temperament of the people and the respective
strength and intelligence of the ruling classes and the proletariat in each case.   In the more democratic countries,
especially those in which the socialist and labor movements
constitute important political and social factors, the necessary transitional reforms, or at least a large part of them,
may be gradually conquered through the direct control
by the proletariat of important organs of the state, such
as municipalities or legislatures, or through the indirect
influence of the growing labor movement.   In other
countries the conquest of the public powers by the working
class may be accomplished by a violent insurrection.   The
wage workers may, in the words of Engels, "seize the
powers of the state" and establish a temporary "dictator-
ship of the proletariat."   Thus the transition from the
system of feudalism to the present order was accomplished
radically but peacefully in England, slowly and incom-
pletely in Germany, rapidly and violently in France.   But
violence is but an accident of the social revolution; it is
by no means its necessary accompaniment, and it has no
place in the socialist program.

And similarly silent is the socialist program on the
question whether the gradual expropriation of the possessing classes will be accomplished by a process of confiscation or by the method of compensation.   The greater
number of socialist writers incline towards the latter
assumption, but in that they merely express their individual present preferences.   Social development, and espe-

cially social revolutions, are not in the habit of consulting cut and dried theories evolved by philosophers of past generations, and social justice is more frequently a question of social expediency and class power. The French clergy was not compensated for the lands taken from it by the bourgeois revolution, and the Russian noblemen and American slave owners were not compensated upon the emancipation of their serfs and chattel slaves. It is not unlikely that in countries in which the social transformation will be accomplished peacefully, the state will compensate the expropriated proprietors, while every violent revolution will be followed by confiscation. The socialists are not much concerned about this issue. Their aim is the establishment of a state in which exploitation of man by man shall become impossible, and when private wealth has been robbed of the character of employing and exploiting capital, its possession by a number of individuals ceases to be a menacing factor in a socialist state.

The "transitional state" thus conceived cannot be bounded by fixed lines of demarcation either in its inception or its termination. As every other period of historical development, it is bound to overlap at both ends. A number of municipalities and states are already wholly or partly under socialist control. Many of the "transitional" reforms of socialism, political and social, have already been realized to some extent in the countries of Europe, America and Australia, and the conceded tendency of all modern legislation is toward the extension of such reforms. In this sense it may well be said that we are in the midst, or at any rate at the beginning, of the socialist "transitional state," although it would be impossible for us to say just when we entered it. And similarly difficult is it to fix the line between the so-called transitional state and the socialist state proper. Theoretically, the reign of pure socialism begins after the entire socialist program has been materialized and society has been reorganized entirely on the basis of coöperative production. But in reality, social ideals are rarely realized in perfect form, and just as the period of feudalism has left remnants of its institutions in a later order, and in some cases down to the present day, so, in all likelihood, many features of our present individualist order will long survive in a state, substantially and preponderatingly socialistic.

The Socialist State

The transition from the present order of individual wealth and competitive industry to a system of collective ownership and coöperative production, by whatever means and in whatever manner accomplished, is bound to be accompanied by very thoroughgoing changes in all relations of men, and by a decided remodeling of the entire social and political structure of society. These proposed changes, with the probable constitution, construction and workings of the "socialist state," have always offered an exceptionally fertile field for speculation.

The modern socialist movement made its first appearance towards the end of the eighteenth and the beginning of the nineteenth centuries, and its philosophy was largely influenced by the general ideological conceptions of that time. The first apostles of the new creed believed with their contemporaries that political and social institutions could be arbitrarily devised, tried, chosen, cast away, and substituted by others. They regarded the evils and shortcomings of modern society as flaws in the social struc-

ture, due to the carelessness of the "founders" of that
society, and saw the remedy for these evils in the simple
expedient of constructing a new society on a more rational
and equitable plan. The early socialist literature is,
therefore, replete with detailed and minute descriptions
of proposed social organizations wherein universal brother-
hood is the rule, bliss and prosperity are the heritage of
all, and justice reigns supreme. And as the authors of
these social utopias were not bound by material impediments and freely drew upon their fertile imaginations, their
schemes are more or less realistic or fantastic according
to their individual temperaments and bent of mind. The
most noteworthy representatives of this early school of
socialism are Morelly, Gabriel Mably, Charles Fourier,
Etienne Cabet, Robert Owen and Wilhelm Weitling.

But the detailed painting of the society of the future
or the "socialist state" is by no means confined to the
pioneers of modern socialist thought. The temptation to
evolve a ready and complete scheme of a new social order,
based on socialism, for the purpose of proving or refuting
the "feasibility" of the socialist ideal is so great, that
socialists and anti-socialists alike still very frequently
resort to that expedient. Conspicuous instances of such
society builders on the socialist side are Edward Bellamy
("Looking Backward"), William Morris ("News from
Nowhere") and Laurence Gronlund ("Coöperative Commonwealth"); while the opposite side is ably represented
by the merciless destroyers of the "socialist state" of the
types of Eugen Richter ("Sozialdemokratische Zukunftsbilder"), William Graham ("Socialism Old and New"),
Victor Cathrein ("Socialism: Its Theoretical Basis and
Practical Application"), and those latest valiant con-

querors of the Socialist Dragon, David M. Parry
("The Scarlet Empire") and W. H. Mallock. Nor can
it be said that the drawing of such detailed descriptions
of imaginary forms and workings of a socialist society is
altogether a waste of time; such pictures are not without
usefulness as food for reflection and interesting speculation,
and some of them no doubt contain sparks of true genius
which may perhaps even find practical application in times
to come. But all such descriptions are nevertheless mere
guesses for which none but their authors are responsible;
they are not part of the generally accepted socialist program or philosophy.

"Never," said the veteran leader of the German Social
Democracy, Wilhelm Liebknecht, on the occasion of the
debate in the Diet already alluded to, "never has our party
told the workingmen about a 'state of the future,' never
in any way other than as a mere utopia. If anybody says:
I picture to myself society after our program has been
realized, after wage labor has been abolished and the exploitation of men has ceased, in such or such a manner,
well and good; ideas are free, and everybody may conceive
the socialist state as he pleases. Whoever believes in it,
may do so, whoever does not, need not. These pictures
are but dreams, and social democracy has never understood them otherwise."

And it is difficult to see how any forecast of future conditions could be much more than a dream. If we look
back from the pinnacles of the twentieth century to conditions of the early part of the nineteenth century, we shall
be astounded at the unprecedented radical revolution
accomplished within the last hundred years in all domains
of our social, political and industrial life. The old pur-

suits, habits and views of our fathers have been mercilessly cast aside. New fields of endeavor have been explored, new truths discovered, new relations established, new worlds created. The globe has a vastly different aspect from that of a hundred years ago, and the nations that people it are vastly different beings. The modern man differs in all his habits and mode of life from his forefathers of but a few generations ago.

It will not be seriously contended that these present conditions could have been more or less accurately forecast and divined at the beginning of the present régime even by the most sagacious and best-informed social philosopher. For even if such a philosopher could reckon with the probable development of the forces then existing, he could certainly not take into account the tremendous effect of the new discoveries and inventions since made, the application of steam and electricity in the industrial processes, the introduction of the railroads, steamships, telegraphs, telephones, and the countless modern machines and contrivances which have served to revolutionize our entire system of production and communication and with it all our habits of life and thought. To the placid and rational philosopher of the beginning of the nineteenth century, an account of our present civilization would have been a much wilder and more incredible dream than the most fantastic socialist utopia seems to-day to our wise bourgeois philosopher.

And still the task of the man who might have assumed a century ago to forecast present conditions would have been mere child's play in comparison with that of the dreamer who undertakes to-day to describe the details of the life and organization of the "socialist state."

The forces of industrial development have by no means reached their zenith, they are still multiplying and multiplying in an ever accelerating ratio. The wider the basis of existing industrial forces, the greater the rate of economic progress; this is the simple working of the theory of geometrical progression as daily demonstrated in our industrial life. The last fifty years have witnessed more industrial progress than the three centuries preceding them, and the coming fifty years will perhaps eclipse the last five hundred years.

The task of the would-be socialist forecaster is besides greatly complicated by another element. The developments of the last century, immense and radical as they have been, have not very materially affected the basic principles of modern industrial organization. But the industrial development of the future, as conceived by socialists, will consist not only in the natural increase and multiplication of the productive forces, but also in a radical reorganization of the methods of production and distribution, and the resultant changes must thus of necessity be more thoroughgoing and less calculable.

And finally, all speculation on the nature and aspect of the socialist state suffers from another inherent weakness. They tacitly assume that the "socialist state" is a fixed and definite phase of social development, whereas in fact it is anything but that. Socialism stands for an order of society in which private ownership in the means of production has substantially given way to a system of collective ownership. Such an order of things may quite conceivably be established in some of the most progressive countries in a short time, say within twenty-five years — our era is one of rapid developments, Such a country would in that case quite properly claim the designation of a "socialist state." But with the establishment of socialism, the general progress of that country would not halt, and the succeeding centuries would continue to change its institutions, life and customs. The socialist state in its maturity will be an entirely different organization from the socialist state in its infancy, and similarly the socialist organization of one country may be radically different from that of the other, and still the social prophet must have in mind a fixed and uniform "socialist state."

Modern socialists indulge but little in fantastic forecasts of the future order of things; they fully realize the general futility of such speculations for the practical purposes of the socialist movement. The socialist criticism is directed against existing evils, the socialist program is a program of immediate relief, and the socialist demands are made on the present state. The socialists are concerned only with the immediate effects of their proposed measures on the welfare of the present population, and if they venture at all to inquire into the future, they limit their inquiries entirely to such immediate effects, to conditions "on the day after the revolution." Such inquiries are very useful as serving to illustrate the constructive sides of the socialist philosophy.

Much valuable work on such lines has recently been done by Karl Kautsky ("The Social Revolution," Second Part), and Anton Menger ("Neue Staatslehre"), and very creditable attempts in the same direction have also been made by Annie Besant and G. Bernard Shaw (in the "Fabian Essays"), Oswald Koehler ("Der Sozialdemokratische Staat"), B. Malon (in "Précis de Socialisme"), and the American writer, John Spargo ("Socialism"). And as the socialist movement gains in power and the socialist ideal becomes more realistic, the socialist thinkers are bound to bestow greater and more serious attention to the elaboration of that feature of their philosophy.

The great distinction between the works of these contemporary socialist writers and their utopian precursors is, that while the latter based their speculations on an entirely arbitrary conception of an ideal state, the former take for their starting point the present actual state. They realize that the so-called "socialist state," as far as we can conceive it to-day, is nothing but the present state with such modifications as the realization of the proposed socialist reforms naturally and necessarily imply, and their forecast is but an analysis of such probable changes. But with all this candor and caution it is still impossible to arrive at scientific and indisputable conclusions as to conditions of even the immediate future. The conclusions of each author are bound to contain some element of speculation and to reflect to a large extent his individual views and inclinations. It is in that spirit and with that understanding that the following chapters are offered.

Production and Distribution of Wealth Under Socialism

The organization of wealth production under socialism offers but little difficulty. The prevalent methods of production, as indicated in a previous chapter, have already become largely social in many important industries.

In the modern corporations, trusts and other combines, the capitalists have created industrial organizations very much akin to the socialist ideal, and have demonstrated the feasibility and advantages of coöperative and planful production on a large scale. By the simple process of combining the greater number of plants in a given industry under one head, discarding the less efficient of them and strengthening the more important, the trusts have largely eliminated the element of waste in production; and by consolidating the management and supervision of the work, and perfecting the specialization and division of labor, they have vastly increased the productivity of the latter. The state, with its larger powers and resources, will be able to increase the advantages of trustified production very considerably.

But a socialist régime, once having assumed the administration of the trusts, will be bound to change the nature and to extend the benefits of these institutions still further. The modern trusts, while social in their methods of work, are not public, but private institutions, and are operated entirely for the benefit of their individual owners.

It is not in the interests of the individual trust magnates to extend production beyond the limits of the present demand; the general purchasing power of the consumers remaining unchanged, such an increased output could only result in a decline of prices. The policy of the trusts is, therefore, on the whole, to limit production. A socialist administration, on the other hand, has a vital interest in extending production in order to enhance the national wealth and to provide employment for a larger number of its members. Since it is not producing for profit, the effect of an increased output on the price of the commodity will not enter in its calculations, and since the purchasing power of the population will be increased in proportion to the growth of productivity, there will be no danger of an industrial crisis.

The members of a socialist state, furthermore, will · be

interested in such trustified industries not only as consumers, but also as employees, and hence they will naturally introduce such reforms in the management of these industries as will benefit them in the latter capacity. Under capitalism the greater productivity of labor in trustified industries is accompanied by loss of work for large portions of former employees. Under socialism it will necessarily lead to a progressive diminution of their hours of labor. Under capitalism the profits of the trust magnates are the sole aim and motive of production, and the safety and welfare of their employees are of but secondary importance. Under socialism production will be carried on principally for the benefit of the producers themselves, and it is reasonable to expect that every known device will be applied to make industry safe, pleasant and attractive.

The modern trusts, thus transformed into coöperative enterprises on a large scale, will in all likelihood become the starting point of the socialist system of industrial organization, and the system will be extended from one industry to the other as fast as the conditions will permit. But this will probably not be, at least for a long time to come, the exclusive form of industrial organization. There are certain industries dependent on purely personal skill, such as the various arts and crafts, that from their very nature are not susceptible of socialization, and other industries, such as small farming, that will, at least for many years to come, not be proper objects for socialization. These may continue to exist in a socialist society as individual enterprises side by side with the larger coöperative works.

On the whole, however, it is safe to assume that by far the greater and most important part of wealth production will be conducted by coöperative establishments. In the

I

countries of the most advanced industrial development, the large plants employ even to-day the greater part of the wage-working population, and there are but few important industries that are not ripe for concentration and consolidation. And since the large coöperative establishments, with their natural economies and advantages, will hold out greater attractions to the workers than the majority of the small individual enterprises, there will probably be but few who will choose to remain outside of the prevalent industrial organization.

The rational organization of labor, the elimination of duplicate plants, of the "middlemen" in industry and commerce and of other waste entailed in a system of competition, the disappearance of all workless "incomes" and of all the purely parasitic types who are to-day maintained and supported by the competitive system or maintained for the special interests and comforts of the ruling and leisure classes, — all these changes necessarily involved in a system of socialism, will increase the productive forces of society and augment the national wealth immensely.

How will that wealth be distributed? With this question we have approached what is considered as the crucial point of socialism by the opponents of that philosophy. The impracticability or impossibility of the "socialist scheme of wealth distribution" is the burden of most of the "scientific" refutations of the socialist theory, and curiously enough most of these criticisms are based on a careless reading of the great theoretician of modern socialism, Karl Marx.

In common with Smith, Ricardo and other representatives of the classical school of political economy, Marx holds that the value of a commodity is determined by the labor time expended in its production, the labor time in question being defined as "the labor time socially necessary to produce an article under the normal conditions of production with the average degree of skill and intensity prevalent at that time."[1] This simple statement of fact has been almost uniformly interpreted by the astute critics of Marx as the socialist "plan of distribution," and many valuable reams of paper have been consumed in ingenious objections to that plan.[2]

In fact, however, Marx occupied himself just as little with the distribution of wealth in a future socialist state of society as Darwin occupied himself with the ultimate physical type of man. As a true man of science, he limited his researches to the past developments and existing facts and tendencies. In formulating the labor theory of value, Marx simply stated a fact, a law applicable to the present system of producing wealth — nothing else.

"Marx," says Frederick Engels, his foremost interpreter, "deals only with the determination of the value of *commodities*, that is to say, with the value of articles which are produced in a society consisting of private producers, by each private producer for his individual account and for the purpose of exchange. This value in its definite historic meaning is created and measured by human labor embodied in the separate commodities. . . . It is this simple fact, daily enacted before our own eyes in the modern capitalist society, which Marx states. . . . Whatever other values may be mentioned,

[1] Karl Marx, "Capital," English Edition, Vol. I, p. 11.
[2] See William Graham, "Socialism New and Old"; Victor Cathrein, "Socialism: Its Theoretical Basis and Practical Application"; Schaeffle, "Quintessence of Socialism."

this much is certain, that Marx is not concerned with these things, but only with the value of commodities; and that in the whole chapter on Value in his 'Capital' there is not the slightest hint whether and to what extent *this theory of value is applicable to other forms of society.*"[1]

And Karl Kautsky adds: —

"There could be no greater error than to consider that one of the tasks of a socialist society is to see to it that the law of value is brought into perfect operation, and that only equivalent values are exchanged. The law of value is rather a law peculiar to a society of producers for exchange."[2]

But what then, may be asked, is the socialist plan of distribution of wealth?

The plain answer to this inquiry is: The socialists do not offer a cut and dried plan of wealth distribution.

As a proposition of abstract justice and fairness there is no reason why any discrimination at all should be made in the distribution of the necessaries and material comforts of life between the members of the community. The increased productivity of labor and the consequent augmentation of wealth are due to the concerted efforts of men in all fields of endeavor, physical and mental, in generations past as well as present, and the precise share of each individual in the general wealth of the nation is altogether insusceptible of measurement.

It must be granted that some individuals are stronger, wiser, more gifted and skillful than others. But what of that? Is there any moral ground for punishing the

[1] "Herrn Eugen Dühring's Umwälzung der Wissenschaften," pp. 209, 210.

[2] Karl Kautsky, "The Social Revolution," Chicago, 1903, p. 129.

cripple, the invalid, the decrepit, the imbecile, the unfortunate step-children of nature, by reducing their
rations of food or clothing? Is there any moral sanction for rewarding the man of physical strength or mental
gifts by special allowances from the storehouse of human
society? Do humane parents discriminate in that manner
between their strong and weak, their fortunate and unfortunate children? Is the title of the stronger and "abler"
to greater material reward based on equity, or is it rather
a survival of the barbaric "fist right" of the dark ages?

To the socialists the old communistic motto: "From
each according to his ability, to each according to his
needs," generally appears as the ideal rule of distribution
in an enlightened human society, and quite likely the time
will come when that high standard will be generally
adopted by civilized communities.

The productivity of labor is increasing with such
phenomenal rapidity that we may well foresee a time when
society will, with comparative ease, produce enough to
afford to all its members, without distinction, all necessaries and even luxuries of life, and when there will be
just as little justification for a quarrel over the method of
distribution of material wealth as there is to-day for a
quarrel over the use of air or water. To the wise skeptics
the statement may seem extravagant, but when we compare the wealth and productivity of modern countries to-
day with those of half a century ago, we shall easily realize
that we are by no means dealing with pure utopian dreams.

But just and feasible as this ideal method of distribution may be, it is to-day nevertheless a mere ideal, a hope
to be realized in the more or less distant future. It is not
a part of the present program of the socialist movement.

Modern socialists recognize that the methods of distribution under the new order of things must take for their starting point the present methods, *i.e.*, payments of varying wages or salaries for services rendered.

Here again we run counter to a deep-rooted popular conception or rather misconception of the socialist program. One of the pet schemes of the early socialist experimenters was the substitution of "labor certificates" or "time certificates" for money. By this means they expected to fix the value of each commodity with reference to the labor time contained in it as it were automatically, to eliminate the "unearned increment" of the capitalist and the profit of the middleman and to give to each producer the full equivalent of his labor. The scheme was on a par with that of the "equitable labor exchange banks," the communistic societies and the other social experiments of the utopian socialists. They all proceeded from the belief that a small group of men could dissociate themselves from the rest of society, establish a miniature socialist commonwealth, and induce their fellow-men to follow their example by the practical demonstration of its excellence. Modern socialists have long discarded all miniature social experimentations and arbitrary social devices as utopian and puerile, and the continued dissertations of many distinguished critics of socialism about the "socialist plan" of the suppression of money and the abolition of money payments for services, only go to demonstrate how little they are abreast with the developments of socialist thought.

Money and wages are both the products of a certain phase of economic development. Neither was known before the rise of private property, and in all likelihood both will at some time in the distant future lose their usefulness and disappear. But these reflections again belong to the sphere of dreams of the golden future, — they have no room in a sober and realistic program of social reform.

"Money," says Kautsky, "is the simplest means known up to the present time which makes it possible in as complicated a mechanism as that of the modern productive process, with its tremendous far-reaching division of labor, to secure the circulation of products and their distribution to the individual members of society. It is the means which make it possible for each one to satisfy his necessities according to his individual inclination (to be sure within the bounds of his economic power). As a means to such circulation, money will be found indispensable until something better is discovered." [1]

Incentive Under Socialism

Next to the assertion that it would curtail individual liberty, the most popular objection to the proposed system of socialism is that every such system is bound to paralyze social progress by depriving the individual initiative of the incentive to exert itself usefully in behalf of society.

This argument assumes: first, that individual initiative is the chief lever of human progress, and second, that the love of material gain is the principal, if not the only, motive which impels men to strive for the highest degree of excellence in the various fields of private and public endeavor. Since socialism is based on a system of more or less equal and secured incomes, and excludes the possibility of large pecuniary rewards, it is argued that under such a system the man of genius will have no inducement

[1] "The Social Revolution," p. 129.

to exert his utmost skill, the common mortal will work reluctantly and indifferently, and social stagnation will inevitably result. Let us examine this argument.

What constitutes modern civilization is the sum total of all our achievements in industry, in science, in the arts, and in the various organs and institutions of public life and activities which are comprised under the general designation of politics.

There is no doubt that a large share of these achievements is due to the individual initiative and the creative genius of exceptional men. But let us not overestimate the importance of this factor in social progress. Our civilization owes on the whole much more to the collective endeavors of man than to the individual genius of men, and the general improvement in our culture, refinement of work, and mode of life, is vastly more the result of a process of social growth to which the large multitudes of human beings have for many generations contributed their unknown and imperceptible mites, than the merit of the great individual inventors, discoverers or leaders. "Social achievement," says Professor Ward, "has consisted in the establishment of a social order under and within which individual achievement can go on and civilization is made possible." [1]

The art of book printing, the use of gunpowder, and the application of steam and electricity have all been invented or perfected by individual geniuses, but the more substantial arts of plowing, cooking, tailoring and housebuilding have been invented, developed and perfected by the human race as a whole. What is still more significant, however, is this, that while the collective inventions belong to an ear-

[1] Lester F. Ward, "Applied Sociology," Boston, 1906, p. 38.

lier age and the individual inventions to a later age, we have undoubtedly reached a period which is characterized by the process of the gradual passing of the individual inventor, initiator or hero, and of the return to a system of social progress through collective effort.

And nowhere is this process more distinctly noticeable than in the most vital sphere of human activity, industry. Industrial development depends almost entirely upon the efficient organization of the mechanism of production (which includes a proper division of labor, organization of management, and use of effective machinery), and of transportation and exchange, and in all these domains collective achievements are rapidly supplanting individual enterprise. The modern mass production based on the factory system forces the organization and division of labor along lines practically indicated by the machine; and while there is still much room left for the exercise of human ingenuity in the arrangement and rearrangement of details, such arrangements and rearrangements are in most cases the result of simple experience, almost of mathematical calculation, and not the work of an exceptional genius. Nor are the other modern industrial categories, the corporations and trusts, the stock exchanges and banks, the system of credit and the national and international markets, the individual invention of an industrial genius. They are the products and forms of gradual industrial development; the entire industrial community, employers and employees, have imperceptibly built them up in the course of centuries, and they are still busily engaged in the process of developing and perfecting these institutions without marked individual initiative or leadership. And in the domain of the invention and perfection of machinery, this peculiar territory of the individual genius, the element of personal initiative is gradually and steadily receding to the background.

The laws of mechanics are being explored with ever increasing accuracy and planfulness for the practical requirements of industry, and the new improvements in the tools of production are now but rarely in the nature of great and unexpected inventions; more often they are merely the successful solutions of preconceived problems by means of well-defined scientific methods. The hustling, up-to-date experimental laboratory is rapidly crowding out the dreamy inventive genius. What we call "Edison" to-day is not the Thomas A. Edison who early in life made the astounding inventions in telegraphy, but the well-equipped, well-organized electrical laboratory at West Orange, New Jersey, with the number of trained scientific workers engaged in it.

And what has been said of the industrial process applies with almost equal force to the domain of science: the factory system with its specialization, division of labor, and collective production, is the recognized form of modern scientific research almost as much as it is the form of the modern manufacture of market commodities. Scientific work is, as a rule, not done by individuals but by groups of workers; not at home, but in laboratories, clinics and libraries, and scientific discoveries like mechanical inventions are most often the results of planned and collective labor. Left to his own individual resources, the modern scientist would be almost helpless.

Nor does our public life form an exception to this general tendency of our times. The great individual legislators, as Moses, Solon, Lycurgus, and even Napoleon,

have been superseded by the many-headed bodies of popular representatives in the legislative chambers; the great
free-lance statesmen have made room for the chosen leaders
of strong political parties, and the success of a modern
battle depends not so much on the military genius of the
individual commander as on the proper organization and
equipment of his army. In the recent Russo-Japanese
war the demoralized Russian army and navy did not
produce a single military or naval "genius," whereas in the
well-organized and well-equipped Japanese army and navy
every general and admiral was a "hero." In one domain
after the other the individual genius and arbiter of human
destiny, the "hero" of Carlyle is being dethroned and
subordinated to the collective human fraternity. The
domain of the arts is to-day practically the last resting
place of the " superman."

Individual initiative and talent thus by no means play
such a determining part in the world's progress as the
critics of socialism claim. But on the other hand the socialists readily admit that they play some part. There
always were and probably always will be persons of extraordinary gifts and abilities who may contribute vastly
more to the store of human welfare and happiness than the
average man. Without them the world would probably
not relapse into a state of barbarism, but it will fare much
better with them and their services. But what of it?
Is there any real danger that under a system of socialism
these superior individuals would disappear or refuse to
give the benefit of their special talents to society? Is the
striving for wealth actually the most powerful incentive of
the creative genius? The theory seems plausible enough
as regards the leader in industry, the business man, but

how about the scientist, the artist, the statesman? This is a fruitful source for reflection and comparison.

The manufacturer, banker or other active capitalist undoubtedly strives for material wealth. But wealth is for him only secondarily, if at all, a means of procuring physical or intellectual enjoyment. To him wealth represents power, and above all, it is the test of his success in his chosen vocation. To say of a man engaged in industry or commerce that he has made a large fortune is to say that he has proved himself efficient and successful in his career; to say of him that he has lost his fortune is equivalent to asserting that he has proved himself the inferior of his rivals, that he is inefficient, and that his life work has been a failure.

The man of science, on the other hand, would gain or lose but little in the esteem of his contemporaries and in his own self-respect by the gain or loss of a fortune. The test of his success is not the amount of money he has made, but the extent of the recognition accorded to him and his work by the learned fraternity. Scholastic honors and academic titles are to him what money is to the business man; his incentive is not the love of money but the desire of recognition.

Again, the reward of the artist is neither money nor academic titles. As an artist he strives primarily for public applause and glory, for these are the true tests of his success and efficiency in the side of his existence which he values most, his art.

So likewise, the statesman cares most for influence and authority, the soldier for military honors and preferment, and the priest for the respect and reverence of his fellowmen.

Of course, it may well happen, and no doubt often does happen, that the scientist, the artist, the statesman, the soldier and the priest are anything but indifferent to material wealth. They may prefer an easy and comfortable existence, they may sometimes be goaded on to create by sheer poverty and want, and they may even occasionally be grasping and greedy. But these will then be features entirely independent of their respective gifts and talents, and by no means a stimulus to their best application. "It is not true," again observes Ward, "that men of genius depend upon adversity and dire necessity as a spur to activity. This is all a popular illusion which the entire history of human achievement disproves and should dispel. The instinct of workmanship, if it be in no other form than fear of the hell of ennui, is the great and unremitting spur that drives and goads all men to action." [1]

The real incentive moving all men to bring forth the best that is in them is just that best that is in them: their desire is to excel and to earn the recognition of their fellowmen in such a form in which such recognition is most fitly expressed. And the business man, whose apparently sole motive is money making, forms no exception to this rule. To-day, when industries are conducted for private gain and in competition between the individual capitalists, accumulated individual wealth is, as we have seen, the only measure of the business man's efficiency and success. But when the industrial organization passes into the hands of society and becomes a part of its general administration, the distinction between service in that branch of the government and any other branch of it

[1] "Applied Sociology," p. 245.

will naturally cease. The director of industries will become a "statesman" just as any other public functionary, and will be just as much moved by motives of a more ideal nature as the latter. Our post office has been nationalized, and its operation has become an administrative function, while the express business of the country has remained the individual enterprise of competing capitalists. The salary of the Postmaster-General, who is a public officer, is a mere pittance in comparison with the revenues of the head of one of our large express companies, and still the government has been able to secure for the administration of its Post-Office Department men at least as capable as the highly paid managers of the express companies.

A socialist society will not destroy the individual incentive in industrial life; it will merely change its character by substituting a more ideal standard for the present standard of pecuniary gain.

And as for the scientist, artist and statesman, a socialist régime cannot possibly affect their creative work adversely by cutting down their money reward, since that reward, as we have shown, never was their prime incentive. The golden age of Athens knew nothing of immense fortunes and heavy money rewards, but it produced a sculpture, drama, literature and architecture never surpassed in history.

"To undertake to state the influence which the communistic elements in Athenian life had upon the extraordinary development of Athenian art and literature in the fifth century before our era," says Professor Seymour, "would be dangerous. But any reader may see that the artist and dramatist were not stimulated by any material rewards or prizes. Æschylus had no income whatever, so far as we know, from his plays, and the architect's pay was only twice that of the stonecutter." [1] Nor, we may add, did the great statesmen and orators of that period, as Pericles and Demosthenes, receive large pecuniary compensation.

On the other hand, there is every reason to believe that a socialist régime will offer larger opportunities for the unfolding and development of true genius and for its pure artistic exercise than present society does.

Our modern capitalist society does all in its power to suppress genius and ability, but does not entirely succeed. Capitalism reduces one part of the population to the condition of uncultured, exhausted wage slaves, and forces the other into a wild, all-absorbing race for material wealth; still the exceptional gifts of some break through these formidable obstacles. Capitalism subverts all art and science to the worship of the golden calf; it subordinates the beautiful to the practical, the true to the profitable, and strips life of all poetry and noble inspiration; still, art and science are not entirely dead. The capitalist manufacturer cheats the inventor, the capitalist publisher robs the author, the capitalist art dealer exploits the painter, — the inventor dies in the poorhouse, the author and artist live in beggary; but the inventor continues inventing, the scientist continues studying and the artist continues creating.

Under a state of socialism education and culture will be equally accessible to all, and the citizens will have more leisure to cultivate their gifts. What greater stimulus

[1] "Socialism and Communism in Greece," by Thomas D. Seymour, LL.D., in *Harper's Monthly Magazine* for November, 1907.

can human society offer for the full development of the fine arts and true sciences?

The elaborate and painstaking investigations of Odin, Galton, de Candolle and Jacoby, all collated by Mr. Ward in his scholarly work on "Applied Sociology," show conclusively that modern economic conditions smother scores of native genius for every one they allow to mature. Analyzing the economic conditions of 619 well-known men of letters between the years 1300 and 1825, de Candolle finds that 562 of them had been brought up and had lived in ease and material comfort, while only 57 had spent their youth in comparative poverty; and M. Odin, commenting on the results of this analysis, observes: "This means by the sole fact of economic conditions in the midst of which they grew up the children of the families in easy circumstances had at least forty to fifty more chances of making themselves a name in letters than those who belonged to poor families or to families of insecure economic position." [1]

But, it is argued, all this may be very well as far as the men of exceptional genius and abilities are concerned, but how about the plain ordinary workingman, the "common laborer" who can neither expect the special homage or approval of his fellow-men for his obscure work nor, under a system of advanced socialism, a commensurate pecuniary reward — what will be his incentive to work conscientiously and efficiently?

This question introduces a distinct feature of present conditions into a state of society based on an entirely different order. To-day our industries are managed by

[1] A. Odin, "Genèse des grands hommes," etc., Paris, 1895, p. 529, quoted in Ward's "Applied Sociology," p. 204.

individual capitalists for their private profit and with but
little regard for the health, comfort or needs of the employees; work is exhausting, monotonous, repulsive and
often dangerous. In a system of coöperative labor, the
workingman will naturally be considered above everything else; his hours of labor will be shortened as much
as practicable, his occupation will be more varied, the
dangers of employment will be reduced to a minimum,
the workshop will be clean, bright and hygienic; in a
word, labor will be made attractive.

"Because," observes J. Stern, "the workingman considers as a burden the work which ties him to a mechanical, monotonous and cheerless occupation in squalid
workshops during inhumanly long hours and for which
he receives starvation wages; because the office clerk
prefers to play truant rather than to busy himself the
entire day with matters that do not appeal to his mind
or heart; because men are reluctant in the exercise of
a calling which was forced on them against their wishes
and inclinations; because generally the present class state
imposes on most persons activities which have no charms
for them and only hold out the promise of pecuniary reward — because of all that — are we to infer that the
human being is generally disposed to laziness rather than
to industry? Does not, on the contrary, even the most
superficial examination of persons of all ages and classes
show that love of action, the irresistible desire to unfold
one's strength, to ' do things ' and to create, is implanted
in every healthy human individual, and that to the normal
person nothing is more unbearable than inaction? . . .
In a million of ways the love of action reveals itself as a
mighty power in human life, from early childhood even

K

to old age. Whence comes the passion for all kinds of sports but from the mighty instinct of action? Why do people voluntarily choose strenuous and even dangerous activities, as is shown by numerous instances in life and history? This fear, that without the whip of poverty or force mankind would lapse into a state of inaction, reminds us of the humorous prophecy upon the advent of the bicycle and automobile that men would hereafter have little occasion for the use of their legs, and the latter would become weak, short and crooked like those of the dachshund."[1]

And furthermore, one of the chief causes operating to-day to make labor disagreeable is the lack of variety in occupation.

"The desire for freedom of choice and for change of occupation is deeply implanted in human nature," says August Bebel. "Just as constant and regular repetition without variation will at length make the best food disliked, an employment that is daily repeated becomes as monotonous as a treadmill; it blunts and relaxes. The man performs a given task, because he must, but without enthusiasm or enjoyment. Now, every one possesses a number of capabilities and inclinations, which only require to be roused, developed, and put into action to give the most satisfactory results and enable their possessor to unfold his whole and real being. The socialistic community will offer the fullest opportunity for gratifying this need of variety. The enormous increase in productive power, combined with growing simplification in the

[1] J. Stern, "Der Zukunftsstaat — Thesen über den Sozialismus, sein Wesen, seine Durchführbarkeit und Zweckmässigkeit," Berlin, 1906, p. 30.

process of production, will permit a considerable limitation in the time of labor, while it facilitates the acquirement of mechanical skill in a number of different branches." [1]

The Political Structure of the Socialist State

We cannot, of course, attempt a detailed forecast of the political organization of the future socialist state without embarking upon the domain of speculation. But we may, nevertheless, profitably endeavor to discern the bold outlines of the political structure of the socialist state, at least in the early periods of its existence, provided we always bear in mind the following two fundamental propositions: —

1. The machinery of government of every state must be adapted to the character and objects of such state.

The modern state is the state of the capitalist extracting profits from the working members of the community, and the modern government is, in the words of Karl Marx, "but a committee for managing the common affairs of the capitalist class."

The socialist state, on the other hand, is a classless state of coöperative producers, and its government must be a "committee for the managing of the common affairs" of the members of that state. In other words, the main functions of the socialist state will be of an industrial character, and since there will be no separate economic classes with fixed and conflicting interests, the state will represent the citizens. It will be a democratic state.

2. Every new political organization evolves from the

[1] "Woman," p. 134.

organization immediately preceding it and retains all of its features except such as have become useless or incompatible with the new order of things.

The French Revolution has not done away with the entire political structure evolved under the monarchy; it has merely modified it in a few substantial points. The United States has retained more features of its pre-Revolutionary political organization than it has introduced new ones since the Declaration of Independence.

The socialist state will probably, on the whole, retain the present forms of political organization with such changes as will be necessitated by the altered character and objects of organized society.

Most likely the present geographical limits of the various states will be left substantially intact. The political ideal of the early socialist writers was a globe studded with small autonomous communities. Thus Fourier's political unit is the Phalanx composed of about two thousand inhabitants, and his scheme of political reorganization contemplates the division of our planet into just two millions of such Phalanxes, each economically and politically independent of the rest. It is a noteworthy fact that the proposed utopian communities grow in size as the authors come nearer to our present era.

"The socialist commonwealth," observes Kautsky on this point, "is not the product of an arbitrary figment of the brain, but a necessary product of economic development, and it is understood more clearly as that development becomes more apparent. Hence the size of that commonwealth is also not arbitrary, but is conditioned upon the stage of that development at a given time. The higher the economic development, the greater the division of labor, the larger the size of the commonwealth. . . .

"The division of labor is carried on ever further; ever more do the several industries apply themselves to the production of special articles only, but those for the whole world; ever larger becomes the size of these establishments, some of which count their workmen by the thousands. Under such conditions a community able to satisfy all its needs and embracing all requisite industries must have dimensions very different from those of the socialist colonies planned at the beginning of the last century. Among the social organizations in existence to-day, there is but one that possesses the requisite dimensions, and may be used as the framework for the establishment and development of the socialist commonwealth, and that is the *modern state.*" [1]

The expectation that the proposed socialist commonwealth will be co-extensive with the modern state, and the assumption that the state will be charged with the management and direction of the industries, have led to the widespread notion that the socialist state will be highly centralized and that the socialist administration will be "paternalistic."

Nothing can be less warranted than these assumptions. The modern centralized state is a product of the capitalist system, and especially of capitalist trading.

We again quote that acutest observer and thinker of modern socialism, Karl Kautsky: —

---

[1] Karl Kautsky, "Das Erfurter Programm," 8th Edition, Stuttgart, 1907, pp. 117, 118, 119. Compare also "The Socialist Republic," by Karl Kautsky, translated and adapted to America by Daniel de Leon, New York, 1900, pp. 10, 11.

"Commerce has always had a tendency towards centralization. It causes the influx of commodities as well as of buyers and sellers to certain points favored by their geographical location and political conditions. Under the capitalist mode of production, which converts all industry into production of commodities, and makes it dependent on commerce, the centralization of commerce leads to the centralization of the entire industrial life. The whole country becomes directly or indirectly dependent on the metropolis, as it becomes dependent on the capitalist class. The metropolis, the center of commerce, also becomes the converging point of all surplus value, of all superfluity of the country, and luxury lures after it the arts and the sciences.

"The economic centralization leads to political centralization, and the center of commerce also becomes the center of government." [1]

Since there is no room in a socialist commonwealth for production for sale or for commerce, there is no economic need for a strongly centralized government. Moreover, the very fact that the socialist state will be charged with much larger functions than the present state, and will exercise a much larger interference in the economic relations of its individual citizens, will make it an almost impossible task to direct the most substantial activities of the state from one central point and through one set of general officers.

While the state as such will probably retain certain general functions, it will no doubt be found more convenient to vest the more vital and direct functions in political organizations embracing smaller territories. The

[1] "Der Parlamentarismus," etc., Stuttgart, 1893, p. 30.

socialists regard the present city or township as the nucleus of such a political unit.

The city is to-day already charged with many functions of prime importance to the welfare of its inhabitants, and those functions could be readily enlarged under a socialist administration. The municipality could well conduct, direct or regulate all industries except those that from their nature require an organization of national scope, such as the posts, telegraphs, railways, mines, and the great trustified industries. It could, besides, have the sole care of the safety, health, education and amusement of its citizens and of the support and maintenance of its aged, invalid and other dependent members.

It is not at all unlikely that these functions may, especially in the case of larger municipalities, be further subdivided, and apportioned among several organized "labor groups" or city districts.

"The single communes," says August Bebel, "form a suitable basis for such an institution, and where they are too large to allow of the convenient transaction of business, they can be divided into districts. All adult members of the commune, without distinction of sex, take part in the necessary elections, and determine to what persons the conduct of affairs shall be intrusted."[1]

And Anton Menger describes his conception of the practical workings of such organizations in the following language: "At first it will be necessary to divide the larger municipalities into local districts in order to facilitate their industrial activities. For the same reason every large municipality in which the industrial life is very complex, will have to organize the members of the same trade

[1] "Woman," p. 130.

or calling into separate 'labor groups.' But these intermediary organizations are to be considered only as administrative organs. The municipality remains the owner and the authority in all industrial activity. Hence the members of the group may assert the right of existence as against the municipality, but they have no claim to a division of the product of the group's labor in any fixed proportion. . . .

"The municipality may establish or dissolve the labor group and may assign to it members, work and material. . . . The managers of the labor group are appointed and discharged by the municipality. . . .

"When the socialist state has become firmly established, the labor groups may be transformed with great caution in the direction of greater democracy."[1]

These ideas are, of course, purely speculative, and there seems to be no valid reason why the managers and foremen of the "labor group" should not be elected by the group members at the very outset as suggested, for instance, by Laurence Gronlund.[2] But the ideas are, nevertheless, valuable as indications of one of the possible arrangements under socialism.

The city with or without political and industrial subdivisions will thus absorb the most important governmental activities under socialism, and the central government will as a result be limited to the management of the "national" industries and to the enactment of general laws and regulations.

For while the city will enjoy a much larger measure of independence under socialism than it does to-day, it is

[1] "Neue Staatslehre," 2d Edition, pp. 199, 200.
[2] "The Coöperative Commonwealth," Boston, 1893, p. 186.

not reasonable to suppose that it will be clothed with complete autonomy or the power to pass legislation of a general character. To confer such powers on the municipality would mean to weaken the state and to paralyze its usefulness as a factor in the industrial life of the nation.

The state being thus retained under socialism, what will be the political form of its administration? Will it be republican or monarchic?

To the American reader the question may seem idle, but it is, nevertheless, true that it has been the subject of considerable differences of opinion in the ranks of the socialists of Europe.

Of the early socialist writers Saint-Simon and Fourier asserted that a constitutional monarchy was not necessarily incompatible with socialism. Karl Rodbertus, the friend of Ferdinand Lassalle, held similar views, and even Lassalle himself was not entirely opposed to the notion of a "social kingdom."

Of the modern writers on socialism Anton Menger seeks to solve the problem by the following theory: —

"Like all great questions of politics between princes and nations, this is a question of power. The answer depends upon the revolutionary strength of the nation and upon the power which the monarchy has attained in the course of its historical development. Thus the socialist state will probably appear in the form of a republic in the Latin countries. On the other hand, the dynasties of England, Germany and other Germanic countries may through a proper policy assure the maintenance of the monarchy after the establishment of the socialist régime for some time, perhaps even for an indefinite period." [1]

[1] "Neue Staatslehre," pp. 171, 172.

What seems to lend some plausibility to this peculiar conception is the fact that the Englishmen, the Germans and the other Germanic peoples attribute but a secondary importance to the form of government of present society. There are no aggressive republicans in England, not even among the socialists, and the socialists of Norway, after the recent separation of their country from Sweden, submitted to the election of another king without violent protest.

The sentiments of the German social-democrats on the respective merits of the republic and monarchy were well expressed by August Bebel in the International Socialist Congress at Amsterdam on the occasion of his famous oratorical duel with the eloquent leader of French socialism, Jean Jaurès.

"As much as we envy you Frenchmen your republic," exclaimed he, "and as much as we wish it for ourselves, we will not allow our skulls to be broken for it: it does not deserve it. A capitalist monarchy or a capitalist republic, — both are class states, both are necessarily and from their very nature made to maintain the capitalist régime. Both direct their entire strength in the effort to preserve for the capitalist class all the powers of the legislature. For the moment that the capitalist class will lose its political power, it will lose also its social and economic position. The monarchy is not so bad and the capitalist republic is not so good as you picture them." [1]

And similarly, A. Labriola, the brilliant young leader of the extreme wing of Italian socialism, declares: —

"Class rule does not express itself in a monarchical

[1] "Sixième Congrès Socialist International," Compte-Rendu Analytique, Brussels, 1904, p. 85.

form of government or in a republican form of government, but in the fact that one group of men exercise the political powers in their own interests. We must learn to understand that there are no political forms which exclude class rule, nor such which make it inevitable." [1]

On the other hand, the Frenchman Benoit Malon affirms categorically: —

"Since the republic is the political form of human dignity, the states which will be founded by emancipated nations, can only be republican. The socialist state must be a federated republic, for federalism alone combines the respect for local and particular needs and the relative autonomy of secondary political organizations (municipalities, etc.) with the great interests of the nations freely constituted." [2]

On the whole it is safe to assume that barring perhaps some peculiar tricks with which history sometimes amuses itself, the socialist states will be republics, with or without presidents or other individual heads. The affairs of the socialist republics will in all probability continue to be conducted by representative assemblies.

The modern parliaments owe their origin to the capitalist régime, but the social development of the last centuries seems to have made them indispensable for the democratic management of the affairs of every large and complex state, and as far as we can see to-day, a socialist régime cannot offer anything better as a substitute. The old town meetings and other direct legislative and deliberative bodies of citizens may be practical for the

[1] Arturo Labriola, "Riforme e Rivoluzione Sociale," Milan, 1904, p. 99.

[2] B. Malon, "Précis de Socialisme," Paris, 1892, p. 297.

regulation of purely local affairs in small communities, but they are entirely inadequate to deal with complex problems of national import. Nor can the institutions of the popular Initiative and Referendum take the place of modern representative assemblies. The process of law-making requires even to-day a large measure of skill, special knowledge and precision. The enactment of a wise law or regulation presupposes a careful deliberation over its main object, and the minute and searching examination of its separate provisions. In many cases the original project is modified and improved before adoption, and the law as finally enacted is often the result of a compromise, more or less satisfactory to all. In all progressive legislation, furthermore, there must be a certain consistency and continuity of idea, — a system; and this feature will be more essential to a socialist legislature, which will have to deal with the most vital problems of the nation, than it is to modern legislative bodies.

But such systematic, planful and elastic legislation cannot be introduced by popular Initiative and cannot be enacted by popular Referendum. The Initiative is in its nature spasmodic and often inconsistent, and the Referendum is too rigid and categorical for a regular engine of the popular will. The Initiative and the Referendum are excellent institutions in conjunction with parliaments. As preventives and correctives of legislative abuses they are indispensable to every true democracy; they cannot, however, do away with representative government.

But if representative assemblies should be retained under socialism, they will at the same time probably be modified very largely to meet the requirements of greater democracy and to comply with the new needs and functions of the commonwealth.

The Initiative and Referendum will probably be established in conjunction with all legislative bodies, and will be coupled with the right of the constituents to recall their representative at all times. The representatives of the people will furthermore be elected by the votes of all adult citizens, male and female, and their powers will naturally be curtailed by the limited functions of a socialist parliament.

What will be these functions, and in what manner will they be discharged?

The functions of national government to-day may be roughly divided under two main heads — those of a general administrative or *political* character, represented by the departments of foreign affairs, national defense, treasury, justice, education, insurance, health, fine arts, etc., and those of a character, prevalently industrial or *economic*, such as the administration of posts, railroads, telegraphs, canals, mines and other national industries and the departments of agriculture, public works, etc.

In the modern state the political functions largely preponderate, and the economic functions occupy but a subordinate position. This is natural in view of the fact that the political functions of the present state are largely exercised for the benefit of the ruling classes. Under socialism the industrial activities of the government are bound to increase, and the political activities to diminish.

The division of the governmental functions into those of a political and those of an economic nature has given rise to the hypothesis that the socialist parliament will remain bi-cameral — the political chamber taking the place of the lower house and the economic chamber that of the upper house.

"Does any one believe that the earth will cease to revolve, if the present upper and lower houses of parliament, whose division does not correspond to anything, shall be replaced by a political chamber and an economic chamber?" queries B. Malon, and he continues: "The political chamber might be elected by universal suffrage as our present representative assemblies; but the economic chamber, the larger and more important of the two, should be the result of professional elections, with proper regard to the special qualifications of the elected, so that it should truly represent the producers and workers of all categories."[1]

Anton Menger suggests a somewhat similar arrangement. "It will be expedient," he asserts, "that legislation in the socialist state shall be enacted by two chambers: one to be elective and to be subject to the democratic tendencies of the people, the other to be aristocratic, but to be composed not of the most useless, but of the really best members of the state;" and such "best members," according to Menger, are to be the highest active or retired state officials and the leading representatives of the sciences, arts and literature.[2]

The notion that the industrial affairs of the socialist state will not be administered by officers elected by general popular vote, but by men chosen by the members of each separate trade and calling for their experience and special qualifications, is generally accepted by the socialists.

Wilhelm Liebknecht suggests that the most important

---

[1] "Précis de Socialisme," pp. 300, 301.
[2] "Neue Staatslehre," pp. 179, 180.

work of legislation and administration be performed by committees of experts instead of parliaments,[1] and Annie Besant, in a somewhat vivid flight of imagination, says: "One may guess that in each nation all the Boards of communal authorities will ultimately be represented in some central Executive or Industrial Ministry; that the Minister of Agriculture, or Mineral Industries, or Textile Industries, and so on, will have relations with similar officers in other lands; and that thus, internationally as well as nationally, coöperation will replace competition."[2]

[1] "Ueber die politische Stellung der Sozialdemokratie," 9th Edition, Berlin, 1893, p. 5.

[2] "Industry under Socialism," in Fabian Essays, American Edition, Boston, 1894, p. 147.

CHAPTER VI

SOCIALISM AND POLITICS

Politics, Representative Government and Political Parties

PRACTICAL politics may be defined as the art or action of guiding or influencing the policy of a government, or the effort to obtain control of or influence over the powers of government.[1]

And it is essential for the first part of this definition that the guidance and influence to which it refers, should not be exercised by the organized government itself, but by persons or parties outside of it. The difference between Administration and Politics is just this, that the former consists in the direct management of public affairs by the persons officially vested with the power and charged with the duty to manage them, while the latter is an indirect management secured through influence or power over the public official.

In absolute monarchies the powers of government are concentrated, at least theoretically, in the person of the autocrat; hence the political influence and functions of the country are confined to the small circle of persons who

---

[1] "In the narrower and more usual sense, Politics is the act or vocation of guiding or influencing the policy of a government through the organization of a party among its citizens." — CENTURY DICTIONARY.

"The administration of public affairs or the conduct of political matters so as to carry elections and secure public offices." — STANDARD DICTIONARY.

144

alone have the opportunity to come in frequent contact with the person of the monarch — the high nobility and the dignitaries of the church. Politics in such countries is conducted principally through the medium of court cliques; its objects are usually the personal advantages and preferment of a set of individuals or a caste; its methods are those of intrigue and conspiracy, and the climax of such politics is a palace or dynastic revolution.

Countries of a constitutional form of government, on the other hand, are bound to evolve politics of an entirely different type. The head of a constitutional government, whether he be designated king or president, is but one wheel in the administrative machinery of the state. His powers are limited by a constitution, and the active and vital functions of government are vested in bodies of popular representatives — the national parliaments, state legislatures and municipal councils. In order to guide or influence the policies of such a government, it is no longer sufficient to gain the good graces of the chief executive; it becomes necessary to enlist the support or obedience of a majority of the representative assembly.

This shifting of the field of political operation entails a chain of radical changes in the methods, aims and objects of modern politics. The representative assemblies are large bodies of men, frequently of divergent views and interests; their power is temporary, and its continuance depends upon the confidence of their constituencies; their deliberations and actions are public and open to the scrutiny of the people; their actions must, therefore, be such as will be reasonably certain to meet with the approval of at least that portion of the population whose support is indispensable to their public careers.

L

Under normal conditions the individual and unsupported political intriguer, plotting for his own preferment or for that of the small clique of his friends or confederates, is thus obviously powerless to influence a popular government to an appreciable degree. He disappears in politics with the disappearance of the absolute state, and his place is taken by the large body of citizens, banded together permanently for the purpose of controlling the government, ostensibly in the interests of the people as a whole according to their views of the needs of the people, but actually in the interest of a given class or section of the population, as we shall endeavor to show presently. The most direct way to control the government which naturally suggests itself to such a body of citizens, is to place men of their own midst in the administration, and its ultimate aim is, therefore, to elect a majority of the representatives in the popular assemblies and of other governmental and public functionaries. Thus arises the modern political party with its strong and ramified organization, its platforms, issues and electoral campaigns. And in practice we observe that the origin of organized political parties coincides in each country with the establishment of a parliamentary régime. "They are a necessary evil in free government," as De Tocqueville puts it.[1]

The British Parliament has largely served as a model for all other constitutional countries, and the life of that body in its modern form, as the real repository of the political power of the country, may be dated from the meeting of the Long Parliament in 1640, when the House of Commons deprived the crown of its two most essential

[1] Alexis de Tocqueville, "Democracy in the United States," p. 186.

prerogatives — the power to levy taxes and the right to dissolve Parliament indefinitely, and to the Bill of Rights, which practically vested all legislative functions of the United Kingdom in Parliament. Prior to the Long Parliament there were no fixed political parties in the modern sense in England, but the next year already witnesses the formation of the first two distinct and well-defined parties of England, the Cavaliers and the Round-heads; and these parties, subsequently known as Whigs and Tories, and still later as Liberals and Conservatives, gradually changing their aims and methods of warfare with the changed conditions of the advancing centuries, reappear as the leading factors in all political struggles of England, from the stormy days of the Long Parliament down to our own time.

In France there were no organized political parties prior to the revolutionary Constituent Assembly of 1789, but when the first National Assembly or parliament met in 1791, after the adoption of a constitution for the republic, it found itself at once divided into at least four distinct political parties — the Royalists, who yearned for a return to the old régime; the Feuillants or constitutional monarchists, the Girondists or moderate republicans, and the Montagnards or radical republicans.

With the accession of Napoleon and the smothering of parliament and constitution, political party life disappears in France, but with the restoration and the new grant of a constitution and parliament, the new political parties of the Moderates and Independents immediately spring into being.

In Germany the modern political parties date partly from the days of the Frankfort Assembly in 1848, and partly from the establishment of the North German Union in 1867.

The colonies of the United States knew little of political parties, and held such institutions in scant esteem. "Throughout the eighteenth century," remarks Henry Jones Ford, "party was regarded as a gangrene, a cancer which patriotic statesmen should combine to eradicate." [1] But immediately following the Declaration of Independence, and even before the formal adoption of the national constitution of the new republic, the Federalists and Anti-Federalists appeared in the public arena as full-fledged political parties, and while these parties have since repeatedly changed their issues and watchwords, and have finally settled on the party names of Republican and Democratic, they rule to-day the politics of the United States as absolutely and effectively as any political parties in the world.

In Italy the modern political parties appear immediately after the accomplishment of the unification of the country as a constitutional monarchy. In Austria, Hungary, Belgium and Holland the grant or conquest of a constitution was in every case regularly followed by the formation of political parties; in Russia the grant of a mere phantom of a constitution was the immediate signal for the spontaneous creation of a number of political parties.

Constitutions, representative government and political parties are thus intimately and indissolubly correlated with each other; they have a common origin, and together they constitute one historical phase in the development of

[1] "The Rise and Growth of American Politics," New York, 1898, p. 90.

our political institutions — the phase corresponding on the whole to the modern or capitalist economic system.

Just as the fixed absolute state is the most appropriate form of government of a rigorous feudal society, so is the flexible representative system the ideal form of government of the modern state of free competitive producers.

The rise of representative government and political parties marks in all countries the ascendency of the modern industrial classes over the landowning classes formerly in power.

It is true we find in history abundant mention of parliaments and popular assemblies antedating by centuries the modern capitalist system, and some of them tracing their origin to hoary antiquity. But while these institutions may have had a remote influence on the shaping and forms of the modern parliaments, they certainly had nothing in common with their present substance and function.

The essential features of every modern representative assembly may be summarized as follows: —

1. It is an independent governmental organ, whose existence and permanence are guaranteed by a constitution which represents the supreme law of the land.

2. It meets at regular intervals.

3. It has the power to grant or veto the taxes or budget of the state.

4. It is either vested with supreme legislative powers or it acts as a check upon the legislative powers of the crown.

5. The cabinet ministers are directly or indirectly under its control.

6. As a rule it is bi-cameral.

7. The lower house, at least, is representative in character, and its members are chosen by and accountable to the citizens entitled to vote.

Neither the mediæval English Parliament, nor any other popular assembly of the early or middle periods of our era possessed these attributes.

"The mediæval Parliament," says Edward Jenks, "represented the *estates* of the *realm*, viz.: nobles, clergy, yeomen or peasants, and craftsmen.

"But two things about it are well worth noticing: —

"(*a*) It was not, in any ordinary sense of the term, a *popular* institution. On the other hand, for many years after its appearance, it was intensely unpopular, both with 'constituencies' and representatives. . . . All hated it, because a Parliament invariably meant *taxation*. The members themselves disliked the odium of consenting to taxes which their constituents would have to pay. Only by the most stringent pressure of the *Crown* were Parliaments maintained during the first century of their existence; and the best proof of this assertion lies in the fact, that in those countries in which the Crown was weak, Parliament ultimately ceased to assemble. The notion that Parliaments were the result of a spontaneous democratic movement can be held by no one who has studied, ever so slightly, the facts of history.

"(*b*) Parliament, at any rate the *representative* part of it, was, in the origin, concerned solely with the granting of *money*. The nobles were, it is true, hereditary *councilors* of the Crown; but the clerical proctors, and the members of the counties and boroughs, could claim no such position. There was no pretense of such a thing in the early days of Parliament. It was *liability*, and not *privilege*, which was the basis of Parliamentary representation; it was the old idea of seizure of the village elders (for ransom), carried out on a magnificent scale." [1]

These rather humiliating functions of the early Parliaments are by no means peculiar to England. The French States-General were convoked by the king whenever he needed money. Their duties consisted in making grants, and their rights in presenting grievances or petitions, and the king as a rule forced the former and ignored the latter. The three Estates of France, the Nobility, the Clergy and the Commons or Third Estate, formed three independent chambers, deliberating and voting separately, the decision of any of the two chambers being binding on the third. And as the Nobility and Clergy were exempt from taxation and otherwise mostly united in interest as against the burgesses and peasantry, the Assembly of Estates usually resulted in a heavy tax imposed by the first two Estates upon the third. Once in a while the rebellious representatives of the "third estate" would refuse to "register" the royal edict for new taxes. In such cases the king would personally appear in the session and compel the recalcitrant commons to register his edicts. This peculiar procedure was for some reason styled "*lit de justice*" — bed of justice.

The mediæval German Diet was composed of the personal representatives of the numerous reigning princes of the empire and a few representatives of the cities. It had no important or useful functions to perform and no real power over the country.

The early Polish Diet was merely a council of the nobles, and the early Russian Assemblies were convoked on

[1] Edward Jenks, "History of Politics," London, 1900, pp. 132, 133.

critical occasion, ordinarily for the purpose of furnishing the government with money and arms.

As to the ancient Teutonic and Anglo-Saxon assemblies, the witenagemotes, they have even less claim to the title of parliament in the modern sense than the mediæval bodies. They were practically nothing but councils of elders or chiefs, with little or no binding powers.

And just as the pre-capitalistic "parliaments" have nothing in common with the modern institution of that name, so have the pre-capitalistic "parties" no affinity with the political parties of the modern type.

Historians sometimes designate as parties the followers of hostile princes contending for a throne, or the scattered adherents of a religious creed or even a scientific theory. In that rather loose sense, parties have, of course, existed at all times. But it requires more than the mere common adherence to a person or theory to make a political party.

No aggregation of individuals can be properly styled a political party unless they are bound together by a common social and political ideal and by planned and organized action aimed at the maintenance or realization of that ideal; the two most vital features of every political party are: unity of principle and unity of action.

And here we arrive at the most baffling aspect of the political party — the mysterious union of principle, which lends harmony and continuity to the modern political organization, and enables it to survive all changing political situations and issues. It cannot be mere casual agreement on abstract ideas and theories, for frequently we see a party as a whole abandon its original views and adopt new and altogether different grounds and issues. The history of the last century is replete with instances of parties which were formed for specific political objects, and remained intact and active long after those objects had been fully accomplished.

Nor can it be mere compatibility of temper that holds vast masses of individuals together in definite political parties, for every political party of any significance unites within its fold men of all conceivable dispositions and inclinations.

The force that cements the members of a political party together is obviously not to be looked for in the intellectual or psychic world. It must be found in the more realistic sphere of our existence — the material interests of the special classes of modern society represented by each of the political parties.

Classes and Class Struggles in Modern Society

One of the cardinal doctrines of modern socialism is the doctrine of the "class struggle."

The inhabitants of every state, as was casually mentioned in the preceding chapters, may always be divided into several groups of persons with reference to their source of income or mode of acquiring the material means of their existence. Within each group the single individuals may strive for the largest possible share of the common income, but as against all the other elements of society, each of such groups is interested in the maintenance and increase of its special revenue or material wealth. Each of such social groups constitutes a separate "class" of society, and the characteristic features of every class are these: its individual members are united in their general economic interest with each other, and as a whole they are opposed to all other classes contending with them for their share of the national wealth.

The existence of classes thus creates the instincts of class solidarity and class antagonism, and the socialists contend that the efforts of each class to maintain or improve its position, and the resultant conflicts between them, constitute the politics of the nations and make their histories.

The doctrine of the class struggle in its present finished form was first proclaimed in " The Communist Manifesto," which was drafted by the principal theoretical founders of modern socialism, Karl Marx and Frederick Engels, in 1848, and is there stated in the following terse and cogent language: —

"The (recorded) history of all hitherto existing society is the history of class struggles.

"Freeman and slave, patrician and plebeian, lord and serf, guild master and journeyman, in a word, oppressor and oppressed, stood in constant opposition to one another, carried on an uninterrupted, now hidden, now open, fight, that each time ended either in revolutionary reconstitution of society at large, or in the common ruin of the contending classes.

"In the earlier epochs of history we find almost everywhere a complicated arrangement of society into various orders, a manifold gradation of social rank. In ancient Rome we have patricians, knights, plebeians, slaves; in the Middle Ages, feudal lords, vassals, guild masters, journeymen, apprentices, serfs; in almost all of these classes, again, subordinate gradations.

"The modern bourgeois society that has sprouted from the ruins of feudal society, has not done away with class antagonisms. It has but established new classes, new conditions of oppression, new forms of struggle in place of the old ones.

"Our epoch, the epoch of the bourgeois, possesses, however, this distinctive feature; it has simplified the class antagonisms. Society as a whole is more and more splitting up into two great hostile camps, into two great classes directly facing each other: Bourgeoisie and Proletariat." [1]

The principal classes in modern society are thus, according to Marx and Engels, the classes of the "Bourgeoisie" and the "Proletariat," and a few words must be said here in explanation of these terms very current in the literature of socialism.

"Bourgeois," literally a "townsman," was originally a term used in opposition to that of *gentle* or *noble*, and signified a manufacturer or tradesman. The class of the "bourgeoisie," in an economic sense, has come to stand for the entire propertied class: it includes the modern manufacturer, money lender, and even the landowner who employs his land for industrial or other business purposes. It is the entire "third estate," less the wage workers.

The term "Proletariat" is borrowed from the political nomenclature of ancient Rome, where it was used to denote the class of free citizens without property or assured means of existence. [2] In a more restricted and technical

[1] "The Communist Manifesto," New York, Socialist Coöperative Publishing Assn., 1901, pp. 10, 11.

[2] The etymological derivation of the term is by no means free from doubt. The Roman grammarians, and most of the modern writers after them, derive it from the word "proles" — descendants, and interpret the original meaning of proletariat as a descendant-begetting or child-bearing class. The Austrian philologist, Stowasser, recently suggested the derivation of the word from "pro-oletarius," *i.e.*, substitute for manure worker, hired slave or common wage laborer.

"*Deutsche Worte*," September, 1901, quoted in *Neue Zeit* of October 2, 1901.

sense, the word Proletarian signifies a workingman who does not own his tools of labor, a wage worker; but in its wider application it embraces the entire propertyless class of workers. Thus we speak not only of the "industrial" proletarian, but also of the "agricultural" proletarian, the farmer who does not own his land, or the hired farm hand; and even of the "intellectual" proletarian, the professional who depends upon an unsteady and uncertain hiring out of his talents for a living.

Such then are the main characteristics of the two principal classes of modern society, the Bourgeoisie and Proletariat, or Capitalists and Workingmen, and the antagonism between them to which the authors of "The Communist Manifesto" refer, is the conflict of material interests which springs from their mutual economic relations.

The principal wealth of modern society is represented by an accumulation of commodities owned by individual competing capitalists and used for the purpose of exchange. The process of modern industry is a process of manufacture and exchange of such commodities. All wealth is created in that process, and all profits are derived through it. The different commodities exchange for each other at their actual value; hence, the accumulation of profit and wealth must not be looked for in the process of exchange, but in the process of production.

The value of a commodity is determined by the average social labor expended on its production, and if the manufacturing capitalist should pay to the laborer a wage equivalent to the products of his labor, there would remain no margin of profit for him, and the hoarding up of individual wealth would be impossible. But, as a matter of fact, the manufacturing capitalist does not return to the

workingman, in the form of a money wage, commodities
of a value representing his full hours of labor, but only
such quantity as will enable him to maintain his existence
according to the established standard of living and
to reproduce his species. Thus assuming that the
quantity of food, clothing and other necessaries of a workingman's life per day are produced in six hours of average
social labor time, his wages will represent the portion of
his labor equivalent to six hours, and if he works ten hours
per day, the product of the remaining four hours of his
labor is appropriated by his employer.

Since the individual capitalist owns the tools without
which no labor can be performed in modern society, and
the laborer owns nothing but his ability to work — his labor power, the workingman is compelled to sell that labor
power to the capitalist for a fixed daily wage. His labor
power is sold to the capitalist to be used for a day of a
duration of eight, ten or twelve hours, according to agreement, and the products of his labor are divided between
him and his employer. The portion of such labor that
falls to the share of the workingman is his wage, and the
portion retained by the manufacturing capitalist Marx
calls "surplus value."

The "surplus value" of the manufacturing capitalist is
by no means his clear profit; as a rule, he is forced to divide it with the landlord, the money lender and the merchant. "Surplus value" is the source of all profits of the
manufacturing and trading capitalists, the rents of the
landowning capitalists, and the interest of the money-lending capitalists. Thus the capitalists of all types depend
upon the production of "surplus value," while the working
class depends upon wages. Since wages and "surplus

value" come from the same source, *i.e.*, labor power, it is clear that the proportion of the one will be relatively larger as the proportion of the other is relatively smaller, and *vice versa;* in other words, the greater the share of capital in the created values, the smaller the share of labor.

The economic interests of capital and labor are, therefore, opposed to each other, and while it is in the interest of the class deriving its income from "surplus value" to maintain the present system of distribution of wealth, the interests of the working class lie in the abolition of that system.

These are the main lines on which the modern class struggles are conducted, but a closer analysis of the process will show that they are by no means the sole lines of modern class division.

The capitalists or bourgeoisie constitute but one class in their common interest to exploit the working class, but among themselves they are separated in many groups with reference to the special interests of the respective fields of their operation. The three main forms of capitalist revenue, rent, interest and profits, spring, as we have seen, from the same source, the "surplus value" of the producing capitalists; and the shares of these three categories of income stand in inverse relation to each other. It is, of course, conceivable that rent, interest and profits may rise simultaneously, at the expense of the working class and the consumers, but they need not and do not always increase in equal proportions, and the total quantity of "surplus value" remaining equal, an increase of rents or a rise of the rate of interest will signify a lowering of profits, and *vice versa*. The three main economic divisions of capitalists, dependent on the three forms of income mentioned, the rent-gathering landowner, the interest-drawing money lender, and the profit-making manufacturer and merchant, are thus by no means united in interest between themselves. The money lender or banker exploits the mortgaged landowner and the borrowing industrial alike, while the owner of the factory site and store property exploits the manufacturer and merchant with equal thoroughness. Nor is the industrial group of the capitalist class always a unit in interests: the interests of the manufacturers usually run counter to those of the sellers, and *vice versa;* and even within the manufacturing class the interests of separate trades are frequently opposed to each other — for instance, where the producers of one certain commodity, a finished article, are the consumers of the products of another class of manufacturers, those engaged in the production of materials.

As compared with the divergent interests of the capitalists among themselves, the interests of the working class are, on the whole, harmonious. The workingmen are frequently forced to compete with each other for employment, which, as a rule, results in a general reduction of wages. But this competition is no evidence of a conflict of interest among different groups of workingmen; on the contrary, its effect is strong proof of the solidarity of their interests; and the recognition of the pernicious effects of their competition ultimately leads the workers to a more compact class organization. No group of workingmen benefits by the fall of wages of another group, no class of workingmen exploits another class; hence, there exists no economic cause for antagonism between the workingmen of the different trades.

We have thus described and analyzed the two main

classes of modern society and their component parts. But
between and besides them there are several economic
groups which cannot properly be classed with the one or
the other — the groups characterized by the general designation of the "middle classes." These consist of small
merchants, manufacturers and farmers, who, while they
own their business, implements or land, and sometimes
employ hired labor, still extract but little "surplus value,"
and chiefly depend for their living upon their own efforts.
The members of the middle class are engaged in a strenuous
and losing battle for the maintenance of their economic
independence against the invading large industries. Their
hope is to develop some day into large and wealthy capitalists, their fate most commonly is to succumb to the
superior means and organization of the great industries,
and to find refuge in the employment of their victorious
rivals or to be forced down to the ranks of the wage laborer.
By their sympathies and sentiments, these men incline
towards the capitalist class, by their immediate economic
interests they are arrayed against it, and at times they
break out in a feeble or more vigorous revolt against om-
nivorous capitalism.

Another middle-class group of considerable importance is that of the "intellectuals" in the direct employ of
the capitalists; the managers, superintendents, foremen,
engineers, accountants, clerks, etc. The economic position of these is similar to that of the proletarian
wage worker, inasmuch as they are also hired by their
employers and paid a fixed remuneration for their
services, but it is different with respect to the size of that
remuneration. The average income of the men of this
class is frequently larger than that of the middle-class

manufacturers, traders or farmers; they are styled "employees," not "workingmen"; they receive "salaries," not "wages," and by their education, social environment, tastes and habits, they feel themselves more akin to the capitalist class than to the working class.

And finally we must mention the variety of the middle class known as the "professionals," *i.e.*, physicians, lawyers, clergymen, teachers, journalists, artists, etc. These constitute a class by themselves. They do not operate with capital, and their incomes are not derived from exploitation of labor, nor, on the other hand, do they as a rule sell their labor or talents to a permanent individual employer in return for a fixed periodical compensation. They are "free" practitioners, who sell their services to whomsoever pays for them from time to time. The men of this group usually find their most remunerative clientele, among the possessing class, and place their skill and talent at the disposal of that class. It is from among this group that the capitalists primarily gather the apologists and defenders of their class interests, their "retainers," to borrow an expression from W. J. Ghent.[1] But the professionals are not permanently tied to the dominant classes. They are alert in perceiving every coming social change, and whenever a new class enters upon a promising campaign to displace the old order, these professionals desert their former patrons in large numbers and place themselves at the head of the new movement.

The Class Struggle in Politics

In the preceding pages we have attempted to outline the main class divisions in modern society. In the general

[1] "Mass and Class," New York, 1905.

M

struggle for social existence, each of these classes of necessity seeks to fortify its economic position by the strong arm of the state. The dominant and possessing class as a whole needs the protection of the state, its laws, courts of justice, police power, and sometimes even its armed force to preserve its "vested rights" and privileges and to maintain its power over the working class; and within the capitalist class each interest group needs the special services and support of the state against the hostile groups of other interests. The transportation industries need charters, grants and franchises, the manufacturing industries want subsidies and protective import tariffs on manufactured articles, while they oppose tariffs on food stuffs; the agricultural landowning class, on the other hand, demands a high tariff on imported food stuffs, but combats the tariff on articles of foreign manufacture; the commercial classes generally strive for a free trade policy; the debtor classes see their salvation in anti-usury laws and debased currency; the money-lending class requires a solid and unchangeable monetary standard; the small manufacturers and traders endeavor to avert the threatening ruin of their economic independence by the enactment of laws against combination and concentration of capital, while the workingmen look to the government for protection against excessive capitalist exploitation. In short, each class and group strives to make the state subservient to its economic interests, to retain or capture the powers of government for its own special purposes.

It is this phase of the class struggle which constitutes modern politics, and the economic classes and interest groups participating in it, correspond, roughly speaking, to the political parties or factions in each country. Thus we find in every constitutional country of Europe, whatever the elements of its political life may otherwise be, at least three definite political parties: the Conservative, the Liberal and the Socialist. In Germany and Austria, they are directly known under those names; in England the political party corresponding in its general features to the Socialist Party in continental Europe is known as the Labor Party; in Belgium and Holland the Clerical Party practically takes the place of the Conservative Party; in France the Conservative and Liberal parties sometimes are known under the names of the Party of Resistance and the Party of Movement, but under whatever name or guise they may appear here or there, they uniformly present the distinctive features of class parties. The Party of the Conservatives is always in substance the party of the landowning class. In countries of feudal antecedents it represents in the first instance the descendants of the landowning and privileged nobility, and its political ideal is the reconstruction of the old régime and the restoration of the political powers of the aristocracy of birth — the party is usually opposed to all progress and reform.

The Liberal Party is the party *par excellence* of the modern bourgeoisie. It represents the interests of industry and commerce. In most countries it is the party in power, and the aims of its politics are to maintain it in power. It favors such moderate and gradual reforms as tend to destroy the feudal remnants in modern European society without in any way endangering the supremacy of the class represented by it. Its political interests and ideals coincide on the whole with the present régime, — it is the party of the present.

The Socialist Party is the party of the workingmen who

have drawn the last conclusion from their struggles with capitalism. Its ideal is a coöperative commonwealth based on the collective ownership of the social instruments of wealth production. Its social ideal is not inspired by the fabulous "golden age" of the past, but is founded on the anticipated results of social progress, — it is the party of the future.

Side by side with these three main parties representing the three principal classes of society, there exists in most countries of Europe a party generally known as the Radical Party. This is the party of the middle class, and its political activity is the expression of the last struggles of a class doomed to economic annihilation between the upper grindstone of capitalist competition and the nether grindstone of proletarian organization and aggressiveness.

Paul Louis characterizes this party in the following language : —

"It is composed of men whose social condition is ill defined, who are neither satisfied nor crushed, but who feel themselves menaced and strive to fortify their position. These men desire to conquer the political power in order to break the instruments of the material or moral domination of the great industries and properties. . . . They demand fiscal reforms which would permit them to tax the large revenues and to place artificial fetters on the mechanical concentration of capital. . . . Nowhere do they constitute a coherent party, for nothing is more fugitive than its contingent." [1]

In the countries of Europe we thus find all principal economic classes and interest groups represented by separate and well-defined political parties. The only excep-

[1] "L'Avenir du Socialisme," Paris, 1905, pp. 105, 106.

tion seems to be presented by the money-lending group of capitalists, who, as a rule, do not form parties of their own. This, however, may perhaps be accounted for by the function of money capital, which can become operative only in connection with the other forms of capitalistic ownership, but has no independent productive existence.

All other permanent political parties of continental Europe are but slight variations of the four types described.

In the United States of America, where the economic development of the country has not passed through the stage of feudalism, and where there exist no remnants of a feudal economy or of a class of privileged nobles, there is, of course, no room for a Conservative Party in the European sense, and the parties of the propertied classes are formed on different lines. The Republican Party is substantially the party of the modern capitalists, corresponding in its main characteristics to the Liberal parties of Europe, while the Democratic Party is largely the party of the middle class, the small business man and farmer, and bears some resemblance to the Radical parties of European countries.

Such then, generally speaking, are the leading characteristics and motive forces of the modern political parties, but in practice their formative processes and workings are by no means so clear-cut and simple.

In the complex relations of modern society, it is sometimes exceedingly difficult to determine the exact line of class divisions. It is not always easy to determine when a man ceases to be workman and becomes a member of the middle class, nor whether he is to be classed as a "middleman" or capitalist; and within the capitalist class especially it becomes more and more difficult to divide its members into definite interest groups. The extensive development of stock companies within the last decades has largely broken down the rigid lines of special interest groups within the possessing class, and the typical capitalist of to-day may and frequently does own at the same time stock in banks, in real estate concerns and in industrial and commercial enterprises.

The economic mainsprings of politics are, besides, as a rule deeply hidden below the surface. With the sole possible exception of the working class in the countries of the most advanced industrial development, there is not a single class or interest group large enough to conquer and hold the modern governmental machinery by its own numbers. Each of the classes contending for the political mastery of the country is, therefore, bound to seek the support of other classes or their individual members, and this it can obviously not receive for the mere and avowed advancement of its naked class interests. To overcome the difficulty, the dominant political parties are thus instinctively led to conceal rather than expose their class character; they make concessions or hold out promises to all classes of the population, and by their official platforms and public declarations they pretend to strive for the common welfare of the whole population. The interests of the classes represented by them are thus generalized into the interests of the entire nation, and their striving for political power masquerades as a struggle for lofty political ideals. These false pretensions are sometimes formulated consciously and intentionally by the shrewd party leaders, but perhaps more often the active political party workers, and especially its passive supporters, fully believe in their sincerity; hence, we find the capitalist and middle-class parties of all countries largely supported by working-men, and, generally speaking, there is hardly a political party whose constituent elements are wholly recruited from one homogeneous class.

"It is not contended," says W. J. Ghent, "that men are always, or even generally, conscious of the economic motive that impels them. Far less is it to be contended that they are aware of the influence laid upon the exercise of that motive by the prevailing economic environment. The consciousness of their motives is often but dim and vague, and that motive which they believe dominant, a mere illusion." [1]

And moreover, the economic motive, while it is the dominant factor, is not the sole factor in politics. In times of threatened foreign invasion, the defense of the country may become a paramount political issue of equal importance to all classes of the population, and when a government represents nothing but the autocratic power of a small clique, and becomes equally oppressive on all classes of society, as is the case for instance in Russia, all political parties may well unite in a common program of opposition. In times of special agitation an ideological sentiment may become a political issue of great force and break down all established party lines. At other times, especially when the dominant class is safely intrenched behind the powers of government without vital disputes between its different interest groups and without the menace of a strong working class political party, politics degenerates into a question of mere individual spoils and patronage.

[1] "Mass and Class," p. 12.

The Socialist Party in Politics

In the general political struggles of the classes, the Socialist Party, as was stated above, represents the working class. This statement, however, requires some qualification and explanation.

The Socialist Party represents in politics primarily the general immediate and ultimate interests of the working class as a whole. Its program consists of a number of planks calculated to strengthen the proletariat in its struggles with the dominant classes and to lessen the degree of its exploitation by the latter, and it culminates in the demand for the complete economic enfranchisement of the working class. Since the power of the dominant classes over the workingmen is based on the ownership by the former of the social tools and instruments of wealth production, the cardinal point of the socialist political platform is the demand for the abolition of private ownership in these means of production.

The socialist ideal is a state of society based on organized and coöperative work of all individuals capable of performing work, and on an equitable distribution of the products of such joint labor among all the members of the community. The Socialist Party, the only party which frankly recognizes the class character of the contemporary state and politics, is at the same time the only party which advocates the abolition of all class distinctions. All other political parties, while they ignore or deny the fact of the class struggle, either stand for the preservation of the present class relations or strive merely for the shifting of power from one of the existing classes to the other. The

Socialist Party alone has thus a certain right to claim that it represents the interests of the whole society.

The Socialist Party is, however, preëminently a working-men's party, for the reason that its ultimate aim coincides primarily with the interests of the working class, while it is a menace to the privileges and immediate economic interests of the possessing classes. Recognizing that the vast majority of men are moved by economic motives, the socialists make their appeal in the first line to the working class, and as a rule the Socialist parties actually recruit their adherents mostly from that class.

But the workingmen are by no means the sole supporters of socialism. Its ranks are continually swelled by members of the middle classes, and by large numbers of ideologists from all classes of society, including those of the capitalists. These bourgeois ideologists come into the socialist movement either because they perceive in its lofty social ideal the realization of justice and freedom, or because they have become convinced, through a scientific analysis of modern tendencies of social and economic development, of the inevitability of socialism. The founders of theoretical socialism were men of that type, and the leaders of the socialist movement in all countries recruit themselves principally from among that class.

The socialist movement did not enter the arena of universal history as a practical political movement. In its inception it was purely a philosophical school indulging occasionally in miniature social experiments, and interfering in concrete political movements only by way of exception. In 1848, Marx and Engels still proclaimed that the "communists (the term then employed for the modern word Socialist) do not form a separate party opposed to other working class parties," and as late as 1867, when the German subjects were granted universal suffrage in elections to the North German Diet, the socialists of that country seriously debated the question whether they should take part in these elections, or scornfully reject "the gift of Bismarck," and abstain from voting.

The reasons for the reluctance of the socialists of the earlier period to engage in politics are quite obvious.

In the first place, the movement in its more modern phase was only in its inception, and the number of its adherents was quite small. But it is numbers more than issues that count in political campaigns.

In the next place, the franchise of the workingmen, the class upon whom the socialists primarily relied for their support, was in most countries of Europe monstrously restricted. In Germany universal manhood suffrage was confined to elections to the powerless North German Diet; but the more important municipal and state elections were then as now based on the "three-class system," [1] which reduced the working-class vote to a minimum, or on a property test, which had the same effect.

---

[1] Elections on the "three-class system" are by "categories." The voters are divided into three classes: the first including the largest tax-payers paying together one-third of the taxes; the next, those paying another third of the taxes in the second largest amounts; and the last class, including the remainder of the people. Each class elects the same number of delegates to the conventions that choose the councilors or deputies. The result, of course, is always to return an assembly representative of the property interests, and quite unrepresentative of the masses.

In the elections of 1893 to the Prussian Landtag 5,989,538 voters took part. Of these only 210,759 constituted the first class, the second consisted of 722,633, while the third class embraced all the remaining 5,056,146. The 933,392 citizens of the first two classes could thus entirely outvote their 5,000,000 fellow-citizens of the poorer classes.

In Italy and Belgium the right to vote in parliamentary elections was restricted to citizens paying direct taxes of specified minimal amounts, and qualified by a property test, with the result that in the former country there were in 1879 only 7.77 electors for each 100 male adults, while in the latter the voters constituted but little above 2 per cent of the population in 1874. Similar conditions existed in Holland, Hungary, Austria, Sweden and Norway. In England the expenses of the electoral campaigns were borne by the electors, as they still are, and were prohibitively high for the workingmen. (Within the last decades the electoral laws in many European countries have been somewhat reformed in the direction of greater liberalism.)

Besides, in most countries it was only the lower house of parliament that was elective, membership in the upper house was mostly, as it still remains in many cases, hereditary or appointive, and the composition of these bodies was frequently such as to blast all hopes of a progressive parliamentary policy. Thus the upper house or senate of Italy was composed of princes of the royal family and other dignitaries of the realm, more than 40 years of age, and chosen by the king from among the archbishops, bishops, ministers of the cabinet, admirals, generals and very heavy taxpayers. In Hungary, the upper house consisted of 3 princes of the reigning house, 31 Roman and Greek Catholic prelates, 11 "standard bearers," 57 lord lieutenants, 3 dukes, 219 counts and 81 barons. What a chance a democratic lower house would have for the coöperation of such a chamber!

Moreover, the early socialist leaders had serious misgivings about the effects of an electoral activity on the *morale* of the socialist masses. The parliamentary elections, they argued, could result in but little, if any, benefit to the working class, but they might tend to divert it from the consistent stand of revolutionary opposition, and from the straight path of education and economic struggle.

But still more than the demoralizing effects of electoral campaigns upon the movement, the socialists feared the corrupting influences of parliamentary life upon the chosen representatives of their party. They were inclined to view the European parliaments, with their limited powers, as assemblies whose principal function was to cultivate in their members the fine art of talking; talking not for the sake of convincing, but for the purpose of shining, and such talk, they reasoned, is calculated to deaden the revolutionary spirit of the orator, to arouse his personal vanity and ambition, and to degrade him into a shallow demagogue. The views on the efficiency of parliamentary activity prevalent among the socialists of that time were very similar to those recently expressed by the French socialist writer, Paul Louis, who says: —

"Never has a great decision capable of briskly accelerating the course of history, emanated from a parliament. Parliaments, even when elected by universal suffrage, occupy a position similar to that of the academies; they regard the past, they defend the existing status; by their temperament, their procedure and byzantine exactness, they soon paralyze all men of action who may penetrate there." [1]

Furthermore, they contended, for the socialist movement parliamentary activity could never be anything but a useless farce. As long as the socialist deputies shall remain in the minority, they will be powerless to influence

[1] "L'Avenir du Socialisme," Paris, 1905, pp. 72, 73.

the actions of Parliament, and when the party shall be strong enough to elect a clear majority of the members of any parliament, the country will be ripe for the social revolution, and the cumbersome machinery of Parliament will become useless.

Besides, their strict and rigid interpretation of the class-struggle theory made them doubt the wisdom of deliberating and coöperating with the representatives of the hostile camps in joint council. "Wer mit Feinden parlamentelt, parlamentirt, wer parlamentirt, paktirt!" tersely decreed the veteran leader of German Social Democracy, Wilhelm Liebknecht.[1]

But as against these possible disadvantages, the socialists were bound to consider the following features of political and parliamentary activity as positive advantages for their cause:—

The times of active electoral campaigns are peculiarly propitious for the discussion of social, economic and political theories; hence they offer an excellent opportunity for the propaganda of socialism among the broad masses of the people, and that opportunity is largely enhanced, if socialism is made one of the direct issues of the campaign. And not only are political campaigns important as mediums of effective propaganda, they are also useful as periodical reviews of the socialist forces. The number of votes which the socialists poll at general elections is one of the surest gauges of the progress made by the movement in each country among the masses of the population, and nothing

---

[1] "Ueber die politische Stellung der Sozialdemocratie," Berlin, 1893, p. 12. The sentence is very difficult to render in English. Its meaning is about as follows: "He who discusses with the enemy, negotiates with him, and he who negotiates, compromises."

stimulates growth so much as the proof of growth. Then, again, parliament is a platform from which the popular representative addresses not only his colleagues, but practically the entire nation, and the socialist deputies thus are afforded a rare chance for the propaganda of their party principles on a large scale.

The practical aim of the Socialist Party, moreover, is the capture of the powers of government by the working class in order that it might transform the state from an instrument of class exploitation into a coöperative commonwealth. But the working class cannot accomplish these tasks unless it is well organized and trained in the art of politics and administration, and practical political activity is best calculated to give it that organization and training.

And finally, the socialists by no means disdain all partial reforms, and parliamentary activity opens to them the opportunity to urge and the chance to pass reforms of actual benefit to the working class.

These, then, were the doubts and questions, the pros and cons which met the socialists at the threshold of their political career, and while the leaders were discussing the theoretical aspects of the problem, the mass, as usual in practical questions, solved it, and, as usual, solved it right. The socialists went into politics yielding to the instincts of the masses, rather than following the reasoned policies of the leaders.

Electoral Tactics of the Socialist Party

The tactics and policies of every party must necessarily be such as will be best calculated to insure its political success at a given time and place. They must be shaped to meet the special conditions of each country and period, and must change with the change of these conditions. Political tactics are never immutable, and they are not even as stable as political programs. But while the tactics of a political party are variable and changing, such variations and changes are as a rule neither. very radical nor very sudden. The policy of every party must in the last analysis be determined by and subordinated to its main aims and objects, its political platform, and as long as the latter remains in force, the former changes but slightly.

These general principles of party policy apply to the Socialist Party with even greater force than to the other parties. The socialist platform is the only political platform which is practically identical in its main features and important details in all civilized countries; the principal aims of socialism are not those of local or temporary reform, but of permanent and radical social reconstruction; the socialist methods of warfare were not evolved from casual and fleeting conditions, but from general and firmly established social and economic relations; hence the main points of socialist tactics are bound to be practically uniform and fixed as long as the present social system lasts. And as a matter of fact, we observe that while the details of socialist policy and tactics vary in every country, and are modified with every economic and political change, its most salient features are identical everywhere, and have undergone but little change since the days when the Socialist Party first established itself in practical politics.

The most striking characteristic of all socialist tactics is the political isolation of the party, its reluctance to fuse or combine with other parties in electoral campaigns. The Socialist Party usually makes independent nominations for public office regardless of the prospects of immediate success in the election. As a rule it does not unite with other parties on a common electoral list or "ticket," it does not nominate non-socialists on its own ticket, it does not support candidates of other parties, and its members do not accept nominations or even indorsements from other parties.

This policy of isolation has its good reasons. In theory it is the logical and inseparable sequel of the class struggle doctrine. Viewed from that standpoint there can be no actual solidarity of interest, at least under normal conditions, between the Socialist Party which strives to overthrow the present régime, and the various parties of the propertied classes which are interested in upholding it. A political union between the Socialist Party and any other party can be accomplished, therefore, only on the basis of a compromise which of necessity entails the concealment or abandonment of the most vital principles of socialism. And the Socialist Party is invariably the loser by such combination. Experience has abundantly demonstrated that whenever a party of the propertied classes has invited the political coöperation of the working class, the latter has, with few exceptions, been used by it as a cat's paw for the furtherance of its own class interests. The working class has never derived a substantial or lasting benefit from such an illogical alliance, but the latter has frequently served to bring in demoralization and disorganization in its ranks. Many young and promising revolutionary movements have been smothered by such compromises with the enemy, and the fate of the numerous short-lived political labor movements in the United States is very strong proof of the truth of this assertion. Nor is even the unsolicited support of the bourgeois parties always without danger to socialism in politics. The socialist candidates elected by non-socialist votes tacitly assume certain moral obligations towards this class of voters, and when elected they can rarely maintain the uncompromising attitude of the purely socialist representative. The socialists are, therefore, inclined to reject such political support, arguing with the Roman poet — "Timeo Danaos et dona ferentes" — I fear the Greeks even if they bear gifts.

But with all that the rule of uncompromising socialist tactics, like every other rule of human conduct, is not entirely free from exceptions. It is apt to be observed most rigorously and inflexibly in the earlier days of the socialist movement in every country, when that movement has not yet passed the phase of pure theoretical propaganda and has not yet become a real factor in practical politics.

"There is no need of compromising while the entire activity of the party is limited to oral and written propaganda and the purely theoretical defense of party principles, which saves them from contamination by any foreign elements," observes S. Kotlyarevski.[1]

And, it may be added, not only is there no justification for a compromising policy in the early phases of the socialist movement, but there is every reason against it. While scientific theories or social philosophies are new, it is always their novel and striking features, the features distinguishing them from the accepted theories and philosophies, that receive the greatest emphasis. And only when such new theories or philosophies gain considerable currency or following, are their main propositions sub-

[1] "Partii i Nauka," in *Polyarnaya Svesda* for January, 1906.

N

jected to a more minute and critical analysis, and their qualifications and exceptions noted. The uncompromising and uncriticising propaganda of new ideas is useful and even necessary in the early stages for their popular dissemination. And a practical movement based on such new ideas has besides a special interest in guarding its pristine purity and complete independence in the critical period of its inception or formation, for it is then that it can be diverted or absorbed by foreign elements with the greatest ease.

But with the spread of the socialist movement and the growth of the Socialist Party, new problems present themselves. When the party becomes so numerous as to constitute a factor of importance in the politics and parliament of any country, but not numerous enough to control them by its own strength, the temptation to enlist the cooperation of other progressive parties for the purpose of accomplishing some immediate practical reforms becomes great. Impatient cries are raised within the party urging political combinations for such purposes, and are met by the warning voices of the more conservative leaders tenaciously adhering to the class-struggle tactics.

How do the socialists generally meet the new situation?

In a preceding chapter we observed that even in our present class state there are certain political situations in which the immediate interests of classes otherwise hostile may occasionally coincide.

In countries of feudal origin it is generally in the common interest of the progressive bourgeoisie and the working class to remove the surviving feudal remnants from the social and political structure of their countries, since such remnants are often an impediment to all social progress, and in the countries of restricted, plural or qualified suffrage, the Radical, Liberal and Socialist parties have sometimes an equal interest in extending the suffrage.

The extension of popular suffrage, more especially, is of the greatest vital importance to the Socialist Party, since the latter can hardly make any political progress, still less conquer the political powers of the country, in the absence of equal and universal suffrage.

This situation is the key to the solution of the problem. The socialists often combine with other progressive parties for the attainment of these common purposes; they combine but rarely for any other purposes.

Thus Ferdinand Lassalle, the founder of the Social Democratic Party of Germany, outlined the tactics of the proposed party in his famous "Open Letter" addressed to the workingmen of Leipsic in 1863, in the following language: —

"The working class must constitute itself into an independent political party, and must make the demand for universal, equal and direct suffrage, the watchword and motto of that party. . . . It must feel and constitute itself as a party entirely distinct and separated from the Progressive (Liberal) Party; it must nevertheless support the Progressive Party in those points and questions in which the interests of the two parties are identical, but turn its back upon it and actively oppose it as often as it abandons these interests." [1]

When the English Reform League was organized for the purpose of securing much-needed reforms in the mode of parliamentary elections, Karl Marx and other members

[1] Ferdinand Lassalle's "Reden und Schriften," Bernstein Revision, Vol. II, p. 413.

of the General Council of the International Workingman's Association took active part in the deliberations of that body together with the bourgeois members of other progressive political parties, and in Belgium, Denmark and Sweden the Socialist Party has at different times formally entered into political alliances with other parties upon the common platform of suffrage extension.

But all such socialist alliances with bourgeois parties, whether made for the purpose of suffrage reform or for any other political object, are never permanent. They are made for a special purpose and are dissolved as soon as that purpose is accomplished.

"We social democrats," said Bebel at the International Socialist Congress of Amsterdam, in 1904, "are broad minded enough to accept from our adversaries all concessions we can obtain from them, when they offer us some real benefit in order to secure our support to-day for the government, to-morrow for the liberal parties, the day after even for the party of the center, which makes a special bid for the workingmen's votes. But the hour after we combat them all, the center, the government and the liberals, as our permanent enemies. The bottomless chasm which separates us from the government as well as from all parties of the bourgeoisie is not forgotten for a minute." [1]

In the countries where an absolute majority is required for election to parliament, and a second ballot thus often becomes necessary to determine the choice in certain districts, the Socialist parties frequently enter into agreements with other parties for the support of their mutual

[1] "Sixième Congrès Socialiste International," Compte-Rendu Analytique, Brussels, 1904, p. 88.

candidates as against the candidates of other parties, on the second ballot. While the excuse for this seeming digression from non-compromising socialist tactics is obvious, the Socialist parties of Germany and other countries have repeatedly endeavored to abolish this practice, but with little success; the socialist voters as a rule insist on exercising their suffrage on all occasions, and the watchword of abstention in any election has never met with their general approval.

In the United States, in which there are no political or economic remains of a feudal system, hardly any restrictions upon universal manhood suffrage, and no second ballots in general elections, there seems to be no reason or excuse for any deviation from the general socialist principle of absolutely independent politics, and the socialists of America have in fact on every occasion declared themselves against all forms of political combination or coöperation with other parties.

Parliamentary Tactics of the Socialist Party

The first entry of socialists into parliamentary politics was characterized by the same diffidence and misgivings that had marked their early participation in electoral campaigns.

Thus, when the first socialists were elected to the old North German Diet, so shrewd a party leader as Wilhelm Liebknecht advocated a purely negative attitude on the part of the socialist deputies towards the positive work of Parliament. "My personal opinion," says he, "was that our elected representatives should enter Parliament with a protest, and withdraw immediately, without, however, surrendering their credentials. With this opinion I remained in the minority; it was decided that the representatives of democracy could utilize every opportunity they might deem appropriate, in order to emphasize in the 'Diet' their attitude of negation and protest, but that they should keep aloof from all practical parliamentary proceedings, because any participation in such proceedings would imply a recognition of the North German Union and of Bismarck's policies, and might tend to obscure the fact that the struggles in the 'Diet' are but fictitious struggles and a mere farce." [1]

These negative tactics were steadfastly adhered to during the first two sessions of the North German Diet, but already the next session witnessed a spontaneous departure from the rigid rule, when several socialist deputies took the floor in the first parliamentary discussion on the subject of governmental labor regulation. And the socialist tactics of parliamentary abstinence have since gradually but definitely given way to the policy of watchful and energetic parliamentary activity. The socialist deputies in the European parliaments have preserved their uncompromising attitude of "negation and protest" practically on the sole subject of the budgets of their respective governments; they vote almost uniformly against their approval, arguing that as representatives of the working class they cannot consistently grant to capitalist governments the means to maintain a class state, which in almost all cases includes a standing army.[2] In all other matters,

---

[1] "Ueber die politische Stellung der Sozialdemocratie," p. 12. Compare also, Robert Hunter, "Socialists at Work," New York, 1908, p. 221.

[2] Recently a strong opposition has developed in the ranks of the Social Democratic Party of Germany to the continuance of the party's traditional attitude of protest against the budget.

however, the socialist groups in the parliaments of Europe are among the most active and alert: the socialist deputies are never tired of introducing legislative measures for the betterment of the social, political and material conditions of the workingmen, for the curtailment of capitalist exploitation, and for the advancement of true social progress.

Thus at the convention of the Socialist Party of France, held at Reims in 1903, the parliamentary representatives of the party reported that they had introduced during the preceding session of parliament no less than forty-six legislative bills, the principal provisions of which dealt with the following subjects: the guaranty of secrecy and liberty of the ballot; the suppression of the religious budget; the old-age pension; the repeal of the laws against vagabondage; the right of government and municipal employees to strike; the monopoly of sugar refineries; the enactment of a labor code; the abolition of the trucking system; the abolition of private employment bureaus; the amendment of the laws on trade unions; the abolition of the standing army; the creation of a department of labor; the introduction of the initiative and referendum in legislative matters; the freedom of hunting and fishing, and the insurance of workingmen against accidents.[1]

In the session of the German Diet of 1900–1901, the representatives of the Social Democratic Party introduced bills for the amendment of the industrial courts act; for tenement house regulation and inspection; for the creation of a national department of labor and of a national factory inspection bureau; for the limitation of the work-

[1] "Parti Socialiste de France," Compte-Rendu du Deuxième Congrès National, Tenu à Reims, September 27–29, 1903, p. 28.

day of all employees in industrial, commercial and other occupations and pursuits, to ten hours; for the prohibition of employment of children under the age of fourteen years; for the extension of legal protection to working-women, especially those pregnant or in childbed; for the prohibition of the manufacture, import and export of matches with white phosphorus; for the extension of the rights of assembly, organization and coalition; for the extension and guaranty of the liberty of the press; for the abolition of the offense of lèse majesté; for the immunity of members of parliament from arrest during parliamentary sessions; for enforcing the responsibility of the Imperial Chancellor to the Diet, and for the reapportionment of parliamentary electoral districts in accordance with the increase of the population.[1]

We have chosen these instances of proposed socialist legislation from the two countries in which the socialist parliamentary groups are the oldest and have had ample time to settle down to fixed parliamentary practices, for the reason that the wide and varied scope of these proposed measures is typical of the socialist activity in the parliaments of all other European countries. Besides the proposed laws of the character of those mentioned, there are numerous other radical measures advocated most uniformly and persistently by socialists in parliaments, among them being those providing for a graduated income and inheritance tax.

But the effort to initiate legislation does not by any means exhaust the parliamentary work of the socialists.

---

[1] " Protokoll über die Verhandlungen des Parteitages der Sozialdemokratischen Partei Deutschlands," abgehalten zu Lübeck, September 22–28, 1901, p. 77.

The socialist deputies take part in the discussion on all legislative measures of social import introduced by the government or other parties, supporting or opposing or urging amendments, according to the nature of the proposed measure; they make full and sometimes very effective use of their right to interpellate the government on its actions, attitude or intentions with respect to matters or occurrences of public interest; they accept membership in the various parliamentary committees, and generally participate in all the detailed work of the parliaments. Thus the attitude of the socialists towards the positive work of parliaments has changed very radically within the last few decades, and the change was by no means arbitrary, but was brought about by the increased political strength of the socialist movement. A movement may well maintain a purely negative and criticising attitude so long as it is numerically weak and politically insignificant. But when the movement grows in strength and extension and gradually becomes a recognized social and political power, it can no longer remain at a dignified distance from the actual and practical struggles of modern industrial and political life — it is forced into the very center of these struggles and is involved in all their details: its progress becomes more persistent and aggressive, its program and practical work become more detailed and specific.

In 1867, when Liebknecht and his associates first formulated their rigorous program of parliamentary abstention, Germany was the only country that had socialist representatives in parliament, and the total number of these representatives was eight. To-day, after just forty years, the socialist parties have over four hundred deputies in the national parliaments of sixteen European countries, and hosts of representatives in minor legislative assemblies and municipal councils all over the world.

The socialist deputies in every country constitute a separate and independent parliamentary group, but they freely support other parties in parliaments in such measures and actions as they consider to be in the interests of the working class or in the furtherance of true social progress. The difference between such political coöperation in parliament and coöperation or combination in electoral campaigns is obvious. In parliaments votes are taken upon concrete and single issues from time to time; each party determines its stand on a given issue in conformity with its general views and the interests of its constituents, and the parties taking a similar stand naturally vote and act together on the particular issue. No compromise or organic fusion is involved in the procedure. The socialists in parliament frequently accept and support compromise measures, but only in cases where the measures contain at least some positive benefit to their cause; they do not indulge in the practice of political "swapping," by which one party often gives its support to a measure which it would otherwise oppose, in return for the similar support for its pet measures by the other party.

Nor do the socialist representatives in parliament make lasting or permanent alliances with the other parties for any purpose.

When the famous "*bloc republicain*" was formed in the Parliament of France as a defensive and offensive union against the monarchists and reactionaries, who were advanced to the foreground by the violent anti-Dreyfus agitation, one wing of the socialist group, the moderates or opportunists, joined the "*bloc*." But that policy proved so unsatisfactory to the socialists of France, and met with such decided criticism from the socialists of other countries, that it was soon abandoned.

Another and much more mooted point of parliamentary tactics presented itself to the socialists of Europe in recent years. In 1899, the "radical" French premier, Waldeck-Rousseau, conferred the portfolio of Commerce and Industry on the socialist deputy, Étienne Millerand, and thus for the first time in the history of modern politics a socialist became a full-fledged cabinet minister. The event came as a surprise to the socialists of France as well as to the socialists of all other countries, and the wisdom of Millerand's entry into the Waldeck-Rousseau cabinet, or, stated in terms of the general principle involved, the wisdom of socialist participation in a bourgeois government, for a time furnished the foremost subject of discussion in the socialist press and in all socialist party circles.

The defenders of Millerand's course, who came to be known as "ministerialists," saw in the entry of a socialist into the government of the country a partial attainment of that "conquest of the powers of government" which is the final political aim of all socialist parties. The offer of a cabinet portfolio to a socialist, they argued, is not a free gift on the part of the government; it is a concession forced from it by the growing strength of the party. It is as much a legitimate object of political conquest as is a seat in parliament, and the socialists having conquered that high position in the administration of the affairs of the country, would prove themselves inconsistent and weak-kneed if they should shrink from its responsibilities instead of utilizing its great opportunity for the advancement of their cause.

On the other hand, the ultra radical wing of the socialist movement in France and other countries was utterly opposed to participation of socialists in bourgeois governments under any and all circumstances. The powers of government in a centralized state, they declared, cannot be conquered piecemeal. As long as the dominant interests in parliament are those of the capitalist class, the government must, on the whole, be a class government, administered in the interests of the possessing classes and directed against the classes of non-possessors, and a socialist member of such a government is bound to become a tool of the bourgeoisie in its struggles against the workingmen. The socialist party can gain no positive benefit from the membership of one of its representatives in a bourgeois cabinet, but it may suffer incalculable harm by assuming responsibility for the acts of a hostile government.

The views of the great bulk of socialists outside of France on the vexed question were admirably expressed by Karl Kautsky in a letter to the "ministerial" French newspaper, *Petite Republique:* [1] —

"The question whether and to what extent the socialist proletariat may participate in a bourgeois government," writes he, "is a question of tactics, which must be answered differently in different countries and at different times, and which I do not dare to answer in absolute and unconditional terms.

"In Switzerland and in England, such a participation would seem to me possible; in Germany, out of the question.

[1] Reproduced in *Die Neue Zeit,* 19th Year, Vol. I, p. 37.

"But just because I cannot give an absolute answer, I cannot assert that the principle of class struggle prohibits a socialist from entering a bourgeois cabinet *under all circumstances.*

"Under normal conditions a socialist who recognizes the class struggle will be as little inclined to enter a bourgeois cabinet as an atheist would be inclined to enter a clerical cabinet, or a republican a cabinet of Bonapartists. His activity in such a cabinet could in the long run hardly have any other effect than to corrupt and to compromise him and his party.

"But I do not mean to say that there may not be *exceptional cases* in which it may sometimes be proper for socialists to coöperate for a *definite purpose* with bourgeois democrats in the same government against a common enemy, without violating the principle of class struggle. Such experiments will indeed always be dangerous, but there may be possible situations which would justify them."

The Millerand experiment has abundantly proved that the exceptional situation of which Kautsky spoke did not exist in his case, and the official career of the first socialist minister has, on the whole, confirmed the apprehensions of the "anti-ministerialists." The socialist parties in France and other countries have now adopted the definite policy of uniformly declining membership in cabinets, and while there are to-day two socialist ministers in France (Briand and Viviàni) and one in England (John Burns), the socialist parties of these countries disclaim all connection with or responsibility for them. Viviani and Burns had ceased to be members of the Socialist Party long before they accepted their portfolios, and Briand was summarily expelled from membership in his party as soon as he entered the cabinet. As showing the prevalence of the fashion of appointing socialists to cabinet positions, it is amusing to note that even Tsar Nicholas II could not abstain from offering to a prominent Finnish socialist, Mr. J. K. Kari, a portfolio in the Finnish cabinet. Mr. Kari, formerly secretary of the Finnish Socialist Party, accepted the offer, and was promptly read out of the party.

"What a strange pass our bourgeois republic has come to at this day," exclaims Jean Jaurès, "when cabinets cannot live without calling in socialists, even when socialists as a party deliberately decline to take office; when the republican majority not only turns to our model socialists to bring about needed reforms, but even has recourse to the renegades of revolutionary socialism to carry out effective measures against the advancing hosts! The Third Republic utilizes our men of energy and even our traitors!" [1]

Political Achievements of Socialism

The practical political activity of the socialist parties is, on the whole, of quite recent date. The social democrats of Germany entered on their first electoral campaign as far back as 1867, but for almost twenty years they stood practically alone in the field of socialist politics. Sporadic attempts at electoral campaigns were made by socialists in Holland beginning in 1880, in Italy in 1882 and in Denmark in 1884; but as well-organized and continuous political parties the socialists entered the political arena in France in 1885, in Denmark in 1889, in Sweden in 1890, in Italy in 1892, in Spain in 1893, in Belgium in

[1] *The Independent*, New York, June 20, 1907.

1894, and finally in Austria, Holland and Norway as late as 1897. In the United States the socialists nominated their first national ticket in 1892. In some of these countries the socialists had occasionally engaged in municipal and other minor campaigns somewhat earlier, but on the whole it may be said that the average period of practical and systematic socialist activity in politics does not exceed twenty years.

This comparatively short space of time has by no means been barren of positive results for the socialist movement and the working class.

The parliamentary achievements of the socialist parties may be divided into such reforms and measures as are directly traceable to socialist initiative and such as are the indirect results of socialist politics.

The reforms of the former class are few and rather insignificant, as must naturally be expected in view of the fact that the socialists as yet constitute but a small minority in every parliament, and a minority generally hostile to the rest of the house. Moreover, in several European parliaments, notably in the German Diet, a fixed and rather large number of seconders is required before a proposed measure may be considered by the house; and in most of such countries the socialist parliamentary groups have not been, until recent years, numerous enough to comply with such requirements, so that their activity was of necessity limited to the support or opposition of measures introduced by the government or by other parties.

Summing up the positive achievements of social democratic politics in the German Diet, Hermann Molkenbuhr [1]

[1] "Positive Leistungen der Sozialdemocratie," *Die Neue Zeit*, 25th Year, Nos. 27, 29 and 30.

claims some direct socialist victories in all the domains of parliamentary legislation dealing with workingmen's insurance, factory laws, industrial courts, the civil code, protective tariff and taxation. Taking the existing German law on accident insurance as an illustration, he shows, by an elaborate analysis of the origin of its various provisions, that no less than twelve of its most substantial amendments have been adopted on motion of the social democratic party, while the party of the center, which habitually poses as the champion of the working class, has only two of such amendments to its credit, the party of the government and the liberal union, each one, the other parties having contributed nothing at all to the amelioration of this important law. In France the socialist deputies have initiated or secured the passage of several favorable measures, among them laws reducing the hours of labor of government employees, extending the powers of municipalities, suppressing private employment bureaus, and several important amendments to the accident insurance law. In Denmark the socialists in parliament have, after persistent efforts of twenty years, recently succeeded in securing the passage of a law which makes it incumbent on the government and municipalities to grant considerable subsidies to labor organizations formed for the support of their unemployed members. In Italy, Belgium and Switzerland the socialist representatives in parliament have at one time or another succeeded in securing the passage of several measures of social reform, while in Sweden, Norway and Austria the socialist parties have within recent years secured largely extended suffrage.

Far more important, however, than the laws directly

initiated in parliaments by socialist representatives, are those numerous measures of social legislation which have within the last two decades been passed by the parliaments of almost all civilized countries as the indirect but nevertheless legitimate result of socialist political action. These measures are as a rule taken by the liberal or even conservative parties bodily or with some changes from the programs formulated by the socialist parties, and are fathered as original proposals of the opponents of socialism in order to destroy the effectiveness of the socialist propaganda. Far-seeing statesmen sometimes meet such "issues" with apparent cheerfulness, even before they have acquired the force of popular demands, and shortsighted governments grant them grudgingly when the general cry for them has practically become irresistible. Prince Bismarck, as was pointed out in a previous chapter,[1] frankly avowed that the object of the broad social legislation inaugurated by him was primarily to avert a popular revolution, and the greater part of the social and political reforms inaugurated since by the several parliaments of Europe clearly owe their origin to similar considerations. In those countries of Europe in which the socialist movement has attained such political strength as to cause alarm to the parties of the dominant classes, the latter regularly shape their policies with special reference to their probable effect on the socialist vote, and the "stealing of the socialist thunder" is one of their favorite manœuvers, especially in time of approaching electoral campaigns. Chancellor Von Buelow has publicly admitted this fact for Germany, and it is more than an accident that the golden era of social legislation in all other countries coincides quite closely with the

[1] "Social Legislation and Socialist Jurisprudence."

o

period of practical socialist politics; that countries in which political socialism is weak, as, for instance, the United States, are the most backward in the domain of social legislation, and that the few labor laws occasionally passed by the American state legislatures are so often nullified by court decisions.

But all the parliamentary victories of socialism, direct or indirect, are but a minor part of the political achievements of the socialist parties. Socialist politics is not restricted to parliamentary elections and activity; it extends to all minor divisions of the state in which the administration is wholly or partly elective, to the landtags of Germany, the cantonal councils of Switzerland, the provincial councils of other countries, the state legislatures of the United States, and above all, the councils of municipalities. And it is the last-mentioned domain in which the socialists have so far achieved their greatest practical triumphs.

The powers of municipalities are, as a very uniform rule, largely restricted by the state, and a socialist administration never has the opportunity to realize all or even a substantial part of its program within the scope of a municipal government. But on the other hand the socialists, while they have so far not succeeded in a single instance in conquering the government of an entire country, province or state, have gained the absolute majority in the councils of numerous municipalities in many countries of Europe and within the very restricted scope of municipal powers they have had the opportunity to experiment in practical administrative problems.

Of the countries with a strong socialist representation in the municipal administration, we must mention in the first place France, where but one wing of the socialist movement, the Parti Ouvrier Français, in 1904, had full control of the administration of 63 municipalities and a grand total of over 1300 municipal councilors in 174 cities and towns. The unified Socialist Party of France has to-day about 3800 representatives and officers in about 500 municipalities. The Italian socialists administer over one hundred towns and cities and have representation in the councils of more than 1200 municipalities; the socialists of Belgium have majorities in the councils of 22 municipalities and a total of 650 representatives in 193 towns; those of Austria had, in 1904, 526 representatives in 178 municipalities; the socialists of Norway elected in 1907 over 1100 representatives in urban and rural communities; those of Denmark have over 400 municipal councilors, and the socialists of England and Sweden have strong representations in the municipal administration of their countries. Even the Socialist Party of the United States has at different times had the control of the administration of several towns, and has about three hundred municipal officers in the different parts of the country.

The work and achievements of these socialist municipalities vary in each country according to the special condition of their inhabitants and the latitude of action allowed to them by the central governments, but a pretty complete picture of such work and achievements may be obtained from a brief description of the main features of "municipal socialism" in the countries where it is most strongly represented.

From the country in which municipal socialism is strongest, France, we have the reports of the mayors of several cities [1] which afford an excellent insight into the workings of "socialist" municipalities.

In Roubaix, a manufacturing town in Northern France, of a population of about 125,000, the socialists were in control of the municipal government for a number of years. The first attention of the socialist council was given to the task of properly bringing up the children of the poor.

"The child and its welfare, its protection against disease, against want and against contamination, its training and its culture," says Felix Chabrouilland, the socialist secretary of the Roubaix municipality, in one of the reports mentioned, "this has been the constant care of the socialist council of Roubaix.

"The socialist officers began their work for the little ones by admitting girl-mothers to the relief offered by the bureau of charities, which up to that time had been piously denied them. For the benefit of infants the socialist officers provided a distribution of layettes to needy mothers. Moreover, the bureau of medical assistance has been reorganized, and the mothers can obtain without cost the services of the doctor and the midwife.

"The child is born. To whom shall the mother intrust it if she must return to the factory?

"Before the socialists came into power, Roubaix had no municipal *creches* (day nurseries). They contented themselves with subsidizing to a slight extent the work of private *creches*.

"In 1894 the first municipal *creche* was started in a

[1] The reports appeared originally in "Le Mouvement Socialiste" and in "Le Socialiste"; they were translated into English and published under the title, "Socialists in French Municipalities," by Charles H. Kerr, Chicago, 1900.

rented building in the heart of a populous district. Some months later $10,000 was voted for building another *creche*, which, opened in 1896, deserves to be taken as a model. A third is now building, and others are under construction. Children are received in the municipal *creches* without any charge.

"The resolution establishing restaurants for school children was passed by the socialist council on the first day of its official existence. These restaurants, the cost of which is borne by the school fund, are open every school day of the year. The great majority of children are admitted without charge. The children enrolled as paying are charged fifteen centimes a meal in the kindergartens and twenty centimes in the primary schools. Since 1892 the school restaurants of Roubaix have served 2,818,601 meals, of which only 20,402 were paid for. The meal consists of a soup, a plate of meat with vegetables, 80 grammes of bread and a glass of beer.

"To give children food of the first quality is an excellent thing. But some of them lack sufficient clothing. Since the socialists have replaced the reactionaries in the mayor's office, the bureau for clothing school children has distributed to the poor children in the secular schools 157,617 pieces of clothing, — trousers, shirts, dresses, caps, pairs of stockings or of shoes, etc.

"By the terms of an agreement made in 1897 and renewed in 1900, the city of Roubaix sends to the seaside hospital of Saint-Pol-sur-Mer, a little place near Dunkirk, the children from its common schools who are enfeebled, anemic — in a word, 'candidates for disease,' whose delicate constitution may be restored by the good effects of a sojourn at the seashore. These children are sent during the summer season, from April 15 to October 15, and remain a month at the sanitarium. Each caravan is composed of not less than 100 children nor more than 160, and their only duty while at the seashore is to take deep breaths of fresh air, play in the sunlight and improve in health. No classes, no lessons, no discipline other than what a parent would impose, but watchful care. Already 1865 little 'candidates for disease,' boys and girls, have been helped by a month at Saint-Pol. There is no doubt on the part of any one acquainted with the facts but that the benefit to the children, moral as well as physical, has been great."

The socialists of Roubaix also largely extended and improved the common school system of the town by establishing a number of new classes, introducing courses of manual training, etc.

Next to the all-important subject of education, the socialist administration of Roubaix bestowed the greatest care upon the matter of public health and the support of the poor. It established municipal bathing houses and disinfecting plants as well as municipal bakeries and kitchens. In its bakeries it baked its own bread for the poor of the town, and distributed it freely at the homes of the latter, while its kitchens provided all needy families with wholesome food, at the lowest possible price.

In addition to this, the socialist municipality paid a pension of 120 francs a year to the aged poor of either sex living at home; it provided a number of cottages for widows with little children to care for, established a bureau for free legal advice and built a new hospital for the sick.

The socialist administration of Roubaix largely benefited the municipal employees, whose hours of labor were reduced to eight per day and whose wages were substantially increased, and it endowed the theaters and the scientific and artistic societies of the town more liberally than its bourgeois predecessors had done.

In the still larger city of Lille, which was likewise under socialist control for a number of years, the municipal reforms introduced by the socialists bear a general resemblance to those of Roubaix, except that some of them, particularly those relating to sanitary measures and hygienic supervision, were carried out on a larger scale. A notable feature of the socialist administration of Lille was the promotion of the fine arts and higher education among the poor. The school of fine arts was reorganized on a higher and more efficient plane; the municipal theater was frequently opened to the workers, and by agreement with the management of the theaters in the city, the administration received four hundred free seats at each performance, which were distributed among the workingmen; popular concerts and lectures were periodically arranged at the expense of the city, and liberal prizes were awarded to poor students of recognized ability.

The examples of Roubaix and Lille are typical for all other municipalities under socialist control in France. In almost all cases the care of the children, the public health, the assistance of the poor and the legal protection of the workingmen are the prime concern of the administration.

The socialists of France ascribe but a secondary importance to the municipal ownership of street cars, telephones, etc., although wherever possible, they regulate the rates of such public service concerns and sometimes even operate them as municipal enterprises.

With all their reforms, the socialist municipalities in France are as a rule far from being extravagant or reckless in their expenditures, and their balance sheets usually show a substantial surplus. The taxes are shifted, as much as possible, from the poor to the wealthy.

In Belgium the powers of the municipal administration are even more limited than in France — the mayor of the city is appointed by the king, and the decisions and ordinances of the municipal council are subject to the veto of the "*deputation permanente*," a bureau of the provincial parliament and of the king. Under these circumstances the socialists in Belgian town and city councils have naturally not been able to introduce very radical innovations in the municipal administration of the country. Thus the principle of the progressive income tax for the raising of municipal revenues has repeatedly been adopted by the councils of socialist municipalities, and has been vetoed by the government as often as adopted. Among the first tasks of a socialist municipality in Belgium is the improvement of the conditions of the workingmen in its employ. A fixed minimum wage, a fixed maximum workday, and insurance against accidents are almost uniformly among the first measures adopted by a new socialist administration in a Belgian town. The schooling of children with the special features of free clothing, free meals and vacation colonies plays as important a part in every socialist municipal administration in Belgium as in France, but in the former somewhat more attention is being paid to the municipal operation of street cars, gas, electricity, waterworks, etc.

The socialist municipal councilors of Belgium have organized a union for the study of municipal problems and the dissemination of information on affairs of municipal administration, with a permanent bureau and a salaried secretary, and their example has been followed by the socialists of Holland.

The socialist municipalities of Denmark proceed substantially along the same lines as those of France and Belgium. Speaking for the town of Esbjerg as a typical example, the editor of the local socialist paper relates in a recent report : "The Socialists hold 12 of the 19 seats in the city council. Our first act, after having gained control, was to assist the poor, and we have managed to make it possible for all poor to avoid public charity.

"We then helped the hungry school children by giving them a free noon-day meal, until the minister of the interior prohibited the appropriation of the necessary means.

"We next had the food paid for by the free poor fund and in turn appropriated money for the fund.

"Later, however, we formed a private organization, which took charge of the feeding of the school children, and strangely enough, the city council was now given permission by the department of the interior to appropriate the required money for this purpose.

"We have endeavored to improve the school system, until we now have free and uniform education in all common schools.

"However, other things have drawn public attention toward Esbjerg more than these. The contractors formerly had a solid organization and as a rule always agreed on bids for public works, and then divided the profits. The socialists soon put a stop to this. We employed workmen direct and bought our own lumber and brick. We built a school and employed our carpenters direct. Then we were boycotted. We could get no more brick at the kilns, and the team owners were forbidden to deliver any material to the building. This strike lasted half a day, after which we bought the required brick at the contractors' own brick kiln.

"The employers' association, however, has since attempted, hitherto without any success, to delay or even stop all work undertaken by us.

"The anti-socialist minority has now resigned in a body, in spite of the fact that they have been represented on all committees, according to their number in the council."

The distinctive features of municipal socialism in Italy are the reduction of the taxes on articles of food, the increase of direct taxes, and the municipal subsidies and support of labor exchanges and coöperative enterprises conducted by trade unions, although the socialist administrations do not neglect any of the customary municipal reform measures.

In the United States Wisconsin is so far the only state in which the socialists have of late years had a substantial and growing representation in the legislature and in the councils of some municipalities, notably in the city of Milwaukee. In the state legislature as well as in the Milwaukee City Council, they form minority groups, but they have nevertheless been able to influence the actions of both bodies in a marked degree. Mr. Carl D. Thompson, a former socialist member of the Wisconsin State Legislature, enumerates a surprisingly large number of positive measures initiated by the Socialist Party and passed by the city council of Milwaukee or the state legislature of Wisconsin.[1]

[1] "The Constructive Program of Socialism," Milwaukee, 1908.

The achievements of socialist politics in the field of positive reform are thus not insignificant. But the socialists do not overestimate them. They consider them as measures calculated to brace and strengthen the working class in its struggle against capital, but by no means as the beginnings or installments of a socialist system.

The work of systematically rebuilding the economic and political structure of modern society on the lines of socialism, can begin only when the socialists have the control of the entire political machinery of the state, *i.e.*, of all the legislative, executive and judicial organs of the government. As long as the socialist representatives in modern legislative or administrative organs remain in the minority, the more radical and truly socialistic reforms advocated by them, the reforms aimed at the dispossession of the privileged classes, are bound to founder on the opposition of the ruling-class majorities in the government. The socialists can expect to carry out their program only by a series of gradual and successive, but systematic and uninterrupted measures, when they themselves are in the majority in the government, either having carried a majority of the popular vote in a successful election, or having been placed in power by a popular rising. The chief aim of socialist activity is, therefore, to develop the numerical strength and political maturity required for the ultimate conquest of the powers of government, and the supreme test of the success of present socialist politics is the measure in which it realizes that aim. And it is in this, their most important function, that socialist politics have achieved their highest triumph.

For whatever might have been the significance of socialist politics as a factor in securing immediate social reforms, it certainly has been of transcendent importance in the creation of the powerful national organizations of socialism. It was the practical political battles of socialism, the concrete attacks on the enemy, the definite issues and war cries, the common victories and defeats that attracted multitudes of European workingmen, and it is these that are beginning to attract the mass of American workingmen to the banner of socialism. If the number of socialist voters of the world has grown from about 30,000 in 1867 to almost 10,000,000 in 1908; if the socialists have become a recognized factor in the public life of 25 modern nations, having representation in the parliaments and administrative organs of 16 of them; if the socialists have elaborated a clear, detailed and sober program of social transformation, and developed in their ranks thousands of thinkers, orators, statesmen, organizers and leaders, the practical politics of the modern socialist parties is largely responsible for these splendid results. Without the unifying and propelling force of political activity, the socialist movement to-day might not have advanced much beyond the stage of the purely literary significance of the early socialist schools or beyond that of a number of incoherent sects.

PART II

SOCIALISM AND REFORM

CHAPTER I

INTRODUCTION

Socialists and Social Reformers

To the outsider one of the most puzzling aspects of the socialist movement is its attitude towards the modern movements for social reform. The socialists are reformers. The socialist program contains a large number of concrete measures or "demands" for the progressive improvement of our industrial, social and political institutions, and much of the practical political activity of socialism is directed towards the advancement of such reform measures.

And still socialists are often found reluctant to co-operate with non-socialist reformers for the attainment of specific reforms. Even when such proposed reforms are apparently in line with the demands of socialism, the separate movements for their realization are not seldom met by them with indifference, sometimes even with active opposition.

The socialists have on that account been charged with narrowness and inconsistency, but these charges are based on an entire misconception of the character of socialist reforms. There is a vital distinction between the reforms advocated by the socialists and those urged by the reformers of all other shades.

The non-socialist reform movements may be divided into two general groups; those inaugurated distinctly for the

benefit of the middle classes, *i.e.*, the small farmers, manufacturers or traders, and those supported by ideologists of
all classes.

The movements of the former variety have for their in-
variable object the strengthening of the position of the
middle class as against the increasing power of large
capitalism. The measures advocated by them often con-
template the arrest of industrial development or even the
return to conditions of past ages. Among such "reform"
measures are the restrictions on combinations of capital
and the provisions against suppression of competition.
Measures of this character are reactionary even though
in their formulation they sometimes coincide with working-
class demands.

The ideologists of the "better classes" represent a less
reactionary but not more efficient type of social reformers.
These kind-hearted but shortsighted gentlemen are
thoroughly convinced of the soundness of our social
system as a whole. They notice occasionally certain
social evils and abuses, and they endeavor to remove them
in what seems to them to be the most direct way. They
happen to encounter an appalling condition of poverty,
and they seek to allay it by alms. They notice the spread
of disease among the poor, and they build hospitals and
sanitariums. They are shocked by the tidal wave of crime
and vice, and they strive to lead the sinners back to the
path of righteousness by moral sermons and model penal
institutions. They find their elected representatives in
public office incompetent and corrupt, and they unite to
turn them out of office and to elect more efficient and
honest men. They treat each social abuse and evil as an
isolated and casual phenomenon. They fail to see the con-

nection between them all. For them, as for the late German-American statesman, Carl Schurz, there is no social problem, but there are many social problems.

The aim of all socialist reforms, on the other hand, is to strengthen the working class economically and politically and to pave the way for the introduction of the socialist state. The effect of every true socialist reform must be to transfer some measure of power from the employing classes. A socialist reform must be in the nature of a working-class conquest.

The socialist reform measures, moreover, are all inseparably and logically connected with each other, and only when taken together do they constitute an effective program of social progress. As separate and independent measures, they would be trivial, and from the point of view of the ultimate aim of the socialist movement, none of them is alone of sufficient importance to warrant the concentration of all efforts for its realization.

The difference between the conceptions and methods of the ideological social reformers and those of the socialists may be best shown by an illustration borrowed from the domain of pathology. A number of physicians are called into consultation on a grave case. The patient suffers from spells of coughing, headaches and high fever. His appetite is poor, and he is losing weight and color.

If the physicians are thoughtless and superficial practitioners, they will regard all these indications as so many separate and independent diseases. They will treat each of the supposed diseases separately or they will have each treated by a specialist in that particular branch of medicine. But if a scientific and experienced practitioner be called into the consultation, he will say to his colleagues: "Gentle-

P

men, your diagnosis of the case is wrong. The patient
does not suffer from a complication of diseases. The
many supposed diseases which you have discovered are not
independent casual ailments; they are all but symptoms
of one grave organic disease — tuberculosis. If you succeed in banishing this organic disease from the patient's
system, the symptoms which you take for independent
ailments will disappear of themselves, but if you persist in
treating the symptoms without attacking the root of them
all, the patient cannot improve."

And so, likewise, it is with the so-called evils of society.
Our social conditions are not healthy and normal, our
social organism is ill. The abject poverty of the masses
with all its concomitant evils — sickness, ignorance, vice
and crime — is appalling, while the extravagant luxuries
of our multi-millionaires only serve to accentuate the utter
misery of "the other half."

The gigantic trusts and monopolies which have developed
within recent years, the periodic crises and chronic strikes
and lockouts, are proof of the pathological condition of our
industries, while boss rule, corruption and bribery mark a
similar condition in our politics.

To the superficial student of society these conditions
present so many separate "evils," each one independent
of the others, each one curable by itself. Hence our
charity organizations, anti-vice leagues and societies for the
prevention of crime; hence our "trust busters," single
taxers, municipal-ownership men and anti-corrupt-prac-
tices advocates; hence our social and political reformers
of all types and specialties.

The socialists, on the other hand, see a clear connection
and necessary interdependence between these evils. They

regard them all as mere symptoms of one deep-rooted
disease of our social organism and do not believe in curing
the mere symptoms without attacking the real disease.
This disease the socialists find in the unhealthy organization of our industries, based on the private ownership of
the means of production and distribution.

Poverty is the direct result of capitalistic exploitation,
and ignorance, vice and crime are poverty's legitimate
children. To maintain its rule, capitalism must dominate
government and public sentiment, hence the constant
incentive for the ruling classes to corrupt our politics, our
press, pulpit and schools.

The ultimate aim of the socialist movement is to convert
the material means of production and distribution into the
common property of the nation as the only radical and
effective cure of all social evils. But this program does
not imply that the socialists propose for the time being to
remain inactive, complacently expecting the dawn of the
millennium.

The scientific physician in our illustration, after having
made his diagnosis, does not idly sit by expecting the
coming of the day when the dread disease shall suddenly
disappear. He proceeds to the proper course of treatment forthwith. By a systematic process of strengthening
his patient's physique, by increasing his powers of resistance, he gradually restores his patient's health. In the
course of the treatment he does not disdain palliatives
calculated to give temporary relief, but all his remedies
are strictly consistent and coördinate, and are applied
with the ultimate object constantly in view — the destruction of the mortal germs of the organic disease.

And the socialists proceed in a similar manner. They

seek to prepare the people for the radical change of the
industrial basis of society, by a systematic and never-
ceasing course of education, training and organization,
but in the meantime they do not reject temporary reform.
They favor every real progressive measure, and work for
such measures wherever and whenever an opportunity
offers itself to them.   But all the socialist reforms are consistent parts of their general program; they all tend in one
direction and serve one ultimate purpose.

To the ordinary social reformer, on the other hand, each
evil is an evil by itself to be cured without change of the
system which produces it, and hence his "practical"
reforms are doomed to failure.   The charity worker may
bring temporary relief to a few hundred poor, a mere atom
in the world of poverty, but he cannot check poverty;
the moral crusader may "save the souls" of some fallen
women and men, but as long as the conditions which drive
them into vice and crime remain unchanged, he cannot
stamp out vice or crime; the political reformer may succeed in a certain campaign, and defeat the corrupt "boss"
or divorce the legislature from the corrupting lobby, but
the next campaign will find a new "boss" at the head
of his party and a new host of capitalist agents in control
of the legislature as long as the industrial conditions
which breed corruption in politics continue. Just as the
middle-class reformers are reactionary and utopian, the
ideological reformers are, as a rule, superficial and ineffective, and the socialists can, therefore, gain nothing by a
union with either.

From this analysis of the aims and nature of socialist
reforms it will be readily seen that socialism cannot attach
an equal importance to all the numerous reform measures

agitated in our days. Its relation to each of such measures depends on the special character of that measure and its efficiency as a weapon in the class struggle. In the following chapters we will endeavor to deal with the subject from that point of view. For the convenience of treatment, we will group the most popular reforms under five main heads, and we will consider the character, achievements, and rôle in the socialist program of each reform group in a separate chapter

CHAPTER II

Industrial Reform

UNDER this general title we will include all direct efforts to improve the present economic conditions of the wage laborers, to diminish the degree of their exploitation and to strengthen their position in the struggles with their employers.

The specific movements coming under this head are those for the improvement of labor conditions and other measures commonly designated as factory reform; the reduction of the hours of work, the abolition of child labor, the regulation of woman labor and all other progressive movements represented by the trade unions and the coöperative societies of workingmen.

The socialists attach the greatest importance to all reforms of this character. They realize that the task of transforming the modern capitalist society into a socialist commonwealth can be accomplished only by the conscious, systematic and persevering efforts of a working class physically, mentally and morally fit for the assumption of the reins of government, and not by a blind revolt of a furious and desperate rabble. Every measure calculated to remove from the workingman some of the cares and uncertainties of his material existence, to improve his health

214

and spirits, to give him some measure of leisure, and some time for thought and study, is bound to enhance his general intelligence, his interest in social affairs and in the progress and welfare of his class.   The adherents of socialism principally recruit themselves from among the better situated classes of the workingmen, and the socialist efforts to raise the economic level of the working class are an organic part of the socialist movement, an indispensable condition of its progress and ultimate triumph.

Factory Reform

The beginnings of factory legislation are to be found in the classic country of modern capitalism, England, where Parliament as early as 1802 adopted the bill introduced by Sir Robert Peel for the protection of the apprentices employed in cotton mills.   The measure was called forth by the inhuman conditions in the English cotton mills, into which thousands of orphans and pauper children of the most tender ages were bound out by the parishes under the old Elizabethan "Apprenticeship Act," without restriction on their hours of labor and without provisions for their health and education.   These unfortunate children were forced to work up to fifteen hours a day, and were crowded in pent-up, unsanitary buildings adjoining the factory.   They were ill-clothed and underfed.   They were growing up under conditions of physical, mental and moral degeneracy, and it was the menace to the future of England's laboring population implied in these conditions which secured the passage of the Peel act.

Viewed from the standpoint of modern conceptions, the act of 1802 was no great achievement.   It limited the workday of the cotton mill apprentices to twelve hours, and compelled the mill owners to clothe their apprentices and to give them a certain limited school instruction. But the great significance of the act lies in the fact that it was the first to break down the bourgeois doctrine of non-interference by the state in the industrial relations of its citizens. It created the "precedent," so indispensable to the Anglo-Saxon mind; it opened the door to factory legislation. And slowly but steadily the principle of state protection for factory workers grew in scope and extension. In England the law of 1802 was followed first by the timid amendments of 1819, 1825 and 1833, and then by the bolder measures of the latter half of the last century, until factory laws became a regular and important function of parliamentary legislation. Starting with the regulation of the labor of apprenticed children, they gradually extended their operation to the "free" working children, then to working women, and finally to all factory workers.

From England the principle of factory legislation spread to the United States, Germany, France and Switzerland, and finally it established itself in all industrial countries.

"Looking broadly now to labor legislation as it has occurred in this country," says Mr. Carroll D. Wright, speaking of factory laws in the United States, "it may be well to sum up its general features. Such legislation has fixed the hours of labor for women and certain minors in manufacturing establishments; it has adjusted the contracts of labor; it has protected employees by insisting that all dangerous machinery shall be guarded; . . . it has created boards of factory inspectors, whose powers and duties have added much to the health and safety of the operatives; it has in many instances provided for weekly payments, not only by municipalities, but by corporations; . . . it has regulated the employment of prisoners; protected the employment of children; exempted the wages of the wife and minor children from attachment; established bureaus for statistics of labor; provided for the ventilation of factories and workshops; established industrial schools and evening schools; provided special transportation by railroads for workingmen; modified the common-law rules relative to the liability of employers for injuries of their employees; fixed the compensation of railroad corporations for negligently causing the death of employees, and has provided for their protection against accident and death." [1]

In reading this seemingly large schedule of labor laws it must, of course, be borne in mind that it enumerates and combines all principal measures enacted in the different states of the Union, and that hardly any single state can boast of a labor code containing them all. On the other hand, however, it must also not be forgotten that the United States is one of the backward countries in the matter of factory legislation, and that many countries of Europe have gone considerably farther in that direction.

But even in the most advanced countries, factory legislation is, on the whole, only in its infancy, and its practical achievements are insignificant compared with what still remains to be done in order to make the work of the factory hand tolerable and safe.

The beginnings of factory legislation were thus introduced by the bourgeoisie at a time when the labor movement had hardly attained the power to speak for itself. The first labor laws were brought about partly as a result

[1] "Industrial Evolution of the United States," pp. 291, 292.

of the struggles between the hostile divisions of dominant classes, each of whom courted the support of the working-men, but probably to a larger extent as a measure of hygiene intended to check the physical degeneration of the working class, whose misery had become so great as to threaten the future of the nation. And it is very significant that Peel's pioneer measure in the domain of factory reform was entitled, "A bill for the preservation of the *health* and *morals* of the apprentices employed in cotton mills."

In some instances, notably in Prussia, the first measures of protective labor legislation were introduced by the rulers as a military necessity. "Thus," relates Adolf Braun, "in an address to Frederick William III in 1836, it was reported that the factory districts were unable to furnish their full quota of soldiers for the army. Shortly thereafter the first Prussian Labor Law, that of March 9, 1839, was enacted. Children under the age of nine years were excluded from work in factories and mines; children under sixteen years were forbidden to work nights or Sundays or more than 10 hours on workdays." [1]

But with the growth of the labor movement and the general improvements in labor conditions brought about by it, the dominant classes have no longer any interest in the protection of the wage workers against the exploitation of their employers, and the task of developing and extending factory legislation falls entirely on the organized workingmen.

Shorter Workday

Prior to the development of modern factory industry, the normal workday of the artisan was one of compara-

[1] Adolf Braun, "Zum Achtstundentag," Berlin, 1901, p. 14.

tively short duration. Speaking of pre-capitalistic England, Thorold Rogers [1] asserts that it was one of eight hours, and his assertion is backed by an abundance of proof.

But with the gradual disappearance of the easy-going artisan of mediæval times, and the advent of capitalist production, the length of the workday and intensity of labor grew steadily, reaching the high-water mark towards the end of the eighteenth and the beginning of the nineteenth century. The golden era of machine invention stimulated production and developed factory industry with an impetuous suddenness and in immense proportions. The ready urban workmen were totally insufficient for the new needs of capitalist industry. Their wives and children and their rural cousins were called into requisition, and their hours of labor were advanced to the limits of physical possibility. At the beginning of the nineteenth century the ordinary workday of the English factory worker seems to have been one of from twelve to fifteen hours, and in seasons of special activity there was no limit to it at all. The effects of such overwork on the physical, moral and mental condition of the factory workers were disastrous in the extreme, and the demand for a reduction of the workday was practically the first manifestation of the incipient labor movement in England. The efforts to reduce the length of the workday have ever since remained a cardinal part of the modern labor movement. These efforts find their expression in the political agitation of the working-class parties as well as in the struggles of the industrial labor organizations in their special fields, and in both domains the labor movement has attained some suc-

[1] "Six Centuries of Work and Wages," p. 327.

cess during the last century. In England the first law limiting the hours of labor to 10 per day, was passed in 1847. The law was loosely framed and poorly enforced, and in 1850 it was superseded by a new bill limiting the hours of labor to 10½ on week days and 7½ on Saturdays. This law originally applied to women, children and men employed in the textile mills only, but its operation was gradually extended by a series of new enactments to practically all factory workers. The hours of labor of textile workers and of children in certain industries were subsequently reduced to 10 per day. In France the workday of adult males, when working together with women and children, is limited to 10 hours, otherwise to 12; in Austria, Germany and Switzerland, the normal workday of adult male factory workers is fixed at 11 hours by law, and several states of the American Union have limited the duration of the normal workday by legal enactment.

Besides these general laws several countries have fixed a minimum workday of varying length for certain special classes of workmen, principally those engaged in the more perilous and taxing occupations and those employed directly by the government.

These, then, are the rather meager results so far achieved by this movement in the domain of legislation. But far larger and more substantial gains have been made in the same field through the efforts of the industrial labor organizations in most of the advanced countries of Europe, Australia and America. In many industries in those countries, nine-hour and even eight-hour workdays prevail.

In almost all modern countries the movement of organized labor to reduce the hours of work has crystallized in the demand for an eight-hour workday, and the movement is, therefore, generally known as the eight-hour movement.

The English trade unions seem to have advanced the ideal of a general eight-hour day for workers of all sexes and ages as soon as their public activity was made possible by the repeal of the Combination Laws in 1824; in Australia an Eight-Hour League was formed in 1856, and a similar organization was called into life in the United States in 1869 under the leadership of Ira Stewart.

In the English-speaking countries, especially, the eight-hour movement has assumed large proportions and importance. "Out of it," says William D. P. Bliss, "has grown in America a so-called eight-hour philosophy, which is held by its adherents to be a complete philosophy of the labor movement and to furnish a program not to be looked at as simply one plank in a labor program, but as a proposition complete in itself, including most socialist propositions and furnishing in its outline a solution of the whole labor question." [1]

A shortening of the hours of labor is a measure of immense importance to the working people, as a factor tending to improve their general condition of health and to raise the average duration of their lives. Long hours of labor are bound to impair the alertness and vigilance of the worker. It is a well-known fact that accidents occur most frequently in the industries in which long hours are the rule, and that they occur with greater frequency towards the end of the workday than at its beginning. But aside from accidents the duration of the workday has a very direct and important bearing on the sickness and mortality of the working class. Dr. J. Zadek, who has made a

[1] "The Encyclopedia of Social Reforms," New York and London, 1898, p. 88.

special study of this aspect of the problem,[1] relates many
striking instances of the effect of a reduced workday on the
health and life of the workers. Thus, after the lace workers
of Switzerland had succeeded in reducing their workday to
11 hours, sickness among the employees decreased by 25
per cent. Up to 1871 the workday of the machine builders
of Great Britain was excessively long, and the average life
of the workers in that trade was 38¼ years; in 1872 the
machine builders secured a reduction of the workday to
nine hours, and seventeen years later the average length of
their lives had risen to 48¼ years!

The adoption of an eight-hour system of work, it is further argued, would benefit the working class and advance
the general cause of human civilization in many ways.
By reducing the hours and quantity of labor of each individual, it would necessitate the employment of a larger
number of workingmen to satisfy the demands of production. The dread army of unemployed, the source of much
social vice and crime and the cause of much disastrous
competition in the labor market, would thus disappear.
A reduction of the hours of labor would result in a material
increase of wages not only on account of the elimination
of competition between workingmen, but also because it
would raise their standard of living. A short workday
would give to the workingman more leisure, *i.e.*, more time
to live, think and enjoy, and such leisure would necessarily
increase his fondness for home and family life, broaden his
intellectual, social and political interests, and develop in
him greater needs and requirements. And it is the habitual requirements of the workingman, his accustomed standard of living, that largely determine his wage. A shorter

[1] "Der Achtstundentag eine gesundheitliche Forderung," Berlin, 1906.

workday would, therefore, also increase the consumptive powers of the working classes, and thus stimulate industry and largely remove the causes of periodic overproduction and underconsumption with the resultant industrial crises and panics.

The formal resolution adopted by the Boston Eight-Hour League, and drafted by Ira Stewart, goes so far as to claim: —

"That less hours mean reducing the profits and fortunes that are made on labor or its results.

"More knowledge and more capital for the laborer; the wage system gradually disappearing through higher wages."

The socialists do not concede to the eight-hour movement all the importance that its most ardent adherents claim for it. They do not believe that the wage system upon which the entire present order is built can be abolished by a gradual reduction of hours and raising of wages, and they even do not admit that the general introduction of an eight-hour workday would be effective in solving the problem of unemployment. The shortening of the hours of labor, as a rule, results in the greater intensity and productiveness of labor, and it is the testimony of many writers on the subject that where a short workday has been introduced, it has been found that the ordinary workingman, owing to his better health, larger energy and more cheerful spirits, could do in eight hours practically as much work as he previously had done in ten. John Rae,[1] himself an employer of labor and one of the most ardent and persuasive advocates of the eight-hour day, largely bases his argument on this observation. But the socialists fully adhere to the

[1] "Eight Hours for Work," London, 1894.

view that a reduced workday would result in an increase
of wages for the other reasons mentioned above, and they
attach the utmost importance to the effect of greater leisure
on the morale and intellect of the working class. Hence
they are among the most active and enthusiastic promoters
of the movement. In countries with a strong trade union
movement they support the eight-hour agitation; in countries where the organizations of the trade unions are weaker
they lead the agitation. Every socialist platform invariably
contains the demand for a progressive reduction of the
hours of labor in keeping with the improved methods of
production, and the socialist representatives in parliaments
and other legislative bodies never miss an opportunity to
urge legislation in that direction.

One of the first resolutions adopted by the International
Workingmen's Association, which stood wholly under
socialist influences, at its first regular convention in 1864,
was to the effect that "the limitation of the workday is the
first step in the direction of the emancipation of the working
class," and that "the congress considers in principle that a
workday of eight hours' duration is sufficient." And when
the first of the new series of international socialist congresses convened in Paris in 1889, it reaffirmed the resolution, and set apart the first day of May of every year for
international labor demonstrations in favor of an eight-
hour workday. "May Day" parades and "eight-hour
demonstrations" have since become prominent features in
the socialist propaganda of Europe and America.

Child Labor

Child labor as an incident of domestic and agricultural
pursuits has probably always existed, but child labor as a

regular and important factor in national industry is an innovation, a blossom of the modern capitalist system of production. It was the machine that made child labor on a large scale possible, it was capitalist competition that made it desirable, and it was capitalist exploitation of the adult workers that made it inevitable. The worst phases of child labor are to be found in the classic country of capitalism and in the classic period of factory development—in England towards the end of the eighteenth and the beginning of the nineteenth centuries.

Describing the conditions of child labor of that period, Mr. William F. Willoughby says:—

"Children of all ages, down to three and four, were found in the hardest and most painful labor, while babes of six were commonly found in large numbers in many factories. Labor from 12 to 13 and often 16 hours a day was the rule. Children had not a moment free, save to snatch a hasty meal, or sleep as best they could. From earliest youth they worked to a point of extreme exhaustion, without open-air exercise or any enjoyment whatever, but grew up, if they survived at all, weak, bloodless, miserable, and in many cases deformed cripples, and victims of almost every disease. Drunkenness, debauchery and filth could not but be the result. Their condition was but the veriest slavery, and the condition of the serf or negro stood out in bright contrast to theirs. The mortality was excessive, and the dread diseases rickets and scrofula passed by but few in their path. It was among this class that the horror of hereditary disease had its chief hold, aided as it was by the repetition and accumulation of the same causes that first planted its seeds. The reports of all the many investigations showed that morality was almost unknown. In the

Q

coal mines the condition of the children was even worse. According to the report of 1842, on child labor, it was estimated that fully one third of those employed in the coal mines of England were children under eighteen, and of these much more than one half were under thirteen. The facts revealed in this elaborate report of over 2000 pages, devoted chiefly to child labor in coal mines, would be scarcely credible if they were not supported by the best of authority, so fearful was the condition of the children found to be. Down in the depths of the earth they labored from 14 to 16 hours daily. The coal often lay in seams only 18 inches deep, and in these children crawled on their hands and feet, generally naked, and harnessed up by an iron chain and band around their waists, by which they either dragged or pushed heavily loaded cars of coal through these narrow ways. In nearly every case they were driven to work by the brutal miners, and beaten, and sometimes even killed. Law did not seem to reach to the depths of a coal pit. Thus these young infants labored their young lives out as if condemned to torture for some crime." [1]

And John A. Hobson, commenting on these conditions exclaims: —

"There is no page in the history of our nation so infamous as that which tells the details of the unbridled greed of these pioneers of modern commercialism, feeding on the misery and degradation of English children." [2]

Nor were the conditions in other countries in the periods of inception of great capitalist production much better. "In the first decades of the last century," relates Dr.

[1] William F. Willoughby, "Child Labor," American Economic Association, March, 1890.
[2] "Problems of Poverty," London, 1891, p. 184.

Herkner, "children of the most tender ages, some of them four years old, were made to work in the industrial centers of the Rhenish provinces, for a daily wage of twopence; their workday lasted 10, 12 and even 14 hours, and often they were made to work in the nighttime." [1]

And even in Switzerland children of six and seven years were employed in the spinning mills, working continually from midnight to noon or from early in the morning till night.

The evils of child labor early attracted the attention of the public-spirited men of all countries, and the first efforts of all factory legislation were invariably directed against this evil. But the process of legislative reform in this field has, on the whole, been slow and quite ineffective. It took the English Parliament fully seventeen years after the adoption of the Peel law to pass the first act prohibiting the employment of children below a minimum age in factories, and that age as fixed by the law of 1819, was — nine years! The minimum age of child workers in England was raised to ten years in 1874, to eleven in 1891, and at present it is twelve years. Of the other countries of Europe, some have entirely failed to legislate on the minimum age of factory workers, and others have fixed it at so low a point that it accentuates rather than relieves the horrors of child labor. Thus, in Denmark, the law forbids the employment of children under ten years. In Belgium, Italy, Russia, Sweden and Holland the age at which children are legally set free for factory work is twelve years. Germany and France do not allow their children to work in factories before the age of thirteen

[1] Heinrich Herkner, "Die Arbeiterfrage," 4th Edition, Berlin, 1905, pp. 24, 25.

years, and Austria and Switzerland before fourteen. In the United States we are confronted in this, as in every other domain of social legislation, by 46 different sets of laws enacted in as many states. The minimum age of juvenile factory workers varies from twelve to sixteen years, but fourteen seems to be the favorite point in most states.

Somewhat more satisfactory results in the field of child-labor legislation seem to have been achieved in the direction of limiting the hours of labor of the youthful factory workers. In England children under fourteen years are only allowed to be employed half time, and the hours of employment of children between fourteen and eighteen years are limited to 12, with 2 hours' intermission for rest. In Germany the hours of children under fourteen years of age in factories must not exceed 6 a day, with an intermission of at least half an hour, and children between fourteen and sixteen must not work more than 10 hours a day, with one hour's interval in the middle of the day, and half an hour in the morning and afternoon. In France children under sixteen may work 10 hours a day in factories. Sweden limits the work of children under fourteen to 6 hours, and under sixteen to 12 hours. In the United States the hours of labor for children are variously fixed at from 8 to 10 per day.

Yet while the legal restrictions on child labor and on the intensity of its exploitation have thus, on the whole, been making slow and laborious progress, the evil itself has been steadily increasing and spreading.

Economically, morally and in every other way, child labor is one of the heaviest curses upon the working class. Originating as a last and desperate resort in the effort to

augment the insufficient income of the head of the proletarian family, child labor has proved in the hands of the
capitalists one of the most effective methods for cutting
the wages of the adult workers. Instead of being a help
to his father, the child has become his competitor in the
factory. The wages of the factory children are ludi-
crously low, ranging from 25 or 30 cents a week in some
countries of Europe to about $2.50 per week in the United
States, and the total earnings of the working children are
rarely enough to make up for the losses in wages which
their competition causes to the adult workers.

And the moral cost of child labor to the working class is
incalculable. It robs the working child of all joys and
privileges of childhood, cripples his body, dwarfs his mind,
takes the very life out of him, and threatens to develop a
generation of dull, cheerless and resistless workers.

"The sucking out of the life juice from these helpless
and defenseless creatures, the destruction of all joys of
life right at the threshold of life, the consumption of the
seed of manhood right from the stem — that, more than
anything else, is the sin of the capitalist rule against the
present generation; it is also a criminal interference with
the future!" exclaims the eloquent Rosa Luxemburg,
speaking on the subject of child labor.[1]

Socialism, which ever strives for the highest physical,
mental and moral development of the working class, and
centers its hopes on the rising generation of workers,
naturally sees in child labor one of the greatest obstacles
to its progress, and combats it by all means at its command.

The socialists favor all legislation for the restriction of

[1] Quoted by Kate Duncker in "Die Kinderarbeit und ihre Bekämp-
fung," Stuttgart, 1906.

child labor, and consistently support every measure tending in that direction. But unlike the ideologist champions of the cause of child labor, who are of late developing considerable activity, especially in the United States and in England, they realize that the evil cannot be wholly cured by mere laws for the abolition or limitation of child labor. The alarming spread of child labor is largely a symptom of the dire poverty of the working class. It is true that in some instances children are sent to work by their parents out of thoughtlessness or cupidity, but these instances may be safely set down as rare exceptions. As a rule the parents of the working class feel very keenly the dreadful sacrifice involved in the offering of their immature and tender-bodied children on the altar of the profit-grinding machine, and only the most implacable need will induce them to do so. Speaking of the beginnings of child work in the English factories, John Spargo remarks: "To get children for the cotton mills was not easy at first. Parental love and pride were ranged against the new system, denying its demands. Accustomed to the old domestic system, the association of all members of the family in manufacture as part of the domestic life, they regarded the new industrial forms with repugnance. It was considered a degradation for a child to be sent into the factories, especially for a girl, whose life would be blasted thereby. The term 'factory girl' was an insulting epithet. . . . Not till they were forced by sheer hunger and misery, through the reduction of wages to the level of starvation, could the respectable workers be induced to send their children into the factories." [1]

It may be argued that if the workingman be deprived

[1] "The Bitter Cry of the Children," New York, 1906, pp. 130, 131.

of the earnings of his children by legal enactment, he
would be compelled in the long run to force up his wages
to a higher level, and thus to make up for the impairment
of the family income.   And there is certainly much justice
in the argument.   But its weakness lies in the proviso —
"in the long run."   Few workingmen's families can stand
a decrease in their meager incomes for any length of time.

Capitalism holds the workers in the grip of a vicious
circle: the poverty of the wage-earning father sends his
child to the factory, and the competition of the child in
the factory increases the father's poverty and makes it
ever harder for him to dispense with the scanty additional
earnings of the child.

To cope effectively with the evil, it is necessary to attack
its very root and source, the poverty of the working class.
The child-labor problem is but one phase of the larger
labor problem and cannot be solved separately.

The socialist demand for greater restriction of child
labor derives its main strength and effectiveness from its
connection with the demands for other industrial reforms
contained in the socialist program.

Woman Labor

In its history, and partly also in its social effects, the
problem of woman labor is somewhat similar to that of
child labor, but its solution presents a different and considerably more complex question.

With the introduction of the machine and of the factory
system, the personal training and physical strength of the
workingman rapidly lost their importance in the process of
production.   What the capitalist demanded was cheap

labor rather than skilled labor, and next to the labor of the child that of the woman was and is the cheapest commodity in the labor market.

The working woman is in the majority of cases not called upon to support a family, as is the workingman. As a rule her earnings are but a subsidiary source of the family income: her wages are intended only to add somewhat to those of her husband or father. The position of the working woman in industry is furthermore not as permanent as that of the man or even the boy — the woman often, though by far not as a rule, quits the factory on her marriage. And finally, the work of the married woman is not as steady as that of the man; it is necessarily interrupted by the periods of pregnancy and childbed. The wants of the working woman are thus comparatively small and her power of resistance is weak. Women rarely organize into compact and permanent trade unions, they seldom strike or revolt, and they are for that reason better objects of capitalist exploitation than men.

"It is," observes Mr. Hobson, "the general industrial weakness of the condition of most women workers, and not a sex prejudice, which prevents them from receiving the wages which men might get, if the work the women do were left for male competition alone." [1]

In the earlier part of the nineteenth century, the exploitation of factory women grew so unbridled and their treatment so brutal that the parliaments and legislatures of the most advanced countries found themselves impelled to take official cognizance of the situation, and to attempt to cure some of the worst evils of woman labor by legislative enactments.

[1] "Problems of Poverty," p. 158.

The first measure in that direction was the English act of 1842, which prohibited underground work for women as well as for children, and that act was followed by several other measures at long intervals, the effect of which was to limit and regulate to some extent the labor of women in industries. Similar laws were also enacted in other countries, but on the whole these laws are even less radical and effective than those dealing with child labor.

The wages of women workers were hardly affected by these measures. They are still much below those of their male companions in the factories, even though their work may be equally efficient. Out of 782 instances selected at random by the United States Commissioner of Labor in 1897, in which men and women worked at the same occupation and performed their work with the same degree of efficiency, men received greater pay in 595, or 76.1 per cent of the instances, and their pay in these instances was 50.1 per cent greater than that of the women.

The average wage of the factory woman in the United States is about $5 per week, while in Great Britain the working woman earns about 11 shillings per week. But it must be remembered that these averages are greatly swelled by the higher pay of women in exceptional positions, and also that they apply to factory work only. The female sweatshop and house workers receive much more wretched pay.

It is, therefore, not to be wondered at that the number of women employed in the industries is growing steadily and rapidly. In the United States, in which the woman engaged in industry was a rare exception at the beginning of the last century, the number of women engaged in gainful occupation rose to almost 4,000,000 in 1890. In

France there were 6,382,658 women engaged in the different industries of the country as against 12,061,121 men, and in Germany the rapid growth of the number of women engaged in the factories alone is shown by the following eloquent figures: —

1895	664,116
1899	884,239
1904	1,119,713
1905	1,180,894
1906	1,244,964

These figures include the female children. In England half of the grown-up women are, according to Mr. John A. Hobson, wage laborers.

The socialists are not opposed to woman labor as such. They recognize that woman occupies a legitimate and lasting position in industry and that the growing importance of her rôle in all spheres of the social, political and economic life of modern nations is fully in keeping with the march of social progress. But they combat the special evils and abuses of woman labor. And these abuses are many.

The woman, when not burdened with a family of young children depending on her care and guidance, is just as fit to work as the man; but the woman with a large family, and the woman in a condition of pregnancy, or immediately after childbirth, has enough useful and necessary work to perform at home. Her work in the factory under such conditions is not a proud assertion of the rights of woman, but a pitiful and tragic surrender of her maternal duties and feelings to the cruel exigencies of dire poverty. And her work under such conditions causes incalculable physical and moral harm to her and her progeny.

The small pay of the working women, furthermore, constantly tends to drag down the wages of their husbands, fathers and brothers to an even lower level.

The efforts of the socialists are, therefore, directed primarily towards raising the wages of the adult male worker, the father of the workingman family, to a point where they would be sufficient to meet the necessary requirements of all members of his family, including those of his young children and their mother. Only thus can the inhuman evils of forced woman labor be effectively cured.

For the remaining female workers in industry, the socialists demand equal pay for equal work, and they strive to interest the working women in the organizations of the workingmen, and to secure their coöperation in the struggle for the improvement of the conditions of labor of both sexes.

The abuses of woman labor and the exploitation of child labor are logical and necessary accompaniments of the competitive system of industry. It lies in the nature of capitalism to stimulate competition in·the labor market by opposing sex to sex, age to age and nationality to nationality, and as long as the system endures, its inherent abuses cannot be entirely removed. Socialism alone offers a complete cure for the evils of woman and child labor. But even such imperfect and partial remedies as may be secured under the present system will be effective only if obtained in pursuance of a consistent program of labor reform in all of its branches and as a result of a strong and planful movement on the part of the workers organized industrially and politically.

The Trade Union Movement

In their efforts to secure radical and lasting industrial reform, and we may add, in their expectations of the ultimate realization of their entire program, the socialists thus rely not on their own strength, but also on the coöperation of the industrial organization of the working class. This industrial organization is represented chiefly by the trade union movement, and the rôle of that movement in the progress of industrial reform and the reciprocal relations between it and the socialist movement, are questions of large moment in the practical work of socialism.

Trade unionism and socialism have a common origin, and are both the products and expression of an advanced stage of the class struggle between capitalism and labor.

In England, France, Italy, Australia and the United States, the modern trade union movement preceded the socialist movement; in Germany, Austria and Russia, the trade unions are largely the creation of socialists, while in Sweden, Norway, Denmark, Belgium and Holland, both movements developed almost simultaneously. In the Anglo-Saxon countries the trade unions have developed a greater numerical strength than the socialist parties, while in the countries of continental Europe the reverse is true. On the whole, however, the total strength of the two movements is approximately equal, as the following figures taken from the leading countries will show:[1] —

[1] The figures for the trade union membership are taken from the paper of Louis de Brouckère on Socialism and Trade Unionism submitted to the Stuttgart International Congress, 1907, and those for the socialist vote are largely compiled from the official reports of the various socialist parties to the same Congress. The Belgian socialist vote has, since June, 1908, substantially increased. The figures for England,

Country	Socialist Vote	Trade Union Membership
Great Britain	342,196	1,866,755
Belgium	500,000	148,483
Denmark	76,612	92,091
Sweden	26,083	114,935
Norway	24,744	18,600
Germany	3,251,005	1,822,343
Austria	1,041,948	322,049
Servia	30,000	5,074
Bulgaria	10,000	8,300
Italy	301,525	347,839
Spain	9,000	36,557
Holland	65,743	30,000
France	1,120,000	800,000
United States	423,969	2,500,000
Total	7,222,825	8,113,026

Stating the proposition in general and broad terms, the trade unions fight the special and economic battles of the workingmen, while the Socialist Party represents the general interest of the wage earners in the field of politics. But on closer examination the distinction is by no means as clear and definite as it seems at first sight.

Every trade union represents primarily the interest of the employees in its special trade, but under a highly developed state of factory production the modern trades

Spain and Servia are estimated. Owing to the chaotic electoral system of Russia the strong socialist vote of that country cannot be estimated. Neither the socialist vote nor the trade-union strength are fully shown in the above table, since a number of countries have had to be omitted from it for lack of sufficient data. The total socialist vote is estimated as exceeding 10,000,000; the total membership of the trade unions of the world is about 11,000,000.

and industries have come to be so closely allied and inter-
woven, that the workingmen in any trade can rarely succeed in their struggles unless they are supported by their
comrades in the allied trades and sometimes by organized
labor as a whole. The growing practice of "sympathy
strikes" is evidence of this fact, and the trade unions
tacitly recognize it by forming local, national, and even
international central bodies for the purpose of coöperation
and mutual support on a large scale.   The interests represented by the whole body of trade unions thus gradually
become the general interests of the working class rather
than the special interests of the employees of particular
trades.

With the enlargement of the scope of the trade union
movement, the very character of the movement is transformed: its economic battles partake of the nature of political struggles.

For the distinction between economic and political action is one of degree and method rather than of kind and
substance. The efforts of the organized employees of a
given shop or craft to secure and maintain a reduction of
their hours of labor by the strength of their own organization, are classed as economic struggles. The efforts of
the entire organized working class or a specific and uniform portion of it to secure and maintain the same reduction of work hours through legislative enactment, constitute political action. As the trade unions in every
country grow in numbers and power, they pay ever greater
attention to the more general phases of the labor problem
and are thus drawn into ever closer contact with politics.
The trade unions of every advanced country are actively
engaged in the effort to secure legislation for the limitation

of child labor, the regulation of woman labor, the improvement of the employers' liability laws, the safeguarding of dangerous machinery and for the abatement of the countless other evils of modern factory work. And whenever legislation is threatened which may be detrimental to the interests of labor or tend to curtail the rights or the efficiency of its organizations, the unions engage in an active campaign of opposition to such measures.

"The distinction between the industrial and the political struggles of the proletariat was only temporary," says the well-known socialist theoretician writing under the *nom de plume* of Parvus; "it was always rather superficial and often fictitious; with the extension of the scope and power of the strikes, it disappears entirely. Whoever tries to exclude politics from the trade unions, must retard the very development of the trade unions." [1]

The trade unions of continental Europe fully recognize this political phase of their movement, and they frankly ally themselves with the socialist parties of their countries in all political campaigns. In England the trade organizations stubbornly maintained the attitude of non-interference in politics until such time as they found their very existence menaced by the legislative and judicial powers of the realm. Then they constituted themselves into a political Labor Party, which declared for independent working-class politics and adopted a radical program of political labor reform.

The only large body of trade unions which, at least to some extent, still upholds the fiction of political indifference, is that represented by the American Federation of Labor, and that fiction is becoming so incongruous as to involve

[1] Parvus, "Der Gewerkschaftliche Kampf," Berlin, 1908.

the organization in the most ludicrous contradictions. Thus, while a special clause in its constitution prohibits any affiliation with political parties, and the favorite slogan of the Federation is "No politics in the union," one of the principal objects of the organization, as likewise stated in its constitution, is "to secure national legislation in the interests of the working people," and every one of its conventions devotes entire days to the discussion of political problems and demands. In the election of 1908, the Federation unofficially supported the Democratic Party. The American Federation of Labor is in politics just as much as are the labor unions of all other countries, but it is the only large labor body that has failed to organize and concentrate its forces in one consistent political labor party, and prefers to scatter and waste them in the support of the political parties of the employing class.

Another distinction frequently drawn between the trade union and the socialist movements is that the former stands for mere improvements of the conditions of labor within the frame of the present system, while the latter strives for the entire abolition of the wage system. This distinction is also more imaginary than real.

The object of all trade unions is directly or indirectly to enhance the worker's share of the product, thus correspondingly decreasing the share of the employer. No limit is set to this process, and its logical conclusion, at least in abstract theory, is the entire elimination of the capitalist's profits — the socialization of industries. The only difference between the socialists and the trade unionists on the point is that while all of the former clearly realize this ultimate goal of the class struggle, many of the latter do not. But even that is rapidly changing. The trade unionists of Europe are as a rule permeated with the philosophy of socialism, and the understanding of that philosophy gives them a clearer vision of their task and makes their struggles more effective. In the United States socialism is making its way among the trade unionists slowly but steadily.

Thus the fields of socialism and trade unionism largely encroach on each other, and the line of demarcation between the two movements is often blurred. Still it would be a mistake to consider them as synonymous. Socialism and trade unionism constitute together the body of the modern labor movement, and the separation of the two merely signifies a division of functions. But that division is essential for the success of the movement as a whole. The activity of the socialist parties lies primarily in the political field: they translate the economic struggles of the working class into political action, formulate its general demands, coördinate its special needs, and always emphasize its ultimate aim, while supporting the immediate economic battles of the unions.

The functions of the trade unions, on the other hand, are primarily directed to the sphere of industrial struggle. They protect the individual worker in the factory against the excessive exploitation of the employer, and they advance the general political interests of their members through the medium of the socialist parties. Beyond these separate provinces there is, moreover, a large field of action in which the labor movement can achieve success only by the spontaneous coöperation of both of its wings.

The most striking instance of such joint action is the political mass strike which has of late been resorted to by

R

the workingmen of Europe on a few extraordinary occasions to good purpose.

From this sketch of the objects and methods of operation of the two movements, it will be readily seen that their relations to each other must be of the closest and most cordial character. In Belgium, Denmark, Sweden and Norway, the membership of the socialist parties and the trade unions is practically identical, and the two organizations may be considered as separate committees of the same body created for the performance of different functions. In Germany, Austria, Holland, Italy and Russia, the two movements are very closely allied in all their struggles. In England the Independent Labor Party, one of the leading socialist organizations of the country, forms a constituent part of the political Labor Party in the same way as do the trade unions. In France the party and the trade unions sometimes quarrel, but it is always the passing quarrel of lovers. In the United States alone the great body of organized workingmen, the American Federation of Labor, has so far kept aloof from the socialist movement.

Coöperative Societies of Workingmen

Another movement that has of late years developed great strength, and is coming to be regarded as a factor of growing importance in the struggles between capital and labor, is the movement represented by the coöperative societies of workingmen.

The origin of coöperative enterprises for joint production, purchase, distribution and consumption of commodities, may be traced back to the eighteenth century, but

the modern coöperative societies have as little in common
with their earlier prototypes as the trade unions have with
the old institutions of the masters' or helpers' guilds.

The coöperative movement of our day is a part of the
general labor movement, one of the manifestations, conscious or unconscious, of the general effort on the part of
the workingmen to lessen the exploitation of their class
by capitalism. The movement has developed within the
last fifty years, and it has attained general extension only
within the last two decades.

In this, as in many other practical labor reform
movements, England led the procession. The famous
society of the Rochdale Pioneers, the oldest of its kind,
was founded in November, 1843, when twelve poor weav-
ers met in the back room of a miserable inn, and agreed
to pay 20 pence a week into a common fund until they
should accumulate enough to start in business for their
joint benefit. In a year their number had increased to 28
and their capital had grown to £28. They rented a store
and stocked it with £15 worth of flour, and from these
modest beginnings the enterprise rapidly grew to one of
the most prosperous and powerful business institutions of
the country. In 1876 the Rochdale Society of Equitable
Pioneers numbered 8892 members, and had an invested
capital of £254,000; the year's business amounted to
£305,000, and the society's net profits were £50,500.

Membership in the society is acquired by the purchase
of a share of stock of the denomination of £5, but that
amount may be paid in small weekly installments. Each
individual member may hold as many as 20 shares, but
no member has more than one vote in the meetings of the
society. Out of the net profits a dividend of 5 per cent

per annum is paid on the stock, 2½ per cent is set apart for
an education fund, and the balance is distributed among
the members in proportion to the amount of their purchases.

In 1863 the great Coöperative Wholesale Society,
Limited, was founded as a sort of central agency for a
number of coöperative enterprises. In 1872 the year's
sales of that society already reached the enormous sum
of £1,153,132. The society originally confined itself to
purchasing commodities at wholesale and selling them to its
members (individual associations) at retail, but gradually
it embarked in the field of independent manufacture,
and with its ready market and large capital its efforts in
that direction have been signally successful. To-day the
society operates extensive biscuit, soap, boot and clothing
factories, woolen and corn mills, cocoa works and jam
canneries; it runs a large printing establishment, conducts
building operations, and has a fleet of its own in connection
with its shipping department. It has branches in several
of the principal cities of England and maintains purchasing agencies in several other countries. It is on the whole
one of the largest establishments of the world. In 1905
its capital exceeded £3,300,000; its sales amounted to
£20,785,469, and its net profits were £368,309.

The Scottish Coöperative Wholesale Society is an
enterprise of almost similar magnitude, and a large number of other independent coöperative societies exist in
England, Scotland and Ireland. In 1907 the Central
Board of the Coöperative Union of the United Kingdom
received reports from 1566 societies having a total membership of 2,434,085. The aggregate sales of these societies exceeded £105,000,000, and their net profits were
over £12,000,000.

But notwithstanding its enormous business success, the coöperative movement is less of a factor in the labor struggles of Great Britain than in most other countries of Europe. The British coöperatives are honeycombed with middle class elements and middle-class notions. They are conspicuously devoid of large class ideals, and are held together principally by the paltry material benefits of the movements.

In all these features the coöperative societies of Great Britain stand in marked contrast to those of Belgium, which are closely allied with the socialist and trade union movements.

The oldest of the modern coöperative societies in Belgium is the famous *Vooruit* (Forward) of Ghent. It was organized in 1880 at the initiative of the socialist leader, Edouard Anseele, and its first enterprise was a bakery in a cellar equipped and operated with a capital of 84 francs and 95 centimes. The undertaking was an immediate success, and was enlarged and extended from year to year. At this writing the amount of its annual business exceeds 3,000,000 francs, and its yearly profits are over 400,000 francs. The bakery produces over 100,000 kilos of bread per week. In 1903 the *Vooruit* conducted four drug stores, seven groceries, a bookbinding shop, a cigar factory, a foundry and one of the largest dry goods stores in the city.

Its *Feestlokaal*, or assembly hall, is located in Rue des Baguettes, in the most aristocratic quarters of Ghent. "It was once the property of the most select bourgeois club of the town," relate Destrée and Vandervelde. "When the members of the club found that it was too expensive for them, the workingmen of Ghent purchased it through the intermediary of a dummy, and rents in Rue de Baguettes at once dropped 50 per cent. In the gardens in which the ladies of high bourgeois society had formerly promenaded, hundreds of factory girls are now dancing on Sundays. In the concerts the *Marseillaise* has replaced the *Brabançonne;* the red flag supplanted the tricolor, and on the holidays of labor the peaceful bourgeois, looking from behind their curtains, see the black columns of workingmen marching through the quiet street like the torchbearers of the revolution." [1]

The next coöperative society of importance to be organized in Belgium was the *Maison du Peuple* (House of the People) of Brussels, founded in 1882.

Of the history of this society Louis Bertrand relates the following: "A group of workingmen of all trades decided to create a coöperative bakery. Each member promised to contribute 10 francs in weekly payments of 25 to 50 centimes. In a few months the society had 80 members on its list and 700 francs in its treasury. These 80 members needed about 120 loaves of bread of one kilogram each per day. They hired a cellar containing a bake oven at a rental of 35 francs per month. . . . Only one baker was employed. In the morning he would bake his bread and in the afternoon he would carry it to the houses of the members. This was not an easy matter, for the members lived in all parts of the city and in the suburbs. . . . Gradually the number of members rose from 80 to 250. At the end of four years it had 400 members. It was necessary to rent a larger place and to install modern bake ovens and a mechanical kneading trough.

[1] "Le Socialisme en Belgique," par Jules Destrée et Émile Vandervelde, 2d Edition, Paris, 1903, p. 47.

"In 1886 the coöperative hired a large hall for 5000 francs per year, and placed it at the disposal of the labor organizations and socialists of Brussels. In less than ten years the hall had become too small, and the coöperative decided to build a new one."[1]

To-day the society counts about 21,000 members, which on the basis of 5 persons to the family, makes about 105,000 consumers.

The *Maison du Peuple* operates the largest baking establishment in Belgium, and sells over ten million kilos of bread per year. The society besides conducts various other enterprises, and its building, the new *Maison du Peuple*, is a veritable palace of labor, costing 1,200,000 francs.

The coöperative society *Progrès*, founded in 1886, is in some respects even more influential than either of the two described. Its region extends over the entire industrial district between Charleroi and Mons, and its four magnificent buildings erected in different parts of the district are the principal gathering points of the socialists and organized workingmen of the neighborhood.

All told, the number of coöperative societies in Belgium in 1907 was 2582. Of these 630 were societies for distribution, 209 were productive societies, 21 were societies for coöperative dwellings, 52 were industrial and 1302 were agricultural credit associations. The membership of the distributive societies consisted of 119,581 families, their aggregate sales for the year 1906 amounted to 31,174,552 francs, and their net profits for that year were 3,035,940 francs.

The workingmen's coöperatives of Belgium are all

[1] "Historie de la Coöperative en Belgique," Brussels, 1902.

affiliated with the Federation of Belgian Socialist Coöperatives, founded in 1900 principally for the purpose of wholesale purchases. The rules of all societies thus affiliated with the Federation are practically uniform, and the constitutions of the societies expressly declare "that the society is above all a political socialist group, and that the members by subscribing to the constitution signify their adherence to the program of the Labor Party." The members of the coöperatives and their families form the basis of the Belgian Labor Party, and in times of electoral campaigns they constitute themselves into political committees. Around the coöperatives and in their spacious halls are grouped the trade unions, the socialist organizations, the social and educational clubs of workingmen, and the editorial rooms of the socialist papers. The coöperatives expend a considerable portion of their profits on socialist propaganda in all forms and in the support of the struggles of trade unions. In a word, the coöperatives in Belgium are the center of the socialist and labor movement. In the electoral campaign of 1900 they printed and distributed at their own expense two million socialist booklets.

The development of the coöperative movement in Germany has followed a somewhat peculiar course owing to special historical and political conditions. In the period of the beginnings of the socialist and labor movement in Germany, the problem of coöperative enterprises played a very important rôle. Schulze-Delitsch, one of the heads of the Liberal Party and an ardent apostle of the doctrine of "self-help," headed a large movement for the organization of voluntary coöperative societies chiefly for production, as a complete solution of the labor question. It was a middle-class movement, its theoretical foundation was unsound and reactionary, and the design of its promoters seemed to be to deter the working class from independent labor politics. To this movement Ferdinand Lassalle opposed his famous plan of coöperative productive associations with state credit, a plan which involved the conquest of universal suffrage by the workingmen and the democratization of the state, *i.e.*, working-class political action. The struggle between Lassalle and Schulze on the issue of state credit as against self-help, assumed the form of a struggle between socialism and liberalism. The socialists concentrated their forces on politics, while the liberals gained control of the voluntary coöperative movement. Under the leadership of Schulze-Delitsch and his successors the latter grew up, large in size, but weak and inefficient in spirit. It laid the greatest stress on productive associations, and encouraged associations for credit, but regarded societies for distribution and consumption with a certain degree of suspicion.

The socialists had but little esteem for the coöperative movement under those circumstances.

But in the meanwhile the expiration of the anti-socialist laws in 1890 set free a large quantity of stored-up energy in the radical workingmen of Germany. They inaugurated a vigorous activity in all domains of the labor movement, and among others they entered the ranks of coöperative societies for consumption in large numbers. This influx of socialists so perturbed the leaders of the conservative coöperative movement that in 1902 they expelled by a *coup d'état* 99 societies for consumption on the ground of their social democratic tendencies. In May of the next year these called a convention at Dresden which was attended by representatives of 621 associations for consumption, largely composed of workingmen with socialist tendencies. At that convention was organized the Central Union of German Societies for Consumption, which is now the leading organization in that field. Towards the end of 1907 there were in Germany 2110 societies for consumption, with a total membership of about 1,131,453. Of these the Central Union represented 959 societies, with a total of 879,221 members. The societies affiliated with it thus represented 77 per cent of the entire membership of the German consumptive organizations. They employed 12,783 persons and conducted about 2500 stores, with a total invested capital of 25,000,000 marks. Their business for the year was 303,794,452 marks, and their profits were more than 20,000,000 marks.

With the separation of the radical societies for consumption from the liberal coöperative movement, the relations between the former and the socialists grew closer and more cordial, and to-day both work in complete harmony.

The coöperative movements in the other countries have developed various degrees of strength and usefulness, and their period of greatest growth lies almost invariably within the last two decades.

In Italy a special feature of the movement is presented by the coöperatives of the day laborers, who hire out their joint work under contract, and subdivide it among themselves in separate gangs, supplying the necessary tools out of the common fund and sharing the contract price. The effect of such coöperation is to eliminate the profit of the padrone. In 1906 Italy had 2792 coöperative societies, doing a total business of over 600,000,000 francs.

Eight hundred and fifty-one of these societies were purely consumptive, 454 were productive societies, 350 were coöperative societies for credit, while the remainder consisted of labor, agricultural and mixed societies.

In Sweden the object of coöperative societies is almost exclusively joint farming and building. Out of the 2524 coöperative societies reporting in 1906, all but 382 belonged to that class. The character of the coöperative organizations in Finland and Holland is very similar to the organization of Sweden.

France had in 1904 about 5500 coöperative societies, of which more than 3000 are agricultural associations. Austria, Switzerland, Holland and Denmark have also developed noteworthy coöperative movements. The United States is the most backward country in this field.

Victor Serwy, at that time Secretary of the International Socialist Bureau, computed that in 1901 there were 56,623 known coöperative societies in the world.

Coöperative societies may be divided into a large number of distinct groups according to the objects pursued and methods employed by them, but we are concerned with those of them only that may be fairly said to form a part of the labor movement. These may be divided into enterprises for coöperative production and enterprises for coöperative consumption or distribution.

The productive societies are of special value for trade unions in conjunction with their struggles against their employers, and they often do good service in offering a refuge to blacklisted strike leaders or other active union members. But as a rule they attain a measure of business success only when conducted in conjunction with societies for consumption. As independent enterprises they generally fail. A manufacturing establishment in modern times cannot succeed unless it is provided with the capital which its large competitors command, and employs the same methods as they. And the workingmen-founders of productive associations as a rule do not possess the required capital nor can they employ the countless customary methods of labor exploitation.

The coöperative societies for consumption, on the other hand, have proved themselves almost uniformly successful from the point of view of business.

The socialists do not foster the illusion that voluntary coöperative societies of labor, either for production or for consumption, could gradually and by the strength of their own development, supersede the prevalent capitalist methods of production and distribution. They do not even attach great importance to the coöperatives as factors in the general improvement and elevation of the material conditions of the workers. But they regard them as useful auxiliaries in the struggles of the working class as sources of ammunition in those struggles, and as effective schools for the training of the workingmen in the administration of industries and in the sense of the solidarity of their class.

The general attitude of socialism towards the coöperative movement of the workingmen was defined by the social democrats of Germany in a resolution adopted at the convention of their party at Hanover in 1899, in the following language: —

"The attitude of the party towards the coöperative industrial associations is one of neutrality. It considers the organization of such associations, when the necessary conditions of their success are present, as calculated to introduce improvements in the economic situation of their members, and it also sees in such associations, as in every organization of the workingmen for the protection and promotion of their interests, a proper medium for the education of the working class in the independent direction of its affairs. The party does not attribute to such associations a determining importance for the liberation of the working class from the chains of wage slavery."

CHAPTER III

WORKINGMEN'S INSURANCE

ONE of the greatest evils of the modern system of wage labor is the uncertainty of the worker's existence under it. So long as the wage earner is in normal good health and his employment is tolerably steady, he manages to eke out a precarious living for himself and those dependent on him. In times of prosperity the laborer, and especially the skilled mechanic, may even save up a modest sum for a rainy day.

But suddenly his work is interrupted and his earnings cease. A dull season may throw him out of employment for weeks, or a general industrial depression may close the doors of the factory against him for months. His scanty savings, if he has any, dwindle and disappear with frightful rapidity, and in a short time the worker finds himself confronted with the menace of actual starvation. Or he suddenly falls sick in the midst of great industrial activity, and is rendered physically incapable for a protracted period of time. To the workingman health means not only well-being and happiness, it means his bread and the bread of his family; sickness for him is not only physical discomfort, it is often helpless, bottomless destitution.

But the sick workingman in the midst of his distress is at least comforted with the hope of recovery, with the hope of eventual resumption of his work and life. How much

254

more desperate is the lot of the man crippled in his employment. The workingman whose principal, if not sole claim, to life lies in the deftness of his fingers, in the strength of his arm or in the muscles of his leg, is in constant danger of being robbed of his limbs and strength by his perfidious and bloodthirsty shopmate, the iron monster machine, ever on the alert for a sign of weariness or relaxation on his part, ever ready to assail him unawares. And when the hapless worker has been maimed and invalidated in the service of his fellow-men, our Christian society does not reward him for his sacrifice, does not indemnify him for his loss, does not even extend a pitying hand to comfort him in his misfortune, but casts him aside mercilessly and unfeelingly, and quietly lets him perish, passing on to the next victim.

And if this cruel fate may accidentally overtake any workingman in the prime of his life and strength, a similar lot is almost certain to befall all workingmen at a more advanced age.

"Not less tragic than the position of the unemployed workman," observes Mr. George Turner, "is that of the aged craftsman. The man who does not give the fullest measure of work for his weekly wage is promptly discarded by an economic system depending upon alert competition for its existence. Fortunate it is that sixty per cent do not live to be replaced by active, able-bodied, hopeful young workmen, and to be left destitute. But a large minority meets this fate. Wages of men from forty-five years upwards show a gradual and persistent decline. The roughest forms of labor are the first to suffer; but in skilled trades where deftness of handiwork is the first condition of efficiency and of continued employment, the

attainment of fifty-five years of age is usually accompanied
by a reduction of earnings." [1]

This uncertainty of existence, the constant menace of
unemployment, of sickness, accidents and old age, which
hangs over the head of every modern wage earner like the
sword of Damocles, is intimately linked with the system of
private competitive industries and "free" wage labor, and
as the system unfolds itself, it tends to aggravate the pre-
cariousness of the workingman's life. With the development and perfection of machinery and the growing intensity of work and competition, the "reserve army of the
unemployed" is constantly on the increase, industrial
accidents are more common, the worker is exhausted and
enfeebled earlier in life, and the aged mechanic is rendered
more useless.

The problem of providing against these contingencies
has, therefore, naturally engaged the attention of the
workingmen ever since the rise of the wage system, and
it has become a matter of ever greater concern to them
as that system has developed.

The first practical efforts for the relief of workingmen
in cases of unemployment, sickness, accidents and old age,
assumed the form of private and voluntary enterprises,
undertaken by workingmen, and sometimes by employers
of labor. To the former class belong the trade unions and
other labor organizations which furnish relief to their
members out of work from funds raised among themselves
by means of regular periodical contributions or assess-
ments, and the numerous fraternal and mutual societies
which insure their members in cases of sickness and acci-

[1] "The Case for State Pensions in Old Age," Fabian Society, London,
1899.

dents, and sometimes even provide for annuities in old age. Among the latter class must be counted the special funds of large employers of labor, notably the mining and railroad companies, established for the purpose of aiding their employees in cases of sickness and accidents or of providing them with pensions after a continuous employment of specified duration. These funds are as a rule created with a view of attracting a better grade of workers to the more dangerous and strenuous trades and insuring their steadiness of work. In the United States they have gained but little extension. In some countries of Europe, notably in France, Belgium and England, they play a much more important rôle, but on the whole the practice is so rare, and the benefits of the system are so restricted and insignificant, that they can hardly be considered a serious factor in the movement for the relief of the workingmen against the uncertainties of their existence.

Of much greater value than the employers' funds, are the coöperative societies of workingmen, such as the various Benefit Orders of the United States, the Friendly Societies of Great Britain, the *Sociétés de Secours Mutuels* of France, Belgium and Switzerland, the *Kranken-Kassen* of Germany and Austria, and the mutual aid associations of almost all other countries.

Beginning on a modest scale in the early part of the last century, these societies soon proved themselves so essential to large masses of the working population, and spread with such rapidity that they almost attained the importance of a social institution. Towards the middle of last century the governments of the most advanced countries of Europe found themselves impelled to take official cognizance of their existence and activity.

s

In England the first legislative act affecting the friendly societies dates back to 1793, but that act and the amendatory legislation following it during more than half a century, did not materially advance the standing or powers of these societies, and left the application of such laws optional with the societies. The first laws which undertook not only to regulate but also in some degree to aid and strengthen the mutual insurance societies of workingmen, were the laws passed in Prussia in 1849 and in France and Belgium in 1850. And similar laws have since been adopted by almost every country of Europe and by most of the states in the United States.

From government regulation to government management is but one step, and in the matter of workingmen's insurance this step was readily taken in several countries of Europe. In France a state department for old-age insurance — the *Caisse Nationale des Retraites pour la Vieillesse* — was established in 1850, and it was followed in 1868 by a similar state institution for accident insurance — the *Caisse Nationale d'Assurance en cas d'Accidents*.

In Belgium a National Old Age Pension Bank was established by the government in 1850. In Italy a semi-governmental Bank for the Insurance of Workingmen Against Accidents — the *Cassa Nazionale di Assicurazione per gli infortuni degli operai*, was created by the law of July 8, 1883.

All these instances of workingmen's insurance institutions managed by the government are those of voluntary state insurance, *i.e.*, institutions conducted by the state as a branch of the government for the benefit of those of its citizens who may desire to take advantage of them. The state does not contribute to the insurance funds, and the amount of insurance is determined on the basis of premium payments. The superiority of such state insurance over that of the ordinary insurance companies lies in the greater safety of the investment and in the fact that it excludes the element of profit.

The institutions of voluntary state insurance have nowhere become very effective or popular for the reason that they leave the entire burden of financing them on the class least capable of carrying it — the working class. Voluntary state insurance is, after all, but another form of self-help in insurance, and such insurance has, on the whole, proved entirely inadequate to relieve the needs of the vast masses of wage earners of our day. Comparing the net results of the various forms of workingmen's insurance, voluntary and involuntary, at the close of the nineteenth century, M. Maurice Bellom remarks: "It is impossible to refrain from an exclamation of astonishment and admiration in reviewing the social results of compulsory insurance. . . . The diffusion of insurance which the compulsory organization has caused, the pecuniary advantages which it has secured for the workers, the ease with which it has enabled employers of labor to discharge their liability, and finally the benefits of a better hygiene which it has conferred on the entire community, have won for the system of compulsory insurance the general recognition of the numerous beneficiaries of that system." [1] Within the last few decades the conviction has grown in some of the most advanced countries that the provision of workingmen's insurance against unemployment, sickness,

[1] *Journal de la Société de Statistique de Paris*, 1901, for June, July and August.

accidents and old age, is not a matter to be left to the inclinations or abilities of individuals, but a task to be assumed by organized society as such; that it is the duty of the state to guarantee the existence of the invalids and veterans of its industrial army at least as much as the existence of the invalids and veterans of its military army is now guaranteed.

The first official proclamation of this principle is probably that contained in the French constitution of 1848, which declared "that the Republic should by fraternal assistance assure the existence of its needy citizens." "But," observes Edouard Vaillant,[1] "the victorious reaction knew how to guard itself against all practical consequences of its republican affirmations and declarations."

It was left to the imperial government of Germany to inaugurate and enforce a general system of compulsory state insurance with direct state aid. This revolutionary measure in the domain of workingmen's insurance was first announced in a famous message of Wilhelm I to the German Diet, on November 17, 1881, and we quote from it the following passage bearing on the subject: —

"Already in February of this year we expressed our conviction that the cure of our social maladies is not to be found in the repression of the social democratic excesses alone, but also in the promotion of the welfare of the working class. We consider it our Imperial duty once more to urge the accomplishment of this task on the Diet. . . .

"In this sense the united governments will first resubmit to the Diet the bill for insurance of workingmen against accidents with such amendments as have been suggested in the discussions on the subject at your last

[1] "Assurance Sociale," Paris, 1901, p. 7.

session. Supplementary thereto a bill will be introduced which has for its object the uniform organization of industrial insurance institutions in cases of sickness. But also those who are incapacitated for work by reason of old age or invalidity, have a well-founded claim on the community to a higher degree of state aid than has heretofore been accorded them."

The first institution of compulsory state insurance of workingmen established in Germany in pursuance of the imperial message, was the insurance against sickness created by the law of 1883 and repeatedly amended since. Almost all industrial workers whose yearly earnings do not exceed 2000 marks, and certain classes of commercial and agricultural workers are brought under the provisions of this law. The institution operates through the agency of local sick benefit societies. The employers contribute one-third of the insurance funds and pay the expense of administration, the employees pay the remaining two thirds, the contributions in each case being proportionate to the wages paid or earned.

The minimum aid fixed by law includes free medicine and medical attendance; a money indemnity equal to three fourths of the daily wage, or half of the wage and free hospital treatment; in case of death a cash benefit to the widow or family of the deceased equal to twenty times his daily wage; and sick relief to working women during six weeks after confinement.

The German system of state insurance against accidents was initiated by the law of 1884. That act is a radical advance over the sick insurance law in that it specifically recognizes the loss occasioned by accidents in the industrial process as a legitimate part of the employer's operating expenses, and places the entire burden of the insurance against accidents on the employing class. The affairs of the institution are administered by the joint representatives of the employers and employees, and the rates of insurance are fixed with reference to the degree of the danger of the several trades, and the efficiency of the safeguards adopted by each particular employer. One of the most substantial benefits of this system has been the greater care developed by the employers of labor and the general decrease of accidents to workingmen.

The system of accident insurance embraces practically all wage workers whose yearly earnings do not exceed 3000 marks. ' The compensation includes free medical attendance and a fixed allowance during the period of disability. In cases of total disability the injured man receives an annuity equal to two thirds of his wages, and in cases of death an indemnity is paid to the surviving family.

The third measure of workingmen's insurance mentioned in the imperial message, that of insurance against old age and invalidity, was not realized till 1889. The system differs from the two other forms of workingmen's insurance in that it has been made a more distinct function of the state as such. The old-age pension fund is administered directly by the government, and the latter contributes 50 marks per year for each insured entitled to an annuity. The remaining funds are contributed in equal portions by the employers and employees. This form of insurance is compulsory on every wage earner, sixteen years of age and over, whose annual wages do not exceed 2000 marks. The fund insures an annuity to each workingman after he has become incapacitated for work, or has reached the age of seventy years. The amount of the pension is determined with reference to the average wages of the insured, the minimum being 115 marks, and the maximum about 450 marks per year.

All the three forms of workingmen's insurance are operated in conjunction with each other, and the main object of the copious amendatory legislation on the subject has been to combine them all into a harmonious and complete system.

In comparison with the crude methods of voluntary insurance, the compulsory state insurance of Germany, insufficient as it is, has proved a decided success.

In 1904 the number of German workingmen insured against sickness was 11,418,446, and relief in that branch of insurance was given in 4,642,679 cases, involving a total expenditure of about 240,000,000 marks.

No less than 20,000,000 German workers were insured against accidents in 1906, and about 14,000,000 persons were insured against invalidity and old age in 1905. The total amount of accident indemnity paid in the year mentioned was 142,436,844 marks, while almost 160,000,-000 marks were paid out in workingmen's pensions. On January 1, 1906, 934,983 invalid and aged workingmen were drawing pensions, and the receipts for that year and purpose exceeded 210,000,000 marks, of which the government had contributed about 38,000,000 marks.

In all, the German empire has spent in the twenty-year period, 1885–1905, the sum of about 5,000,000,000 marks on workingmen's insurance.

The example of Germany has been partly followed by Austria, which enacted laws for the insurance of its workingmen against sickness in 1888, and against accidents in 1887. In Hungary the system of compulsory insurance against sickness was introduced in 1891. In Switzerland the principle of compulsory state insurance of workingmen was adopted in the form of an amendment to the federal constitution. That amendment was adopted in 1890 on a popular referendum, and read as follows: —

"The Confederation shall provide, by legislative enactment, for insurance against sickness and accidents, account being taken of existing aid societies. It may declare participation in insurance compulsory on all or on certain specified categories of citizens."

When, however, a concrete legislative bill on compulsory sick insurance was submitted to the referendum of the people, it was rejected by a vote of 330,000 against 143,000, on account of certain unpopular provisions, principally with respect to the proportion of the contributions of the insured.

In Norway a system of compulsory state insurance against accidents was inaugurated in 1894, in Finland in 1895, in Italy in 1898, and in Holland and Sweden in 1901. France has had a system of accident insurance since 1898, and has very recently adopted a law providing for the compulsory insurance of workingmen against invalidity and old age. Similar institutions are in force in the colonies of New Zealand, New South Wales and Victoria. In Great Britain Parliament has recently established a government system of old-age pensions.

The main principles and methods of operation of these institutions in the countries enumerated are substantially similar to those of Germany, but some of them, notably that of Austria, are more liberal in the amounts of the benefits.

Denmark has the distinction of having the only national

system which somewhat approaches the ideal of state insurance against unemployment. It has recently adopted a law regulating the methods of trade unions in the management of funds for the relief of their members out of work, and providing for regular state contributions toward such funds. In Belgium, Switzerland and France, several municipalities have introduced similar measures for the assistance of unemployed workingmen.

In Belgium and Denmark, the subject of compulsory state insurance of workingmen in one form or another is of late being very strongly agitated, and the indications are that these countries will soon fall into line with the general progress of "social legislation."

The practical plan of workingmen's insurance was first formulated by the well-known Austrian statesman and sociologist, Dr. Schaeffle, in 1867,[1] and was elaborated by Professors Wagner, Schmoller and the other representatives of the school of social science known in Germany by the general designation of "socialism of the chair" (*Kathedersozialismus*). But its practical realization and the steady extension of its application is distinctly due to the propaganda of modern socialism. The message of Emperor Wilhelm I quoted above, plainly admits that the fear of the socialist movement was one of the government's motives in inaugurating the era of social legislation, and Prince Bismarck, the prime mover of the measure, was even franker in his public utterances on the subject, as shown in a previous chapter (Socialism and Law).

Factory legislation involves merely reforms in the relations between the individual employers and employees, but social insurance is based on the recognition of the duties of

[1] Adolph Schaeffle, "Kapitalismus und Sozialismus."

the state as such towards its working-class citizens, and is distinctly a socialistic idea. Factory legislation, therefore, may be forced from the government by a strong labor movement, even if that movement has not reached the consciousness of socialism; but social insurance can be achieved, directly or indirectly, only through the presence of a well-defined and aggressive socialist movement. Germany, the classical country of modern socialism, is also the home of social insurance; in the United States, where the trade-union movement is old and strong and the socialist movement is new and comparatively weak, we have a considerable number of factory laws, but not even the first rudiments of social legislation. England was in this respect similarly situated with the United States, until its workingmen turned to socialism and socialist politics. The English old-age pension system has been among the first results of the change.

The socialists do not overrate the value of workingmen's insurance. They do not consider it as a solution of the social problem, nor even as a measure of adequate relief of the more pressing needs of the working class. But they see in it a potent lever for the elevation of the physical and moral standard of the masses.

The uncertainty of the workingmen's life has probably a more deteriorating effect on the morale of their class than any other feature of their existence; it tends to make them timid and conservative and inaccessible to the movement for the elevation of their class on a broad and bold plane.

The effect of a comprehensive system of state insurance is to remove from the minds of the workingmen the haunting dread born of uncertainty, and to develop in them a certain sense of material security and intellectual independence.

The socialists, moreover, regard the system of compulsory state insurance as a large step in the direction of the social transformation of the modern individualistic state.

"In a socialist society," Edouard Vaillant predicts, "social insurance will in its turn disappear in the higher forms of the social institutions based on equality and solidarity, as they are to-day absorbing and transforming the old institutions of public assistance and the partial and incomplete experiments of private insurance. Charity, public assistance and social insurance are the three successive stages through which we have to pass before the emancipation of the working class and the social republic will render them useless.

"Under the capitalist régime it is only through social insurance that the dignity of the workingman and the poor can be safeguarded, and his legal rights, his guaranty against all social risks and all misery, can be established and maintained. And it is because of this, because the time for the complete realization of the plan has arrived, that we must concentrate all our efforts on its establishment." [1]

And the socialists have never relaxed their efforts to

[1] "Assurance Sociale."

For detailed descriptions of the kinds, methods and results of Workingmen's Insurance, consult: —

William Franklin Willoughby, "Workingmen's Insurance," New York, 1898.

John Graham Brooks, "Compulsory Insurance in Germany," Special Report of United States Commissioner of Labor, Washington, 1895.

Dr. Heinrich Herkner, "Die Arbeiterfrage," 4th revised and enlarged edition, Berlin, 1905.

improve and extend the existing system of state insurance. In Germany and other countries in which the system has been wholly or partly established, they work for the elimination of the workingmen's contributions to the insurance funds on the theory that it is the duty of the state to insure the life and existence of the worker, without curtailing his wages for that purpose; they demand the raising of the benefits to an extent sufficient to meet the actual needs of the sick, disabled and aged workers, and they urge the extension of the system to cover the entire wage-earning class.

In countries in which the system of compulsory state insurance for workingmen has not yet been introduced, the socialists are its most ardent, often its sole advocates.

CHAPTER IV

THE POLITICAL REFORM MOVEMENTS

Political Reform

In theory representative government is government "of, for and by the people," and the modern political machinery is an instrument for the expression and enforcement of the popular will.

But in most of the advanced modern countries the political actualities accord but poorly with these theoretical ideals of democracy. As a rule it is not the great masses, but the small privileged groups who dominate the government. A large portion of the people are openly excluded from all direct participation in politics, and for many of those who nominally enjoy political rights, the exercise of those rights is a mere illusion. The elected or appointed public officials are but rarely the disinterested "servants" of their constituents. More often they are the rulers of the nation, exercising the functions of office for the promotion of their own interests or those of their special class and in hostility to the people. The constituents have but little control over their "representatives," and the general tendency of modern political development has been to alienate the government from the people.

Mr. M. Ostrogorski, who has probably made the most searching and exhaustive investigation of political institutions and conditions in the two greatest democracies of our day, England and the United States,[1] makes the alarming but well-substantiated statement that in both countries the political parties, which were originally devised for the realization of the will of the voting masses, have turned into effective instruments for the defeat of that very will. Political parties have become political machines run by political "bosses" on the principle early announced by a prominent American politician, "To the victors belong the spoils." The "victors," within the meaning of that maxim of modern political ethics, are always the party bosses and their henchmen, and the "spoils" are the public offices of trust and confidence, the powers of popular government and all its departments.

The professional politicians in the United States, including officeholders and party bosses of all grades, have developed into a distinct class. Mr. Ostrogorski estimates their number at about 900,000 — i.e., about 6.5 per cent of the voting population, and that class practically controls the politics of the country and constitutes its government. Only from one to ten per cent of the voters take part in the primaries, and the large bulk of the votes in popular elections is manipulated by the professional politicians, either by means of the stultifying clap-trap methods of modern American campaigning, or by direct personal promises and influence, or by the still more direct method of purchase. Mr. Ostrogorski makes the startling assertion that more than 11 per cent of the American voters sell their votes.

It is this perversion of popular government that has given rise to the many modern movements of political re-

[1] M. Ostrogorski, "Democracy and Political Parties," New York, 1905.

form, and as the vices of prevailing political conditions and methods become more acute and apparent, these movements grow in extension and intensity.

The main currents of all such political reform movements may be said to proceed along three distinct lines.

The first of these is directed against the personal incompetence or corruption of individual officeholders or politicians. This is the so-called "good government" movement, which sees the remedy for all political evils in "putting good men into office." The movement by its very nature is bound to be sporadic and ineffective. It is most common in the large American cities, which are the chronic prey of organized gangs of unscrupulous politicians. When these political marauders, intoxicated with power, become too shameless and aggressive, the decent citizens, mostly of the "better classes," periodically rise in revolt, and inaugurate a "good government" campaign. If successful, they oust the corrupt officials, and elect men of their own ranks in their stead. As a rule they do not attempt any radical changes of the conditions which breed and maintain corrupt political gangs in the cities, and as a result their reform régimes are short lived, and soon succumb to a new and more appalling state of political corruption. The recent histories of New York, Chicago, Pittsburg, Philadelphia, Minneapolis and St. Louis offer abundant instances of such movements, and the pathetic struggles and failures of the shortsighted good government reforms of these cities have been graphically described by Mr. Lincoln Steffens.[1]

The more important movements of political reform are those concerned in the permanent improvements of politi-

[1] "The Shame of the Cities," New York, 1904.

cal institutions and methods. These movements have for
their object the extension of the suffrage to classes still
excluded from it, or they aim to increase the political
powers of the people and to strengthen their control over
their chosen representatives. To the former class belong
the movements for the abolition of all forms of restrictions
on adult manhood suffrage, and for the introduction of
woman suffrage; to the latter, the movements for the
direct election of all public officials, for the introduction
of the principle of initiative and referendum in legislation,
the system of proportional representation in government,
and the right of the constituents to recall their representatives.

All these movements have of late made very considerable gains.

Universal Suffrage

The general principle of universal suffrage of all adult
male citizens has been pretty definitely established in
several countries, such as the United States, England,
France and Switzerland, for all political elections; in other
countries, such as Germany and Austria, it is limited to
parliamentary elections, while in the local elections in
these countries, and in all elections in some other countries,
such as Belgium and Holland, the suffrage is qualified by
the age, property, education or social condition of the voter.
The domain of universal manhood suffrage is steadily
extending, and the struggles for the removal of all qualifications on such suffrage are assuming ever larger proportions,
especially in Belgium, Holland, Germany and Hungary.

As part of the general movement for suffrage extension, the movement for the enfranchisement of women has also made large strides within the last generation. Not only has that movement to-day numerous and energetic adherents of both sexes all over the civilized world, but in many countries it has already realized complete or partial practical victories. The women of Finland enjoy the "active" and the "passive" franchise (the right to vote and to hold elective office) in all elections in the same manner as the men, and out of the 200 deputies in the Finnish Diet, 19 are women. In Norway the tax-paying or propertied women have votes in all parliamentary and local elections. Women are completely enfranchised in New Zealand and in the Australian colonies of South and West Australia, New South Wales, Tasmania and Queensland. In the little Isle of Man, which has its own local parliament, women are likewise allowed to vote on equal terms with men. In the other parts of Great Britain and Ireland woman suffrage is restricted to certain elections for local offices. The Frenchmen have conferred on their women the right to vote in elections for school trustees, charity inspectors and members of the industrial courts. In Germany, Sweden, Denmark and Switzerland women are permitted to vote in certain local elections.

In the United States four states, Wyoming, Colorado, Utah and Idaho, have extended to their female citizens the rights of unrestricted suffrage, while most of the other states allow their women to participate in the elections of local school boards and other minor officials.

Wyoming has had the longest experience with the institution of woman suffrage, which was introduced in that state in 1868. In 1893 its legislature attested its appreciation of the beneficial and ennobling effect of the institu-

T

tion on the public life of the citizens of the state, in a concurrent resolution, which among other things recited: "That the possession and exercise of suffrage by the women in Wyoming for the past quarter of a century has wrought no harm and has done great good in many ways; that it has largely aided in banishing crime, pauperism and vice from the state, and that without any violent and oppressive legislation; that it has secured peaceful and orderly elections, good government and a remarkable degree of civilization and good order."

Of the remaining electoral reform movements, the first in order of importance is probably that advocating the system of

Proportional Representation

Under the prevailing systems of election, the majority party may sometimes monopolize all public offices while the minority parties may have no representation at all. Theoretically we may conceive of a situation where a party representing a bare majority of the voters, say 51 per cent, evenly distributed all over the country, may carry every election and fill every seat in the state and national legislatures and all other public offices of the country, while the remaining 49 per cent may have no representation and no voice in the administration at all. But this applies only to countries in which an absolute majority of the votes cast is required for election. In countries in which a mere plurality determines the elections, as in the United States, we may well conceive a situation where the voters are divided into three or more parties of approximately equal strength, and the strongest of them,

representing perhaps 35 per cent of all voters, may control
the entire government. In actual practice, of course,
the party voters are never so evenly distributed, and a
strong minority party as a rule has some representation
in the government. But this representation is uncertain,
and the smaller parties are often left without any representation. In the general national elections in the United
States in 1908, the total number of votes cast for all
parties was 14,882,132. Of these the Republican Party
received 7,677,544, the Democratic Party, 6,405,707, the
Socialist Party, 420,464, the Prohibition Party, 251,660,
the Independence Party, 83,628, the People's Party,
29,108, and the Socialist Labor Party, 14,021.

In the same elections 391 members of the House of
Representatives were chosen. Under a system of proportional representation these members would have been
apportioned among the various parties as follows: —

Republicans	202
Democrats	168
Socialists	11
Prohibitionists	7
Independence Party . . .	2
People's Party	1
	391

As a matter of fact the House was composed of 219
Republicans and 172 Democrats, and none of the minor
parties had any representation whatever on it.

There are several methods by which the principle of proportional representation may be applied to elections. The
one known as the "free list" or "quota plan" is the
simplest and most commonly employed. This system

presupposes large electoral districts and party nominations. To illustrate its practical working let us take the case of a city with 100,000 voters entitled to elect ten members of Congress or other legislative body. Every ten thousand voters of any political faith will thus be entitled to one representative, and no political party polling at least that number of votes will be entirely excluded from representation. Let us assume that there are four parties in the field. Each of the parties may nominate ten candidates, but it will serve the purpose if they nominate one or two more than they expect to elect. The electoral ticket and the votes cast for the different parties will be as follows: —

	REPUBLICAN PARTY	DEMOCRATIC PARTY	SOCIALIST PARTY	PROHIBITION PARTY
	A	H	M	P
	B	I	N	Q
	C	J	O	
	D	K		
	E	L		
	F			
	G			
Votes	37,500	29,900	21,100	11,500
Representatives . .	4	3	2	1

This illustration presupposes a straight party vote, and in that case candidates will be declared elected in the order of their positions on the ballot, the positions having been fixed by the respective parties. This is known as the "block-vote." But the plan of proportional representation does not preclude the voter from expressing his preference for specific candidates of his party. The voter may be allowed to vote for the individual candidates of his choice, and his vote will count both for the candidate and the party, and he may be even allowed to vote on the cumulative system, *i.e.*, cast all of his ten votes for one candidate or distribute them among several candidates in such proportions as he may choose. Where votes are counted for the candidate as well as for the party, each party will receive the representation to which the total number of votes cast for its ticket entitles it, and the candidates receiving the highest individual votes on the ticket will be declared elected.

The system of proportional representation has been introduced in the parliamentary elections of Sweden, Finland and Japan; it is being strongly urged in several other countries for national elections, and is frequently applied in local elections. Belgium has the curious system of proportional representation based on the "single vote plan" and combined with plural voting. The system is the same as shown in our illustration, except that every voter casts one vote which counts for the candidate designated by him on the ballot and for his party, and except also that persons of property or college education have the privilege of voting three separate ballots instead of the one ballot allowed to the other citizens.

The Referendum, Initiative and Right of Recall

If proportional representation is designed to give to each political group of citizens a representation in government in accordance with its numbers, the Referendum seeks to maintain the representatives under the constant control of their electors. By the "Referendum" is meant the right to compel the legislature to submit to the vote of the entire people any law, ordinance or other question

to be adopted, ratified or rejected at the polls. Where
the referendum is in vogue, it is usually set in motion by
the petition of a certain number of voters, ordinarily from
five to ten per cent. If such petition is presented to the
legislature within a specified time after the passage of a
certain act or measure, say within two or three months, the
act or measure in question is submitted to a popular vote,
and the decision of the voters seals its fate. The Referendum was introduced in Switzerland in the early part of the
nineteenth century, it was largely extended by the constitution of 1874, and has since become an established feature
in that progressive little republic. It has also been adopted
in four states of the Union, and it is the uniform method of
amending state constitutions in all states but one. It is
also often resorted to in the local politics of many cities in
America, Europe and Australia.

The benefits of the Referendum as practiced in Switzerland are stated by Mr. John A. Hobson in this language: —

"1. It provides a remedy for intentional or uninten-
tional misrepresentation on the part of elected legislatures
and secures laws conformable to the actual will of the
majority.

"2. It enhances the popular confidence in the stability
of law.

"3. It eliminates much waste of political energy by
enabling proposals of unknown value to be submitted
separately to a quantitative test."

Yet the greatest service of all is the training in the art
of self-government which the referendum gives. Says Mr.
Hobson: —

"It may indeed be questioned whether a people whose

direct contribution to self-government consists in a single vote cast at intervals of several years, not for a policy or even for a measure, but for a party or a personality, can be or is capable of becoming a genuinely self-governing people. Some amount of regular responsibility for concrete acts of conduct is surely as essential to the education of a self-reliant people as of a self-reliant individual." [1]

And Mr. Curti, for many years a member of the Swiss Parliament, sums up his own experience as follows: —

"I am certain that the Referendum has prevented but little of the good we might have done, but it has averted many evils if only by the fact that it always stood warningly before us. I should say that it does not condemn democracy to a standstill, despite its occasional retrogressive movements, but that it lends steadiness to progress itself." [2]

The Referendum, beneficial as its operations may be, is not effective to secure the dominion of the popular will over the representative legislatures without the aid of another modern political weapon — the Popular Initiative.

The Initiative is "the right of a certain percentage of the voters, usually five to ten per cent, to propose a law, ordinance or constitutional amendment for action by the legislature or decision at the polls or both." [3] If the proposed measure is acted upon favorably by the legislature, that disposes of it, but if the legislature fails to enact it, it must be submitted to a popular vote for adoption or rejection.

[1] Quoted from *Equity*, Philadelphia, for January, 1908.

[2] Theodor Curti, "Die Resultate des Schweizerischen Referendums," Stuttgart, 1898, p. 48.

[3] "A Primer of Direct Legislation," *The Arena*, Trenton, New Jersey, 1906, p. 8.

The Referendum alone is merely designed to prevent mischievous legislation, for its workings are negative; the Initiative enables the people to force positive legislation. The Referendum and Initiative complement each other, and in a majority of cases they have been adopted together and as parts of the same political system.

The Right of Recall is the right of the constituents of any public official to withdraw him from office before the expiration of his elective or appointive term. This right is based on the theory that in a democracy every public official is the agent of the people, and may be discharged by the latter at any time and for any reason.

The Right of Recall is usually exercised by a petition for the removal of the objectionable representative or official, signed by a large number of voters within the district from which he has been elected. Upon such petition new elections are ordered, and the name of the objectionable incumbent is submitted to the voters together with the names of any new candidates, so as to give to the voters the opportunity to retain him in office or to recall him.

The system has been introduced in Switzerland, in several municipalities of the state of California, and recently in the city of Seattle, Washington. It is not as popular as the Referendum and the Initiative, and the adoption of the latter often tends to make the measure superfluous, at least so far as regards legislative representatives.

The socialists advocate all political reforms which have for their object the democratization of the modern state, and that not only on account of their general desire for political progress, but also for the special reason that such reforms are indispensable for the progress and success of the socialist movement. All restrictions on popular suffrage are primarily designed to disfranchise the propertyless working class, the main source of the political strength of socialism, and all methods of disproportionate representation work most disastrously on minority parties and new political movements.

The social democrats of Germany under Lassalle's leadership entered the political arena with the motto of unrestricted suffrage for all adult citizens, and that motto has remained the battle cry of militant socialism in all countries of restricted suffrage. In Austria, Russia, Belgium and Sweden, the socialists have been the leading spirits of all movements for suffrage extension, and in other countries they have often been its sole champions.

Socialism and Woman Suffrage

A similarly unmistakable stand have the socialists always maintained on the subject of woman suffrage. "As soon as the Socialist Party was born," attests Mrs. Zetkin, "it adopted the demand of equal rights for man and woman in its political program. The social democracy is the organization of woman suffrage *par excellence* in Germany. In the many thousands of meetings in which the party year after year proclaims its theories and explains its program, the justice of woman suffrage is always emphasized. The proletarian movement of women especially has repeatedly unfolded all over the empire an exclusive propaganda in favor of the fullest and highest political rights of the female sex. Bebel, von Vollmar and other socialist representatives have time and time again made earnest pleas for woman suffrage in the General German

Diet and in the different provincial diets. And the social democracy has not satisfied itself with mere talk in favor of woman suffrage. It has repeatedly proposed positive legislation on that subject. As the first and, up to the present, the only political party of Germany, the Social Democrats already in 1895 offered a resolution in the Imperial Diet which declared that all elections to Parliament and to the provincial diets should be based on the universal, equal, direct and secret vote of all adult citizens, without distinction of sex." [1]

For the socialist movement the demand for woman suffrage is not a mere sentimental proposition of abstract justice. The working woman has become so large and important a factor in modern industrial life that the workingman can hardly carry on his economic and political struggles without her coöperation. For the upper and middle class woman suffrage is a convenience and an advantage; for the woman of the working class it is an immediate material necessity.

It is for this reason that the breach between the bourgeois "suffragists" and the working women advocates of suffrage is constantly deepening. The suffragists of the upper and middle classes favor woman suffrage qualified by a property test because such test would not exclude them from voting, and also because they regard such limited suffrage as a partial victory for the general principle of woman suffrage.

The proletarian suffragettes, on the other hand, see in such qualified woman suffrage only a means of strengthening the political power of the possessing classes, thus cor-

[1] Clara Zetkin, "Zur Frage des Frauenwahlrechts," Berlin, 1907, p. 19.

respondingly diminishing the political strength of the propertyless working class.

The question of woman suffrage was thoroughly examined by the last International Socialist Congress held at Stuttgart in 1907, and the resolution adopted on the subject thus defines the socialist attitude towards the general movement for woman suffrage: —

"It is the duty of socialist parties of all countries to agitate most energetically for the introduction of universal womanhood suffrage. The socialist parties repudiate limited woman's suffrage as an adulteration of, and a caricature upon, the principle of political equality of the female sex. It fights for the sole living concrete expression of this principle; namely, universal womanhood suffrage, which should belong to all women of age and not be conditioned by property, taxation, education, or any other qualification which would exclude members of the laboring classes from the enjoyment of this right. The socialist women should not carry on this struggle for complete equality of right of vote in alliance with the middle-class women suffragists, but in common with the socialist parties, which insist upon woman suffrage as one of the fundamental and most important reforms for the full democratization of political franchise in general."

CHAPTER V

In the last chapter we dealt with such reforms as affect primarily the character of government. Here we will consider some reforms bearing on the functions of government and the manner of their discharge, and for lack of a more expressive term, we will designate these by the common title of " administrative reforms."

Under this head we will examine three significant movements of recent times: the movements for government ownership of certain industries, for the shifting of the burden of taxation on the possessing classes, and for the abolition of standing armies. The three movements are but loosely related among themselves, and the socialist attitude to them is different in each case.

Government Ownership

The movement for the transfer of ownership in certain industries of a public or quasi-public nature, such as railroads, telegraphs, telephones, street cars, waterworks and gas works, to the central government or to municipal governments, has made very substantial progress within the last few decades, and its ideas have found very extended application. Switzerland, Belgium and the Australian colonies, Prussia and Russia own the greater part of the railroads of those countries; in Saxony all railroading

284

is government monopoly, and in Austria, Holland and Norway the governments are gradually and steadily absorbing the private lines. All of these countries began with private ownership of the roads, and gradually transferred such ownership to the government.

Still more marked is that process in the case of the telegraph. "With the exception of the sale of the experimental line from Washington to Baltimore," says Professor Parsons, "no country has changed from public to private ownership, but every country in the world that began with private telegraphs has changed to public ownership, except Bolivia, Canada, Cuba, Cyprus, Hawaii, Honduras and the United States." [1]

Germany, Bulgaria and some of the Australian colonies introduced their first telephones as government monopolies, and have retained them as such, while Great Britain, Belgium, Austria, France, Switzerland, Sweden and Norway have acquired all or portions of the telephone systems of their country from the original private owners.

The field of municipal ownership is even more extensive than that of national ownership. Municipal ownership of water and gas works is practically the rule in most countries of Europe, and in the United States more than half of the cities and towns own their own waterworks, and several cities have acquired their gas works.

Municipal street railways have received the largest extension in Great Britain, where the municipalities own and operate more than 40 per cent of the total mileage. The movement for the transfer of all privately owned street cars to the municipal governments has of late met with

[1] Frank Parsons, "The City for the People," Equity Series, Philadelphia, 1901, p. 207.

more or less substantial success in all modern countries
except the United States.

From the fact that socialism advocates the public ownership of all means of production, and that its political program demands the national ownership of railways and
telegraphs, and the municipal ownership of street cars
and gas and water works, the inference is often drawn that
the growth of government ownership as here described is a
direct or indirect achievement of the socialist movement.
This notion is as erroneous as it is widespread and popular. The socialists do not claim any credit for the present-day institutions of government ownership, nor have
they any illusions as to their significance and benefits.
Government ownership under the present régime does not
represent an advanced phase of industrial development
or the climax of industrial concentration. It is in no sense
an installment of the socialist coöperative republic.

National ownership of railroads, telegraphs and telephones has been in most cases introduced by the governments for reasons of military expediency or for the sake
of revenue. In other cases it was brought about as a concession to the interests of the middle classes.

Similarly, municipal ownership, where not brought
about by a socialist administration, is as a rule but a device for municipal revenue. Government ownership, both
national and municipal, has some very decided advantages
over private ownership, and on the whole, it assures better
service to the public and better treatment of the employees.
But these advantages are to a large extent offset by the
fact that government ownership tends to strengthen the
powers of the modern class state, and to curtail the freedom
of combination and coalition on the part of the employees.

What the socialists demand is not government ownership, but public ownership, and the distinction is very
material under present conditions, as pointed out by
Professor Parsons, who says: —

"*Public* ownership and *government* ownership are by
no means synonymous. Where legislative power is per-
verted to private purposes — where the spoils system
prevails and the offices are treated as private property —
where government is managed in the interests of a few
individuals or of a class, anything that is in the control of
the government is really private property, although it
may be called public property. If councils and legislatures are masters instead of the people, they are likely to
use the streets and franchises for private gain instead of the
public good. If the government is a private monopoly,
everything in the hands of the government is a private
monopoly." [1]

In fact, the movement for the national or municipal
ownership of public utilities is the most striking illustration of a reform movement which may be revolutionary
or retrogressive according to the source from which it
emanates.

The socialists of all countries favor the municipaliza-
tion or nationalization of public utilities, but that only as
a measure to be carried out by an administration controlled
or at least strongly influenced by the working class.
Their demand for municipal or national ownership of the
industries mentioned is coupled with the further demand
for the democratic administration of those industries, and
for their management in the interests of the employees
and the public. On the other hand, the most reactionary

[1] "The City for the People," p. 17.

capitalist governments may utilize it for the purpose of strengthening their grip on the people, and the middle-class apostles of municipal or national ownership of the type of Hearst or Bryan in the United States or the "radical" bourgeois parties of Europe, see in it primarily a means of decreasing the taxes of property owners and reducing the rates of freight, transportation and communication for the smaller business men.

In Germany, where the socialists have had ample opportunity to watch the practical workings of government ownership, they passed judgment on the institution in the following terse resolution adopted at their annual convention of 1892: —

"State socialism, so-called, inasmuch as it aims at state ownership for fiscal purposes, seeks to substitute the state for the private capitalist, and to confer on it the power to subject the people to the double yoke of economic exploitation and political slavery."

Tax Reforms

The support of the modern state in all its branches, civil and military, involves the expenditure of immense funds, and the problem of raising these funds has ever been the hardest bone of contention between the governments and the governed. All moneys for the support of the government necessarily come from the people in the form of taxes, and the distribution of the burden of taxation among the various classes of the population always depends on the methods employed in its levying.

The two main contending methods of taxation are the direct and the indirect. A direct tax is a tax imposed on the very person of the citizen who is expected to pay it, and one that cannot be shifted by him; an indirect tax is a tax on real estate or commodities, formally imposed on the owner, manufacturer or merchant, but actually borne by the tenant or consumer. Instances of the first class are the poll tax, the income tax and the inheritance tax; instances of the latter class are the real property tax, the import duties on raw material or manufactured goods of foreign importation, and the excise duties on articles of domestic manufacture, such as tobacco, liquors, etc.

The ruling classes and the modern state as a rule favor the indirect tax, while the socialists have always been strongly opposed to it.

"The indirect tax is the instrument through which the bourgeoisie brings about the complete exemption from taxation of capital, and burdens the poorer classes of society with all the expenses of the state government," asserted Ferdinand Lassalle in his famous "Workingmen's Program" in 1862, and this conception is still the generally accepted socialist view on the subject. The socialists have always consistently advocated the system of direct taxation, and among the most universal planks of their practical political programs are the demands for a progressive income tax and a progressive inheritance tax.

A progressive income tax is a direct tax levied upon the excess income of each citizen above a certain minimum, and progressively graded according to the size of the income. The tax has the merit of placing the onus of maintaining the government upon the classes who derive the greatest benefits from it and who can bear the burden with the greatest ease.

In England the progressive income tax was first intro-

U

duced in the period of the Napoleonic wars as a temporary makeshift, but the system has since established itself in the country firmly, and the revenue from that source was almost £36,000,000 in 1902. From England the progressive income tax has spread to Italy, Switzerland, Germany, Austria, Hungary, Denmark, Holland and Australia. France at present taxes only the incomes of corporations and business associations, but a general and rather high income tax is now proposed by the government. In the United States a progressive income tax was in force, and yielded excellent results during the closing years of the Civil War, and until 1872, when it was repealed. In 1894, a new income tax law was passed by Congress, but the law was declared unconstitutional and void by the Supreme Court, the far-reaching decision having been rendered by a vote of 5 to 4, after one of the justices had changed his expressed views on the question. Several states of the Union, however, levy an income tax on their citizens.

A progressive inheritance tax is a tax on those acquiring property by inheritance or by will. The tax is sometimes levied only on collateral heirs, and usually it is progressively graded either in accordance with the size of the inheritance or with the degree of remoteness of the relationship between the deceased and the heir, or both.

The progressive inheritance tax, and especially the collateral inheritance tax, furnish large parts of the state revenues in most of the Australian colonies and in Switzerland, where the tax is in some cases as high as twenty per cent of the estate. England, Germany, France, Austria, Italy, Spain, Belgium, Holland, Denmark, Switzerland, Russia, Roumania, Australia, Canada, and most of the states of the Union, all have inheritance taxes, but in most of these countries except France and Australia, the tax rate is rather insignificant.

Socialism does not consider the direct income and inheritance taxes within the frame of modern capitalist society as a means of equalizing the distribution of wealth, but it favors them as effective instruments for the abolition of indirect taxes, which diminish the purchasing power of the working class and lower its standard of life.

The "Single Tax"

Another movement of tax reform which has developed considerable strength within the last quarter of a century, especially in the English-speaking countries, is that based on the so-called Single-Tax theory.

The theory was first fully and clearly formulated by Henry George in his famous work "Progress and Poverty," published in 1879, and it has since been elaborated and restated in numerous books, pamphlets and periodicals.

The principal features of the proposed reform are tersely stated by the originator of the movement himself in the following language: —

"We propose to abolish all taxes save one single tax levied on the value of land, irrespective of the value of improvements in or on it.

"What we propose is not a tax on real estate, for real estate includes improvements. Nor is it a tax on land, for we would not tax all land, but only land having a value irrespective of its improvements, and would tax that in proportion to that value.

"Our tax involves the imposition of no new tax, since we already tax land values in taxing real estate. To carry it out we have only to abolish all taxes save the tax on real estate and to abolish all of that which now falls on buildings or improvements, leaving only that part of it which now falls on the value of the bare land. This we would increase so as to take as nearly as may be the whole of the economic rent, or what is sometimes styled the 'unearned increment of land values.'" [1]

This single tax on land values is proposed by Mr. George and his followers not merely as an improvement on the prevailing methods of taxation, but as a cure of all social evils of our times.

The root and source of all human poverty and misery, according to the conception of the single taxers, lies in the fact that the valuable land in all civilized countries is monopolized by a comparatively small class of landowners, who appropriate all benefits derived from it, and impose a high tax for its use and occupation in the form of rent.

This system makes it possible for a number of men to hold large areas of land for speculative purposes, thus withdrawing it from actual use. And as land is in the last analysis the source of all wealth, the withholding of any part of it results in the curtailment of wealth production for the nation.

Furthermore, so long as land was free to all, everybody could gain his subsistence by agriculture or by industrial pursuits on a small scale, but so soon as land becomes private property, it is only the man who can afford to pay a high rent — the capitalist — who can engage in any industry, while the poor man is compelled to sell his labor for the best price obtainable.

[1] Henry George in "Financial Reform Almanach" of England for the year 1891.

And lastly, rent being an arbitrary tax on production, it draws from the profits of capital and wages of labor alike, impoverishes both, gives rise to industrial crises, and produces an unjust distribution of wealth which is building up immense fortunes in the hands of a few while the masses grow relatively poorer and poorer.

"The taxation of the processes and products of labor on the one hand," says Mr. George, in the article already mentioned, "and the insufficient taxation of land values on the other, produces an unjust distribution of wealth which is building up, in the hands of a few, fortunes more monstrous than the world has ever before seen, while the masses of our people are steadily becoming relatively poorer. These taxes necessarily fall on the poor more heavily than on the rich; by increasing prices, they necessitate larger capital in all business, and consequently give an advantage to large capitals; and they give, and in some cases are designed to give, special advantages and monopolies to combinations and trusts. On the other hand, the insufficient taxation of land values enables men to make large fortunes by land speculation and the increase in ground values — fortunes which do not represent any addition by them to the general wealth of the community, but merely the appropriation by some of what the labor of others creates.

"This unjust distribution of wealth develops on the one hand a class idle and wasteful, because they are too rich, and on the other hand a class idle and wasteful, because they are too poor — it deprives men of capital and opportunities which would make them more efficient producers."

It is the conviction of the disciples of Henry George that a single tax on land values as advocated by them would gradually lead to the abolition of private ownership in land.

The only country in which some general application of the tax on land values has been attempted is New Zealand, and while it is claimed by the friends of the reform that the system has on the whole had a stimulating and beneficial effect on the industries of the country and has succeeded in curbing wild land speculation, predicted benefits of a fundamental character have so far failed to materialize. It must be added, however, in justice to the advocates of the measures, that the New Zealand system of land taxation is by no means a full application of the single-tax theory. On the other hand, at least one of its principles, that of taxing vacant and unused land most heavily, has of late found direct or indirect recognition in the systems of taxation of several countries, states and municipalities.

The socialists have but little sympathy for the single-tax theory. They do not agree with the economic premises on which it is based, and they consider the proposed reform as entirely impotent to cope with the evils which it seeks to combat, and in some respects even as distinctly reactionary.

The single-tax philosophy was evolved by Henry George a generation ago in the then little developed far West, and it is entirely adapted to the industrial conditions which surrounded him at the time. It presupposes a system of industry based mainly on agriculture and small manufacture, and is sadly out of place in a system of gigantic factories.

Land values occupy but a secondary position in modern industrial wealth. If the up-to-date large capitalist were to be taxed on the value of his factory site to the full extent of its rental income, but be relieved from all taxes on the factory buildings, implements, stock and other property and income, he would practically escape taxation. On the other hand, an accessible or even free factory site would not enable the propertyless wage worker to equip a costly modern plant and to set up in business on his own account in competition with his present employer. It is the private ownership of the machine, even more than the private ownership of land, that holds the working class in bondage.

The single taxer recognizes but one form of economic exploitation — rent. The socialist, on the other hand, asserts that the source of all exploitation is the "surplus value" (the unpaid part of the workingman's labor) from which all rent as well as interest and profit are derived.

The single taxer would abolish the landlord, the monopolist of "land values," but continue the existence of the capitalist and wage worker; the socialist strives to wipe out all class distinction and to introduce complete economic equality. The single-tax theory professes to be an absolute and scientific truth applicable to all ages and conditions alike, while socialism professes to be a theory growing out of modern economic conditions, and expecting its realization from the steadily growing concentration and socialization of industry. The single taxer, lastly, is an earnest supporter of the competitive system of industry, while the socialist is as ardent a collectivist.

Thus the two social theories differ very materially in their views, aims, and methods.[1]

[1] Compare, Morris Hillquit, "History of Socialism in the United States," 4th Edition, New York, 1906, pp. 272, etc.; also A. M. Simons, "Single Tax vs. Socialism," Chicago, 1899.

Abolition of Standing Armies

One of the greatest evils of the modern state is the standing army. Capitalist society cannot be maintained without a host of soldiers. In their world-wide competitive struggles, the capitalists of each country strive not only to preserve and extend their own markets, but also to invade those of the rival nations and to conquer new markets. This feature of the modern capitalist system of production and exchange inevitably leads to clashes between competing nations, and the specter of war is ever hovering among them. The modern capitalist state is powerless without a strong army or navy. It must always be ready for offensive and defensive military action, and it must always make a display of military strength to curb the bellicose designs of its neighbors. It must prepare for war, if it wants war; it must prepare for war, if it wants peace.

A strong army moreover has within recent times become essential to the maintenance of capitalist government for another reason and for another purpose. With the increasing intensity of capitalist exploitation, the outbreaks of revolt on the part of the working masses tend to become more violent and frequent, and where these outbreaks are of such a character that the local authorities are either powerless to cope with them, or disinclined to interfere with them, the army is the most effective instrument for their suppression. To the capitalist government the army is an organization for the protection of the ruling classes from "all enemies, foreign and domestic," and the protection from "the domestic enemy" is often its more important function.

The vast dimensions of the standing armies of the most powerful countries of Europe are shown by the following figures: —

Russia	1,500,000
France	746,000
Germany	650,000
Great Britain . . .	550,000
Austria	470,000
Italy	290,000

And even in the United States, which up to recent times has been practically free from the curse of militarism, the development of industry and foreign commerce and the growth of the class struggles have of late years given rise to a movement on the part of the ruling classes to increase and strengthen the army and navy. The recent military law of the United States Congress aims to consolidate the federal troops and the various state militia organizations into a standing army of 250,000 soldiers, while the agitation for a huge navy is steadily increasing.

The military and naval organizations of the modern states are an intolerable economic drain upon the nation. The "Nouveau Manuel du Soldat," taking the statistics of the year 1899 as the basis of calculation, figures the loss of productive value caused by militarism in Europe as follows: —

The total military expenses of the European powers for 1899 were $1,436,864,218. In the same year those countries had in the field 4,169,321 men, who, if employed at productive work, would produce every day, at an average of only 60 cents per day per man, a total of $2,501,592.60. Europe had in its armies 710,342 horses which could produce $284,136.80 per day at an average production of 40 cents per day. The expenditures and wasted productive values of the army upon that basis thus amounted to $2,272,523,038 per year on the basis of 300 working days!

This burden has vastly grown since 1899. In Germany alone the military budget has increased from about 920,000,000 marks in 1899 to 1,300,000,000 in 1906–1907. Karl Liebknecht estimates the present total military cost of Europe at 13,000,000,000 marks, or about $3,250,000,000 per year.[1]

The standing armies and the navies are besides a prolific source of general brutalization and demoralization of the people.

By drafting the young men of the nation into the army, the state withdraws from the productive ranks of the population its most vigorous and useful members, compels the rest of the people to support them in useless idleness during their protracted term of service, and at the expiration of the term it sets them adrift, often with crippled minds, corrupted morals and impaired social usefulness.

"When, after a satisfactory test, the young man becomes a soldier in the standing army," observes Vaillant, "he ceases to be a citizen. In order that he may become a passive instrument in the hands of his superior, he is deprived of all civil functions and political rights upon entering the military life. For him there is no right and no law. He is merely a thing of the military state. It is the rule without exception, the rule established in order that it may not be tempered by the possible humaneness of the

[1] Dr. Karl Liebknecht, "Militarismus und Antimilitarismus," Zürich, 1908, p. 43.

superior officer. The military rule takes possession of the young man and arbitrarily disposes of his actions, his liberty, his life. If the brutality and arrogance of the officer do not break his resistance and will, he is tried, convicted, sent to prison or to death by a court martial. This is 'justice' for him, these are the tribunals where his superiors, constituting themselves his judges and executioners, take their revenge for his lack of discipline. In fact, it is necessary that the army be entirely separated from the people, so that it may serve against it, against the working class, as the police force and bodyguards of the capitalist class and the government. For this purpose, especially in an army through which all the children of the working class pass, it is necessary that a discipline of terror and of death steady the arm of the soldier in civil as well as in foreign war." [1]

The rapid *tempo* of technical progress in all matters of military organization and equipments leads to constant revolutions in the system of armament and forces upon the nations burdens which exhaust their material strength. The governments of the principal countries of Europe seem almost to have the sole function of securing and feeding their soldiers, and the tremendous growth of the national debts and indirect taxes necessitated by the standing armies has brought many countries to the verge of national bankruptcy. It was this state of affairs which compelled the youthful czar of Russia in 1898 to emit his desperate cry for universal limitation of armament, which was euphemistically styled a "peace message," and it is this condition of things which accounts for the modern "peace conferences" of the governments.

[1] Edouard Vaillant, "Suppression de l'Armée Permanente," Paris, p. 12.

The working class, which furnishes the large bulk of the army and contributes the greater part of the funds for its support, is naturally opposed to all wars and standing armies, and the socialists, as the political spokesmen of that class, have always carried on a strenuous propaganda against wars and standing armies. But socialists have but little enthusiasm for the official "peace conferences" held under the auspices of the present governments. The object of these conferences is not to abolish standing armies, but merely to decrease their size, and that not below the point required for the suppression of the "domestic enemy," the working class.

Socialism stands for the abolition of all wars and all armies, but it recognizes that within the modern social system this is an unattainable ideal. The practical socialist program, therefore, advocates what the socialists consider the next best step, — introduction of a national democratic militia system instead of that of the standing army.

There is but one country in the world in which that system has found almost complete application, and that country naturally is the one that may be called the experimental laboratory of all social reforms — Switzerland.

The militia system was introduced in Switzerland in 1874. Subsequently that system was supplemented by the institutions of the *Landwehr* and *Landsturm*.

The militia proper, or the *Élite*, consists of all able-bodied male citizens between the ages of twenty and thirty-two years; the *Landwehr* is composed of all men between the ages of thirty-two and forty-four years, while all citizens, between the ages of eighteen and fifty years, who for one cause or another do not belong to either of the two classes, constitute the *Landsturm*.

The cavalry exercises every year, all other corps of the *Élite*, or active army, every two years, while the members of the *Landwehr* are called under arms for the purpose of military exercise and maneuvers once in four years. The Federal Council of the republic is the head of the army.

In 1902 the total military forces of the Swiss militia were as follows: 153,649 in the *Élite*, 88,813 in the *Landwehr*, and in the *Landsturm*, 43,368 soldiers under arms, and 237,275 in the non-armed or auxiliary service. In other words, the little republic with a population of about 3,000,000 had an active army of 285,830 trained men, and in case of emergency could rely on 523,105 citizens for its defense. And the total military budget of Switzerland is less than thirty million francs per year.

The militia system of Switzerland is the socialist model of existing military organization, though the socialists do not consider it perfect, and strongly advocate certain improvements, especially the election of officers and the military education and training of the youth as part of the general educational system.

The militia system has been criticised as too cumbersome, irregular and scattered for offensive action, but in the eyes of the socialists this feature is one of its greatest merits. The militia is primarily an instrument for self-defense, just as the standing army is mainly an instrument of aggression.

But the principal virtue of a true democratic militia is that it leaves the military power in the hands of the people and prevents the ruling classes from turning it into a tool of oppression and despotism. The only people that is really free is an armed people, and the people as such can be properly armed only under a general militia system.

"I ask you to observe," said Edouard Vaillant, speaking in support of his bill for the introduction of the Swiss militia system in France, before the Chamber of Deputies, "that when we advocate the institution of militia, we do not pretend to propose a measure of socialism. The militia is the military organization of the city, which without distinction between military and civil functions, has become at once military and civil. It is the present city transferred to the camp, it is the citizen-soldier, and the soldier-citizen, always a citizen in all his functions, be they military or civil." And again : —

"The armament of the people is the necessary complement to universal suffrage and to the development of a true democracy. The militia has in all history been the institution of democracy, appearing with its victories, disappearing with its defeats." [1]

This positive side of the militia system, the arming and training of all male citizens, makes the reform of almost as great importance to the working class of the countries free from standing armies as to the workingmen in the most military states.

[1] "Suppression de l'Armée Permanente," pp. 25, 26.

CHAPTER VI

Crime and Vice

THE alarming growth of crime and vice in modern times has advanced a problem which society can no longer ignore. Up to very recent years the views of the good and virtuous people on the criminal and the prostitute were exceedingly definite and simple. The one was a malicious enemy of law and order, to be mercilessly run down and punished for his deliberate malefactions; the other was a shameless creature, an outcast of society, to be loathed and despised. And it is only within the last decades that more sober views on the subject have begun to assert themselves. The application of scientific methods to the investigation of social phenomena was gradually extended to the domain of crime and vice. Attempts were made to discover their true nature, origin and causes and to devise rational methods for checking their growth. The new science of criminology was thus born, and as is the case with every social science, especially during the period of its inception, several divergent schools of thought were soon developed within it.

Of such modern schools of criminology the most popularly known and most sensational is that established by the famous Italian criminologist, Cesare Lombroso, the school of "criminal anthropology." The main doctrine

of this school is that the criminal is distinguishable from
the normal human being by certain physical and psychic
peculiarities, which stamp him as an *uomo deliquente*,
delinquent man or born criminal.

These peculiarities are of an atavistic nature, and are
either inherited or gradually acquired through a definite
process of physical degeneration. The proof of this
theory rests on the results of extensive investigations into
the family histories of numerous criminals, on physical
measurements and autopsies of delinquents, and on fine
observations of the general mental traits and moral conceptions of the criminal classes. The habitual criminals,
according to these observations, as a rule spring from an
ancestry tainted with drunkenness, epilepsy and insanity;
they have no conception of right and wrong, and their
physical construction and appearance show a reversion
to the peculiarities of primitive men.

Lombroso's theories were extended by the brilliant
coterie of his disciples, and finally Dr. B. Tarnowsky, of
the St. Petersburg Military Medical Academy, transferred
them from the field of crime to that of vice. To the type
of the "born criminal" was added that of the "born prostitute," both possessing largely the same characteristics.

The conception of the born criminal leads necessarily
to that of the incurable criminal, and the school of criminal
anthropology thus practically proclaims the hopelessness
and futility of all social attempts to curb crime and vice.
The doctrines of that school bear a close resemblance to
the pseudo-scientific arguments of the old-time advocates
of slavery and the modern opponents of woman's rights
— all of them seek a sanction for revolting social conditions
in the alleged physical inferiority of the victims of those

conditions, and all of them fail to take into account the social and historical influences which contribute so largely to the development and modification of the physical, mental and moral type.

A substantial improvement on the one-sided views of the school of Lombroso was introduced by the well-known Italian criminologist and socialist leader, Enrico Ferri.[1] Ferri admits the existence of a criminal type to be distinguished by physical symptoms, but he regards such symptoms merely as evidence of pathological traits, inherited or acquired, which predispose the subject to a career of crime. In his view such criminal inclinations are by no means irresistible — they may be overcome by other agencies. Ferri recognizes three main factors as causes of crime; the physico-psychical constitution of the individual, his natural environment, and his social environment. He distinguishes five different classes of criminals: —

1. *Born criminals*, or persons with a hereditary taint predisposing them to crime;

2. *Insane criminals*, or such who commit crimes while insane;

3. *Criminals through passion;*

4. *Criminals through circumstances*, whose crimes are accidental and are due to their social surroundings, and

5. *Habitual criminals*, who have become such after the first offense, through prison life and associations, and through the relentless persecutions of organized society.

The last two classes, according to Ferri, embrace about 75 per cent of all criminals. But the criminals through passion are also largely the products of the conditions of the modern struggle for existence, and even the born and

[1] "Crime as a Social Phenomenon."

x

the insane criminal types are to a large extent developed by social conditions.

"The anthropologist who recognizes the hereditary or acquired biological anomalies of these criminals," says he, "does not thereby deny the indirect social origin of the greater part of these anomalies themselves." [1]

Similar views are held by many eminent criminologists, especially of the Italian school. The social cause of crime is still more emphasized by the "positive school of criminology," whose leading exponent is the well-known German criminologist, Franz von Liszt. That school does not ignore the individual characteristics of the criminal as a factor in the commission of crime, but it attributes to them a secondary importance only.

"The individual conditions of crime are often the direct products of its social conditions," observes von Liszt. "The misery of the masses is the fertile soil not only for the growth of crime itself, but also of that degeneration based on hereditary taint which in its turn again leads to crime. . . . Every crime is the product on the one hand of the peculiarities of the individual criminal, and on the other, of the social conditions which surround the criminal at the time of the deed — in other words, it is the product of *only one* individual factor and of *countless* social factors."

And again: —

"It is an established fact that a protracted industrial depression always results in the increase of crime generally, and especially of offenses against property, principally theft; in the decrease of marriages and births of legitimate

[1] Enrico Ferri, "Kriminelle Anthropologie und Sozialismus," *Neue Zeit*, 14th Year, Vol. II, No. 41.

children with a corresponding increase of illegitimate births; in the rise in the infantile death-rate, the increase of suicides, the lowering of the average life and in a series of other disquieting phenomena. A close examination would show that the influence of industrial conditions on criminality is more far-reaching than commonly supposed. Thus the geographical distribution of criminality in each country is largely based on the industrial conditions of the different sections of the country. . . . Thus also the strong increase of offenses against property in December, January and February may be accounted for by the decreased opportunities for work in the cold season and the greater need of food, clothing and fuel. . . . The 'industrial conditions,' whose favorable or unfavorable influence on criminality must be primarily considered to-day, are the *general condition of the working classes,* not only their financial, but also their physical, mental, moral and political condition." [1]

The socialists most generally adhere to the views of von Liszt and the positive school of criminology.

Crime and vice do not owe their existence to the modern capitalist society. Crimes against the person are as old as human passion, and crimes against property and the vice of prostitution are probably as old as the institution of private property. But if capitalism has not created crime and vice, it has created the conditions for their wholesale development and ever increasing extension. For if the misery of the masses is the fertile soil of crime and vice, capitalism is the hothouse of popular misery.

Whether crime and vice in their devastating triumphal

[1] Quoted by Paul Hirsch in "Verbrechen und Prostitution als soziale Krankheitserscheinungen," 2d Edition, Berlin, 1907, pp. 22, 23.

march brand the bodies and souls of their victims with visible marks of infamy, and whether they choose their victims in the prime of their lives, in their cradles or in their mothers' wombs, is a matter of little moment: the modern social relations are such that they cannot fail to produce destitution and physical and mental degeneracy and crime and vice as specific expressions of such destitution and degeneracy. All conditions surrounding the modern workingman's family, and especially the family of the most poorly paid workingman, tend to drive its members to break the established social canons of law and morality. The exhausting labor of the workingmen and working women sap their physical and moral strength; their helpless and hopeless condition in cases of unemployment, sickness or physical disability render them desperate; their repulsive "homes" rob them of the sustaining influences of family life and drive them to drink and to the rude life of the street; the heartless treatment of their employers and of "organized society" as a whole makes them morose and embittered; their misery is so deep, their temptations are so strong, and their powers of resistance so weak, that it should be a matter of surprise that so many of them escape the clutches of crime or vice.

And just as the heartless system of exploitation breeds crime and vice in the classes of the exploited, so does the senseless system of competition and the headlong race for profits breed the crimes so prevalent and growing in the ranks of the exploiters themselves: fraud, bribery, corruption and numerous similar offenses.

Crime and vice cannot be entirely eliminated from the capitalist system of society. They may be diminished, but not by police measures nor by prison methods, not by supervision nor by segregation, not by any system of punishment or moral preaching, but by removing the worst features of those social conditions that breed crime and vice. The socialists are by no means indifferent to the efforts to check the growth of crime and vice, but they recognize the absolute impotency of purely penal reforms to accomplish that end, and they see the only remedy against the dreadful double scourge of human society in the realization of their general program of industrial and social reform.

Intemperance

Intemperance as such is not a modern problem. The use and abuse of alcoholic drinks are as old as written history, and the movement to combat the evil dates back several centuries.

The first temperance society is said to have been founded by Margrave Frederick V in 1600, and it is instructive to learn that the noble members of that society were bound by a pledge, good for two years, not to drink more than seven bumpers of wine with any meal, nor more than fourteen bumpers a day. They were, however, permitted to quench any surplus of thirst with beer and to drink one glass of whisky on the side. By this ideal of abstention may be gauged the ordinary drinking habits of our forefathers in the good old times when knighthood was in flower.

But on the whole, drinking in those times seems to have been the sport of the nobles rather than the vice of the masses.

It was only with the advent of the cheap corn whisky

in the sixteenth century that strong alcoholic beverages became accessible to the rising class of the proletariat, and since that time the drink habit among the working people has grown so enormously that alcoholism has become a problem of the modern labor movement.

The use of alcohol affects the poor much more injuriously than the men of the wealthier classes, even though the latter may be addicted to it no less than the former. The ill-nourished and weak organism of the workingman offers but little resistance to the ravishing effects of alcohol. The workingman will often succumb to a quantity of the beverage which will not disturb the equilibrium of a man of the better-situated classes.

Moreover, the workingman's income is as a rule barely sufficient to cover the necessaries of his life. He can procure his drink only by depriving himself of more substantial nourishment, thus undermining his body in two directions.

On the whole it may be truthfully said that intemperance is one of the heaviest scourges of the working class and one of the greatest obstacles to all progressive labor movements and to socialism.

The excessive use of alcohol enfeebles and brutalizes large masses of the workingmen. It renders them incapable of study, training and organization, indifferent to the struggles of their class, and inaccessible to its aspirations and ideals.

The alcoholic habits of the working class are deeply rooted in the material conditions of their lives. They are largely caused and stimulated by their industrial and social surroundings.

Mr. Emanuel Wurm, in an able report on Alcoholism

before the German Social Democratic Convention of 1907,[1] mentions the following causes which combine to stimulate drinking among the workers: —

1. The dwelling conditions of the poor.

Says Frederick Engels on this point: "Returning from the factory, the workingman finds a home without any comforts, damp, unattractive and filthy; he stands in need of exhilaration; he must have something to make his work worth while, to make the prospects of the morrow tolerable. . . . His social instinct can find satisfaction only in the liquor saloon; he has no other place to meet his friends."

2. Mental exhaustion caused by overwork.

Modern factory work with its monotonous operations is bound to produce a condition of mental fatigue from which the worker is but too apt to seek refuge in alcoholic stimulants.

3. Conditions of work creating an abnormal thirst.

Under this head come the industries in which the employees are forced to work under a high temperature, or in which the shops are constantly filled with fine particles of dust, or in which the nature of the work generates offensive fumes and gases.

4. Insufficient and unwholesome nourishment.

"The whisky habit is not the cause but the result of misery," said Justus v. Liebig, as early as in 1860. "It is an exception to the rule when a well-nourished man becomes addicted to whisky. But when a man earns less than is required for the quantum of food necessary in

[1] "Protokoll über die Verhandlungen des Parteitags der Sozialdemokratischen Partei Deutschlands," abgehalten zu Essen, September, 1907, pp. 345, etc.

order to restore his labor power, he is compelled by rigid and inexorable necessity to seek refuge in whisky." [1]

The insufficient nourishment of the workingman is due to low wages, high food prices, and also to the unskillful preparation of his food. The workingman's wife has as a rule never had an opportunity to cultivate the household arts, and seldom has the time to practice them.

Various other causes contribute to develop the drink habit among workingmen, most of them having their roots in the modern industrial conditions. And as is the case with almost all social evils of the day, the cause and effect of alcoholism move in a seemingly unbreakable vicious circle — misery causes drunkenness, drunkenness increases misery.

For a long time the socialists of all countries were rather indifferent to the temperance movement. They were fully alive to the dangers of the evil habit for the working class, but they had little faith in the cures offered by the ideological temperance advocates. High taxes on spirituous liquors, wherever tried, have failed to check the drinking evil and have only resulted in greater inroads on the meager budget of the working families. Prohibition has proved as impotent to cope with the evil, and as a rule has only served to encourage smuggling and illicit stills. Nor were the socialists inclined to expect substantial results from a purely moral crusade against alcoholism. The generally accepted socialist view was that the evils of alcoholism could be lessened only by the betterment of the material conditions of the workers, and could be removed only with the abolition of the wage system.

"As every other evil of the capitalist mode of production,

[1] Quoted by Wurm in report mentioned.

alcoholism can be checked only to a certain extent through the class struggle. It can disappear totally only with the disappearance of the system which has created it and which always reproduces it," declared Kautsky in 1891.

But of late the socialists of many countries have considerably changed their views on the problem of alcoholism and on the value of the modern temperance movements. They have gradually come to realize that in the matter of abstinence from or temperance in the use of alcoholic drinks, the purely moral factors of will power and determination play a large part. In their campaigns against the drink evil they still lay the greater stress on the betterment of the material conditions of the workers, but they also recognize the value of a purely educational propaganda against the abuses of alcohol.

To the Social Democratic Party of Austria belongs the merit of having stated the proposition most clearly and tersely in a resolution adopted in 1903, and from which we quote the following portion: —

"This convention declares that alcoholism has a disastrous effect on the physical and mental powers of the working class, and that it is a strong obstacle to the organizing work of socialism. No means to remove the evils arising from alcoholism should, therefore, be neglected. . . .

"The principal means in this struggle will always be the elevation of the material conditions of the proletariat, but a necessary supplement to this is the task of enlightening the workers on the effects of alcohol and of shattering their prejudices in favor of the drinking habit."

The socialists of Germany declare it to be the duty of organized labor to see to it that the workingmen, and especially their children, be enlightened by oral and written

propaganda on the dangers arising from the use of alcohol
and the drink-treating habit.

A similar stand has been taken by the socialists of
Switzerland and Holland. In Sweden the socialist program contains a plank demanding that the public schools
include in their curriculum a regular study course on the
evils of alcoholism. In Norway the Socialist Party demands the imposition of heavy taxes on all alcoholic
beverages. In England the Labor Party favors the local
option system. In Belgium the socialists have banished
all alcoholic drinks from their numerous meeting places
and recreation halls, while the socialists of Finland demand
the unconditional prohibition of all manufacture and sale
of alcoholic drinks.

The socialists of the United States for the first time took
official notice of the alcohol problem at their national
convention of 1908, and expressed their views on the
subject in the following resolution: —

"We recognize the evils arising from the manufacture and
sale of alcoholic liquors, especially those which are adulterated, and we declare that any excessive use of such
liquors by the working class postpones the day of the final
triumph of our cause. But we do not believe that alcoholism can be cured by an extension of police powers under the
capitalistic system. Alcoholism is a disease, and it can be
cured best by the stopping of underfeeding, overwork and
underpay, which result from the present wage system."

The Housing of the Poor

The dwelling conditions of the working people, especially
in the large cities and in factory towns, present a problem

of growing importance. Herded together like sheep, large families of human beings of all ages and sexes live in one or two small squalid rooms, without sufficient air or light. Here they cook, wash, dress, eat, sleep, quarrel and curse, make merry and make love in the constant company of each other and in an atmosphere of filth, irritation, cruelty and misery. The congested tenements are not only prolific sources of drunkenness, but also veritable breeding places of sickness, and of all species of vice and crime. The foul air of the "slum" dwellings is surcharged with the germs of death; the dread white plague and all other infectious diseases feed principally on the unfortunate inhabitants of the tenements, and the mortality of the children of this nether world is appalling. The miserable surroundings of these "homes" drive the children into the streets, the men into the liquor saloons and the women into the arms of vice. Tenement life in the slums demoralizes the present generation of the workingmen, and breeds a race of feeble, apathetic and cheerless men and women which is the greatest menace to our progress and civilization.

With the concentration of industries and the massing of ever larger numbers of workingmen in the manufacturing centers, the menace of popular congestion has within the last generation become particularly apparent and acute. Many movements for the reform of the housing conditions of the poor have sprung up, many measures of relief have been proposed.

The first impulse of the tenement-house reformers is to go at the solution of the problem in what seems to be the most direct way. They wish to physically destroy the slum or to eradicate its worst evils: to wash, sweep and

air the squalid rooms; to break through windows in their
dark walls to let in air and sunshine, and finally to distribute the unfortunate tenement dwellers over a wider
area by removing many of them from the congested spots
into the more cheerful, healthy and sunny suburbs.

These purely mechanical reforms have been tried and
are being tried to-day in all of the worst slum centers of the
world.

More than forty years ago Miss Octavia Hill of London
inaugurated a movement which has for its object the training of tenement dwellers in the habits of cleanliness, order
and decency in their households, and the movement has
found many enthusiastic adherents in some of the large
industrial cities of England, Scotland and the United
States.

Laws providing for the construction of tenement houses,
with better provisions for air, light and sanitary arrangements, have of late been enacted in numerous countries.

" Model " tenements have been built in large numbers.
The Peabody fund and the Guinness trust in England, as
well as numerous other philanthropic institutions in almost
all advanced countries, have erected many thousands of
such "model" tenements.

Several great municipalities of England and Scotland
have attempted to provide for the housing of their poor
directly. They have purchased and torn down their
worst tenements and have erected in their stead sanitary
dwelling houses, and let them to the poor at cost.

Finally, the movement for suburban development as a
cure for city congestion has also assumed large and ever
growing proportions. Almost every large industrial city is
steadily extending the radius of its surrounding rural

territory as an outlet for its crowded population, and multiplying and improving its transit facilities.

All these measures have had a certain beneficial effect on the housing conditions of the city poor. Separately and collectively they have probably served to relieve the congestion of the working population to some degree and to make their conditions of life somewhat more tolerable, or rather, without them these conditions might have grown even more intolerable than they are to-day.

But weighing the positive achievements along these lines of tenement-house reform, we cannot help being disappointed at the meagerness of the results. The slums of the world have not disappeared, nor have they on the whole been appreciably improved anywhere. In comparison with the benefits derived, the time, energy and money expended on those measures seem an almost unproductive waste.

Sermons on household cleanliness and sanitation, as a rule, fall on deaf ears where crowding and poverty mechanically produce filth and indifference.

The "model" tenements have on the whole proved a great success for their philanthropic or commercial founders, a success equal to from 5 to 10 per cent per annum on their investments. But to the masses of the poor they have brought but little relief. The rents in new "model" tenements are as a rule a trifle higher than those in the ordinary ones, just high enough to allow the class of clerks and other better-paid employees to take advantage of them and to shut out those who most stand in need of dwelling reform — the poorest classes of workingmen.

The municipal experiments of demolishing the most disreputable tenements and erecting new and better ones, have also largely failed to accomplish the results hoped for. But too often it has been found that the procedure resulted only in the transfer of the slum center from one spot to another. The evicted slum dwellers as a rule have settled down among their nearest slum neighbors.

And as for suburban development — it also did not and could not materially relieve the evil of congestion. Suburban development means, in the first place, increased means of communication between the city and the suburb, more lines of street cars and railways, and in the second place, more buildings and business in the suburbs. The principal beneficiaries of such reforms under present conditions are, as a rule, the railroad companies, the property owners along the new lines of travel, the land speculators dealing in suburban property, and incidentally also our upper and lower middle classes, who furnish the bulk of all suburban population.

The slum dwellers do not move to the suburbs, they cannot move to the suburbs. The slum dwellers are the hardest worked and poorest paid of the working class. They have not the money to pay the fares to and from their places of work, and they have not the time to spend on travel. Mr. Jacob A. Riis has observed that the housing problem is a transportation problem. That may be true for the middle classes, *for the workingmen the housing problem is not a transportation problem, but a wage problem.*

The trouble with the movement for tenement-house reform, as with all current reform movements, is that it touches the surface, but not the root of the problem. Under our system of civilization, the "slum" is not a local or accidental abuse, but a social institution. Poverty is the inevitable result of our industrial system, and the slum is poverty's logical place of abode.

The first condition for the development of a slum district is its proximity to the factory. The workingman, and the poorer-paid workingman especially, is compelled to live within walking distance of his place of work. The price of land in such favored districts, then, naturally rises, and the landowners find it to their best advantage to build huge and cheap buildings occupying every available inch of ground, and containing many small rooms. These they let for exorbitantly high rent, and the workingman tenant is compelled to crowd his family into as few rooms as physically possible, and to secure one or more roomers besides to help him pay the rent. Then an entire industry adapted to the needs and means of the population develops in the district. In the streets of the slum, in its groceries, eating houses and dry goods stores, the vilest and cheapest of food stuffs and of other commodities converge from all parts of the city and country. The slum is adjusted to the entire household economy of its inhabitants and holds them in its iron grip. It must persist as long as exploitation and poverty continue.

The various reforms heretofore tried have some value as temporary palliatives, and the socialists heartily favor them as such. They advocate municipal construction of model tenements to be let to workingmen at cost, and they advocate suburban development through improved transit lines to be built and operated by the city in the interest of the traveling public and the employees. But they do not expect substantial relief from such measures.

The slum evil can be relieved only by better wages and shorter hours, it can be cured only by socialism.

APPENDIX

Early History

SOME writers on the subject include in the history of the socialist movement all ancient and mediæval manifestations of communistic thought and institutions. But as a matter of fact the modern socialist movement has nothing in common with the utopias of Plato, Campanella and More, or with the prehistoric tribal institutions, early Christian practices or the various sectarian communities of the Middle Ages.

The political socialist movement of our day is primarily a movement of the working class, and has for its object the reconstruction of the present-day system of industry on the basis of collective ownership of the tools of production.

The movement thus presupposes the existence of a competitive individualist system of industry and of a wage-earning class. In other words, modern socialism is unthinkable without its antithesis — capitalism. Socialism is the child of the modern or "capitalist" system of production. And more than that, it is the product of that system at a certain advanced stage. The socialist movement is a protest against the present industrial system, hence it presupposes a state of development of that system to a point where it has become oppressive; it involves a criticism of the system, hence it implies a dissatisfaction with it; and finally, it offers a substitute for the present system, hence it is predicated on the assumption of a state of decline of the capitalist régime.

Thus while the beginnings of the present industrial system may be traced back to the fifteenth or sixteenth century of our era, the modern socialist movement is barely more than a century old.

Socialism, like most other social theories and movements, has passed through several stages of development before reaching its modern aspect.

In its first phases it was primarily a humanitarian movement, and its political rôle was but secondary and incidental.

The early socialists saw only the evils of the new system of production; they did not penetrate into its historical significance and tendencies. The evils of the system appeared to them as arbitrary deviations from the "eternal principles" of "natural law," justice and reason, and the social system itself as a clumsy and malicious contrivance of the dominant powers in society.

To the "unreasonable" and "unjust" social systems of their times they opposed more or less fantastic schemes of social organization of their own invention supposed to be free from the abuses of modern civilization, and thereupon they appealed to humanity at large to test those schemes.

These social schemes were, as a rule, unfolded by their authors by means of description of a fictitious country with a mode of life and form of government to suit their own ideas of justice and reason. The happy country thus described was the Utopia (Greek for "Nowhere"), hence the designation of that phase of the socialist movement as "utopian."

Y

One of the fruits of these theories was the organization of the numerous communistic societies of the early part of the last century. The utopian socialists knew of no reason why their plans of social organization should not work in a more limited sphere just as satisfactorily as on a national scale, and they fondly hoped that they would gradually convert the entire world to their system by a practical demonstration of its feasibility and benefits in a miniature society.

Another practical application of the utopian socialist philosophy is to be found in the conspiratory revolutionary societies which accompanied the socialist agitation of several European countries, notably France, in the thirties and forties of the nineteenth century. The object of these societies was to capture the organs of government and to decree a socialist state of society, a perfectly sane and logical procedure from the point of view of men who believed that systems of society could be created and altered at will.

As with every other movement it is, of course, impossible to locate the exact starting point of modern socialism. In a general way, however, it may be said that the beginning of the modern socialist movement coincides with the period of the great French Revolution.

The first gleams of socialist philosophy appear in the works of the pre-Revolutionary French philosophers of the school of the Encyclopedists, notably in those of Jean Jacques Rousseau, who as early as in 1754 denounced private property as the cause of all crimes.

But a much more definite and elaborate expression of the utopian socialist creed we find in the two works of Morelly: "Naufrage des Iles Flottantes ou la Basiliade." (The Shipwreck of the Floating Islands or Basiliade), 1753, and "Code de la Nature" (Code of Nature), 1753. The former is an utopian novel in metrical form, and the latter is a philosophic essay. Morelly is a keen and farseeing critic of the industrial system of individualist competition, and advocates a somewhat loose form of communism.

Next to Morelly, Gabriel Mably (1709-1785) must be mentioned among the early French socialist writers. Like Morelly, Mably advocated a social system based on the community of property, with the difference, however, that the state of Mably is highly centralized, both in the system of production and distribution.

A more realistic note in the literature of the young socialist speculation is introduced by the French lawyer, François Boissel (1728-1807), whose "Catechisme du Genre Humain" (Catechism of Mankind), which appeared in 1789, the year of the French Revolution, contains the first attempt at a scientific analysis of the modern mode of production.

These three authors are the principal exponents of socialism in pre-Revolutionary France. Their works are purely theoretical, and they did not result in any socialist activity.

The first direct step toward an active revolutionary and socialist movement was made by François Noel Babeuf (1760-1796). Babeuf, himself an active factor in the great French Revolution, was by no means satisfied with its accomplishments. "The Revolution," he argued, "has proclaimed Liberty, Fraternity and Equality, but equality is a mere sham unless it is social and economic as well as political." With the aim of capturing the government of France and establishing social and economic equality, he organized the famous Conspiracy of Equals. The movement is said to have attained considerable dimensions in Paris when it was detected in 1796. Babeuf was convicted on the charge of treason, and beheaded. Years later, Filippo Buonarotti, a friend and disciple of Babeuf, published the history of the conspiracy and the program of the conspirators, and the work played a large part in the movement of the secret socialist societies of later years.

Babeuf was the last representative of the eighteenth-century socialism. The beginning of the nineteenth century produced a series of socialist thinkers and workers who have influenced the shaping of the present-day socialist movement more directly than their predecessors. Of these, two are always mentioned together. They are Charles Henri Saint-Simon and Charles Fourier.

Saint-Simon is a teacher rather than a practical social reformer. The keynote to his philosophy is the demand that society be organized not on a political but on an industrial basis. His last work, "Nouveau Christianisme" (New Christianity) is the most complete exposition of his social views, and contains the germs of the theory of economic determinism which in the hands of Karl Marx subsequently became one of the most powerful weapons in the arsenal of contemporary socialist philosophy.

After the death of Saint-Simon his work was continued by a talented coterie of his disciples, prominent among whom were Olinde Rodrigue (1794–1851), Barthelémy P. Enfantin (1796–1864), Armand Bazard (1791-1832), Auguste Comte, the father of positive philosophy, and Ferdinand de Lesseps, of the Suez Canal fame. The Saint-Simonian school at one time gained considerable influence in the intellectual circles of France, its organ, " *Le Globe*," had a large circulation, and in the revolution of 1830 the Saint-Simonians played a not unimportant part. But the movement ultimately split, principally on the question of woman's rights. Under the leadership of Enfantin the Saint-Simonian school developed a mystic religious cult with certain unconventional practices in the relation of the sexes, which led to the arrest of Enfantin and his followers on the charge of immorality, and to the inglorious end of the Saint-Simonian movement.

If Saint-Simon was the preacher of order and system, Fourier may be called the apostle of harmony.

God created the entire universe on a harmonious plan, reasons Fourier, hence there must be harmony between everything in existence. Endowing human beings with certain instincts and desires, God intended their free and untrammeled exercise, and not their suppression. All human instincts and desires are legitimate and useful, and if existing society curbs the right of the citizen to follow those instincts and desires, it is evidence of a defect in our social system, not in the individual. Fourier advocates the reorganization of society on the basis of autonomous communities of from 1500 to 2000 members. These communities, styled by him " phalanxes," are voluntary associations of citizens for the purpose of coöperative labor and collective enjoyment, with ample provisions for the choice of associates and occupations, variety of pursuits and attractive surroundings of industries. The phalanxes are not communistic enterprises, but rather partake of the nature of modern joint-stock associations, in which capital receives its reward as well as labor and "talent."

Saint-Simon emphasizes the rights and importance of

society, Fourier dwells principally on the rights of the individual citizens as against organized society. The two great utopians may be said to be the prototypes of the two dominant tendencies in the social theories of our times — collectivism and individualism.

Chief among the French disciples of Fourier is Victor Considérant, under whose leadership the Fourierist movement attained some importance years after the master's death. But even more influence than in France, the philosophy of Fourier exercised in the United States of America, where it counted among its most enthusiastic adherents men like Albert Brisbane, Horace Greeley, Parke Godwin, George Ripley, Charles A. Dana, Margaret Fuller and other men and women prominent in the world of letters.

In France, the home of Fourierism, but few attempts at the practical realization of the system were made, but in the United States over forty phalanxes were established between 1840 and 1850, among them the famous Brook Farm and the North American Phalanx. Of the socialist writers and reformers of that period who have largely contributed to the development of the modern socialist movement, we must mention Étienne Cabet (1788–1856), Louis Blanc (1811–1882), Jean Lamennaîs (1782–1854) and Pierre J. Proudhon (1809–1865).

Cabet's utopian novel "Voyage en Icarie" (Voyage to Icaria), published in 1842, gave rise to a popular movement in favor of communism which at one time was said to number several hundred thousands of adherents. The movement resulted in the establishment of the "Icarian communities" in the United States. The first of these communities was established in Texas in 1848, and the last of the series perished in California almost half a century later.

Louis Blanc, who first achieved fame through his work "Organization du Travail" (Organization of Labor), published in 1840, played an important part in the French revolution of 1848 as a member of the Provisional Committee. He was chiefly instrumental in bringing about the famous decree of that committee recognizing the "right to labor," and was indirectly responsible for the establishment of the National Workshops, which under the post-revolutionary administration of the French government turned into a disastrous failure.

Lamennais is the father of Christian Socialism in France. He early advocated the union of the Catholic church with the growing socialist movement of the workingmen. His views were condemned by Pope Gregory XVI, and Lamennais thereafter addressed his appeals directly to the people. His "Paroles d'un Croyant" (Words of a Believer), published in 1834, contains a burning indictment of the selfish rich, and is full of tender sympathy for the disinherited of the world. It was widely read by the workingmen of his generation, and made a deep and lasting impression on his countrymen.

Proudhon, the author of the famous "Qu'est-ce que la Propriété?" (What is Property?) and "Contradictions Économiques" (Economic Contradictions), may be said to be the father of modern "communistic anarchism."

This review of early French socialism would not be complete without a brief reference to the secret societies which made their appearance immediately after the revolution of 1830, and continued with varying degree of strength and success for about ten years. The principal organizations of that cycle are the *Société des amis du Peuple* (Society of the Friends of the People), *Société des droits de l'homme* (Society of Human Rights), *Société des familles* (Society of Families), and *Société des saisons* (Society of Seasons), and the most prominent leaders of the movement were Louis Blanqui (1805-1881), Armand Barbès (1809-1870), Voyer d'Argençon (1771-1842) and Filippo Buonarotti mentioned above.

While the socialism of France during the first half of the last century was thus replete with various movements, schools and thinkers, the movement in England during the corresponding period is practically represented by one name — Robert Owen.

The socialism of Owen differed from that of his French contemporaries just as much as the political and industrial conditions and national temperament and genius of England differed from those of France.

Owen was primarily a practical business man, not a philosopher, and still less a conspirator. His socialist views were developed by his contact with actual industrial conditions, more highly developed in England than in any other European country, and they always bore the imprint of that origin.

Owen's early activity in the field of social reform was more of a philanthropic than revolutionary character: it consisted in the long and patient work of improving the conditions of his own employees in the Scotch manufacturing village of New Lanark, and in this he succeeded so well that within one generation (from 1800 to 1824) the former miserable village, with a degenerate and wretched population, had become a model community of healthy, industrious and happy men and women.

His revolutionary career may be said to date from 1817, when upon the invitation of the committee of the Association for the Relief of the Manufacturing and Laboring Poor, he unfolded his views on the causes of poverty and the needed social reforms. The gist of his views is that widespread pauperism and popular misery are inseparable from an industrial system based on free competition, and that under such a system the increased productivity of labor inevitably leads to the deterioration of the condition of the working class.

He was a great believer in the influence of environment on the formation of human character, and predicted that improved material conditions of the laboring population would result in the physical, intellectual and moral regeneration of the masses.

His activities as a socialist propagandist and experimenter extend over forty years, and are as variegated as intense. He organized the famous New Harmony communities in the United States (1826-1828), and several similar communities in England, Scotland and Ireland. In 1832 he established the Equitable Banks for Labor Exchange, a contrivance for the exchange of commodities by their producers without the intervention of the profit-making merchant and manufacturer, and several years later he formed the Association of all Classes and Nations whose members first applied the appellation of "socialists" to themselves. He was indefatigable in the propaganda of his creed in the United States as well as in England. He delivered several lectures in the Hall of Representatives at Washington, called an international socialist congress in New York, and presided over the first national convention of English trade unions. He was largely responsible for the introduction of the infant-school system, and is considered the father of factory legislation.

Owen's influence was, however, mainly personal, and he left no school or movement behind him.

In Germany the first manifestations of socialist thought and activity are connected with the names of the celebrated philosopher Johann Gottlieb Fichte (1762–1814), who in his "Geschlossener Handelstaat" (Closed Trading State) advocates the state regulation of production and distribution of goods, and the tailor Wilhelm Weitling (1808–1871), who may be considered the connecting link between present-day socialism and its earlier forms.

Weitling seems to have imbibed the theories of French communism in his early traveling days, but he instilled into them the life and faith of the active propagandist and enthusiastic apostle. Like Owen he extended his activity to all spheres of radical social reform known in his day, organizing coöperative enterprises, workingmen's study clubs, a communistic settlement, trade-union organizations, etc. His main theoretical works are: "Die Welt wie sie ist und sein sollte" (The World as It is and as It Should Be), 1838, "Die Garantien der Harmonie und Freiheit" (The Guaranties of Harmony and Freedom), 1842, and "Das Evangelium des Armen Sünders" (Evangel of a Poor Sinner), 1846.

Weitling is the first socialist to make a more direct appeal to the working class, although the modern socialist conception of class struggle is still foreign to him. Weitling's fields of activity were Switzerland and the United States, but his influence also extended to Germany, Austria and the colonies of German emigrants in other countries.

In the meantime, the industrial development of Europe had proceeded with giant strides, and with it also the scientific study of the character and tendencies of the existing industrial régime. The fantastic theories and hypotheses of early socialism, like those of so many other young sciences, had to be greatly modified. Socialism had to be given a new, more realistic and sounder foundation, and this task was accomplished towards the middle of the last century by the twin founders of modern socialism, Karl Marx (1818–1883) and Frederick Engels (1820–1895).

The socialism of the new school, known as Marxian or Scientific socialism, proceeds on the theory that the social and political structure of society at any given time and place is not the result of the free and arbitrary choice of men, but the logical outcome of a definite process of historical development, and that the underlying structure of such foundation is at all times the economic system upon which society is organized.

As a logical sequence from these views it follows that a form of society cannot be changed at any given time unless the economic development has made it ripe for the change, and that the future of mankind must be looked for, not in the ingenious schemes of inventive social philosophers, but in the tendencies of economic development.

The Marxian socialists base their hopes on the tendency of modern industries towards centralization and socialization, the inadequacy and wastefulness of the individual and competitive system of production, and the growing revolt of the working classes against the iniquities and hardships involved in that system.

Modern socialists address themselves not so much to the humane sentiments of society at large as to the self-interests of the working class, as the class primarily concerned in the impending social change. They do not indulge in miniature social experiments or in political conspiracies, but direct their efforts towards the education and political and industrial organization of the working class, so as to enable that class to steer the ship of state from individualism into collectivism, when the time shall be ripe for it, and to hasten that time.

This phase of the socialist movement may be said to date from the publication of the celebrated "Communist Manifesto." The "Manifesto" is a brief pamphlet written conjointly by Marx and Engels. It has since been translated into almost all modern languages, and has remained to this day the classical exposition of modern socialism.

The "Communist Manifesto" appeared in 1848. The great revolutionary movement of that year and the long period of European reaction following upon its defeat, temporarily paralyzed the young socialist movement inaugurated by Marx and his comrades. For almost fifteen years the movement was confined to a few scattered circles of "intellectuals" in the different countries of Europe and did not penetrate into the masses anywhere. The general political and social awakening which marks the beginning of the sixties of the last century in all principal countries of Europe and in the United States of America, did not pass without affecting the working classes. A strong labor movement grew up in the most advanced countries of Europe, and a large portion of it fell under the spiritual leadership of the socialists.

The first fruit of these renewed socialist and labor ac-

tivities was the organization of the International Workingmen's Association (commonly styled the International)
in 1864. The International was organized in London by
some representative English trade unionists in conjunction
with a number of political refugees of various nationalities
with whom the capital of England was fairly teeming just
then. Its constitution and declaration of principles were
drafted by Karl Marx, and the latter instrument was a
concise exposition of the socialist philosophy winding up
with the declaration — "No rights without duties; no duties
without rights."

The International extended over England, France,
Germany, Austria, Belgium, Holland, Denmark, Spain,
Portugal, Italy, Switzerland, Poland, Australia and the
United States of America, and at one time was considered
a great power in European politics. Its active career embraced a period of about eight years, from 1864 to 1872,
during which time it held six conventions. These conventions were largely devoted to the discussion of social
and labor problems, and served to impress the socialist
movement of the world with a uniform and harmonious
character.

The dissolution of the organization was brought about
by a number of factors, not the least of which was the fate
of the Paris Commune.

The Commune, proclaimed in Paris on March 18, 1871,
in its inception had no connection whatever with the International or the socialist agitation of the time. Its name
was not intended to imply any sympathy with the doctrines
of communism, but was merely meant to signify the communal or municipal autonomy of Paris. The proclamation
of the Commune was a result of the revolt of the Parisians

against the excessive centralization of government in France.

Originally the movement was rather conservative, but in the course of the struggles between the Parisian Communards and their Versaillian adversaries it became more and more radical in character. The Parisian populace, after the Prussian siege of 1870, consisted largely of workingmen and small shopkeepers reduced to a state of extreme poverty and suffering, while many of the wealthier citizens fled from Paris after the proclamation of the Commune, to seek protection from the national troops stationed at Versailles. The Commune, therefore, assumed the character of a struggle between the Parisian proletariat and the French bourgeoisie, and the International threw its entire moral influence to the support of the former. When the Commune was defeated, after a stormy existence of about two months, the defeat and the general European moral opprobrium which attached to the memory of the Parisian revolt, strongly affected the standing of the International.

But the deciding blow to the life of the International was dealt by the growing spirit of anarchism within its ranks.

Up to about 1869 the International was under the undisputed control of the Marxian wing of socialism, but in the later years of its existence the school of " communistic anarchism " steadily gained ground in the councils of the society under the leadership of the apostle of the new creed, Michael Bakounin (1814–1876). Bakounin, a Russian by birth and a revolutionist by temperament, had passed through a very picturesque revolutionary career before he joined the International. He abominated the evolutionary doctrines and "tame" methods of Marxian socialism, and revolted against organization and discipline. He advocated the immediate rising against the obnoxious powers of modern civilization, and proclaimed the principle of "complete individual liberty restrained only by natural laws." He was eloquent, enthusiastic and magnetic, and the desperate conditions of the laboring population of Europe, especially in the Southern countries, furnished a large and very receptive audience for his promises of quick and easy salvation.

Anarchism threatened to become a power in the International, and Marx and his friends decided to avert the danger by sacrificing the organization. In 1872 the seat of its general council was transferred to New York, and three years later the International was formally dissolved.

The International, however, had accomplished its purpose, and during its activity the socialist movement of Europe had developed to such dimensions that it became impossible to confine it within the bounds of one central organization. From this point we shall have to follow the varying fortunes of the movement in the different countries in which it has developed.

Chief among such countries is, of course,

Germany

In Germany the present-day socialist movement runs in an unbroken chain from the days of the agitation of Ferdinand Lassalle (1825–1864). Of extraordinary eloquence, profound learning and indomitable energy, Lassalle was probably the most powerful popular tribune produced by the nineteenth century.

His active work in the cause of socialism is practically

confined to the last two years of his life. But during that short period he succeeded in thoroughly rousing the phlegmatic working class of his country by his ringing speeches and powerful writings. In his social views he was a disciple of Marx, but the principal issues of his agitation were the demands for universal suffrage and for the establishment of coöperative workshops with state credit.

In 1863 he organized the General Workingmen's Association, which at the time of its founder's death numbered only 4610 members, but grew considerably in later years, notwithstanding one serious schism within its ranks.

In the meanwhile a new socialist party, more strictly Marxian, was organized in 1869, under the leadership of Wilhelm Liebknecht and August Bebel, and the six years following are marked by a bitter feud between the rival organizations. The feud was terminated in 1875 by the amalgamation of all socialist organizations at the Gotha convention, and the present Social Democratic Party of Germany was thus born. Since then the progress of the socialist movement has been rapid and steady, and even the unrelenting government persecution under the Exception Laws did not succeed in checking its growth. These laws were designed to suppress all forms of socialist propaganda, and their enforcement was attended by the imprisonment and exile of large numbers of the most active socialists. They were enacted in 1878 after two attempts by irresponsible individuals on the life of the Emperor, and were abandoned in 1890 after their futility had been demonstrated in practice. The growth of socialism in Germany can be best appreciated by a comparison of the socialist vote in the parliamentary elections of that country, which was 101,927 in 1871 and over three and one quarter millions in 1906. The Social Democratic Party of Germany is to-day numerically the strongest political organization in the country.

France

If the socialist movement of Germany may be considered a model of orderly and methodical growth, that of France has had, on the contrary, a most bewildering and stormy career.

With the fall of the Paris Commune the movement in France had received a blow from which it recovered but very slowly. For a number of years after 1871 the only manifestation of socialist activity was to be found in the students' circles organized by Gabriel Deville and Jules Guèsde, and the main efforts of these circles were directed towards the propaganda of socialism among the trade unions. In these efforts they gained a partial success in 1878 when the general trade-union congress of Lyons pledged its support to some socialist candidates, and several large trade organizations indorsed the entire socialist program. The arrest of Guèsde and thirty-three other labor leaders in 1879 for participation in a political labor conference, and the brilliant defense of Guèsde on that occasion, largely served to increase the sympathies of the working population for socialism, and the general trade-union congress of Marseilles, held in the same year, unreservedly declared itself in favor of the movement.

But this declaration, made by the delegates under the influence of the events immediately preceding the convention, did not seem to have the unanimous support of their constituents. At the following convention, held in Havre in

z

1880, the discussion was resumed, and resulted in a split. The organized workingmen divided themselves into two separate organizations distinguished from each other as "collectivists" and "coöperativists" respectively. And the socialist movement in France has ever thereafter progressed through a process of alternate fusions and divisions. The first schism in the ranks of the socialist movement proper took place in 1882, when the strict adherents of Marxian socialism, led by Jules Guèsde, Paul Lafargue and Gabriel Deville, separated from the *Possibilist* or opportunist socialists, headed by Paul Brousse and Benoit Malon. The former organized the *Parti Ouvrier* (Labor Party), and the latter, the *Federation Française des Travailleurs Socialistes Revolutionaires* (French Federation of Socialist Revolutionary Workingmen). To these must be added the *Parti Revolutionaire* founded by the veteran of the French Revolution, Blanqui, upon his release from his last term of imprisonment in 1879, and after his death directed by the well-known communard, Edouard Vaillant.

The number of socialist parties was further augmented by a split within the ranks of the *Possibilists*, the more radical wing of which organized an independent party in 1891 under the name of *Parti Ouvrier Revolutionaire Socialiste*, and under the leadership of Allemane, and also by the formation of numerous local groups of "independent socialists" whose membership included such prominent socialists as Étienne Millerand and Jean Jaurès.

The period between 1898 and 1901 is marked by efforts to bring about the union of socialist forces. These efforts were partly realized in 1900, when a national congress of all French socialist parties and organizations was held in Paris.

But in the meanwhile a new issue presented itself to the socialists of France. The events attending the Dreyfus agitation had forced socialists to the front in national politics, and one independent socialist, Étienne Millerand, was given a portfolio in the cabinet of the new premier, Waldeck-Rousseau. Millerand's entry into the "bourgeois" cabinet had the approval of the more liberal or "opportunist" wing of the socialist movement under the leadership of the eloquent Jean Jaurès, but was strongly condemned by the more orthodox faction headed by Jules Guèsde. And on this new issue the socialist organizations of France now grouped themselves. The "ministerialists" combined into the *Parti Socialiste Français*, while the "anti-ministerialists" united into the *Parti Socialiste de France*. Both parties continued a separate though not always antagonistic existence until 1905, when they united into one, largely through the good services of the International Socialist Congress held in Amsterdam in 1904. The new party is the first in France to bring together all of the more important socialist organizations under one administration, although some minor groups of "independent" socialists still remain in existence.

The first socialist campaign in parliamentary elections in France was made in 1885, when the combined socialist parties polled about 30,000 votes. The successive growth of the socialist parliamentary vote is shown by the following round figures: —

1887	. . .	47,000
1889	. . .	120,000
1893	. . .	440,000
1898	. . .	700,000
1902	. . .	805,000
1906	. . .	1,120,000

Russia

While the modern socialist movements in Germany and France, as well as in all other European countries, are primarily economic in their character, and are supported principally by the industrial working classes, the movement in Russia was in its inception preponderatingly political and ethical, and was represented principally by men and women of the better-situated and cultured classes. This difference in the character of the movement is accounted for by the difference between the social and economic conditions of that country and the rest of Europe at the period of the birth of socialism in Russia. At a time when the modern industrial régime was fully developed, and the system of representative government firmly established in the other principal countries of Europe, Russia was a purely agricultural country with a population of peasants just liberated from serfdom, with no manufacturing class or industrial proletariat worth mentioning, and with an almost Asiatic form of autocratic government. The socialism of Russia was not the direct result of economic development, not a form of class struggle between the classes of capitalists and workingmen: it was partly an expression of political revolt against absolute czarism, and partly a reflex of the economic socialist theories with such modifications as comported with the peculiar conditions of Russia.

The first expressions of socialist thought in Russia coincide with the agitation for the emancipation of the serfs, and its best-known representatives of that period are a famous coterie of publicists and critics among whom we must mention Alexander Herzen, an expatriated nobleman of considerable wealth, who conducted an active agitation for Russian freedom from London principally by means of his magazine *Kolokol* (Bell), and Nicholas Chernyshefsky, the editor of the influential magazine *Sovremennik* (Contemporary), who was deported to Siberia in the prime of his life, to return thence an old man and a physical and mental wreck.

The next phase of the socialist movement in Russia is that designated as "Nihilism." The word was coined by the well-known novelist Ivan Turgenief as a term of ridicule of the new current of Russian thought which developed strongly around 1860 to 1870, and whose main characteristics were a crude materialism and the negation of all established beliefs.

"Nihilism" was an intellectual rather than a political or social movement, but its effect was to promote socialism in two ways; it created a negative attitude towards the old order of things in Russia, and it developed a thirst for positive knowledge among the youth of both sexes, driving large numbers of them into the universities of Western Europe, principally those of Switzerland, since they could not quench that intellectual thirst at home. These young and receptive Russian students were powerfully attracted by the awakening socialist movement of Western Europe, and also came under the influence of their own exiled countrymen, Michael Bakounin, Alexander Herzen and Peter Lavroff, the foremost Russian representative of scientific socialism at that time. The socialist sympathies of these Russian students were so manifest that their government finally took alarm, and in 1873 summarily recalled them to their fatherland under pain of exile. The effect of the order was hardly gratifying to the government:

the students returned in large numbers, but they returned as active socialist propagandists.

At this stage of the movement Russian socialism was perfectly peaceful. The activities of the young propagandists were principally educational; their main effort was to raise the intellectual level of the illiterate peasantry composing the great bulk of the population. They spread in the villages, settled among the peasants, whose habits, language and even dress they tried to imitate, and conducted the work of socialist propaganda side by side with that of general education. But their activity provoked severe government persecutions; the "political offenders" were hounded down, executed, imprisoned or exiled to Siberia, frequently without so much as the formality of a trial. Within five years the young movement found itself practically checked: the socialist propagandists, reduced in numbers and rendered desperate by the relentless and cruel police persecution, abandoned the peaceful methods of propaganda. A seeming accident determined the succeeding phase of Russian socialism.

In 1878 a young woman named Vera Sassulich shot at General Trepoff, the military commandant of St. Petersburg, as an act of revenge for his brutal treatment of a political prisoner. Vera Sassulich was placed on trial for the offense, but was triumphantly acquitted by the jury amid the plaudits of the better part of the population. Encouraged by the success of Sassulich, deprived of all means of peaceful activity, and rendered desperate by the relentless police persecutions, the socialists turned to methods of force and conspiracy.

A sudden and radical change took place in the Russian revolutionary movement. The old type of peaceful propa-

gandist and dreamer disappeared, and instead of him there
arose the sullen and determined terrorist. The Russian
socialists engaged in mortal combat with the autocratic
government, and the embodiment of that government, the
czar, in person. The struggle lasted but a few years, and
it was the strangest ever witnessed in history. A mere
handful of idealists, without substantial support on the part
of any class of the population, was arrayed against the
rulers of Russia, supported by a powerful police, a vast
army and unlimited resources; and still the struggle was
fierce, just as fierce on the one side as on the other. The
"white terror" of the government was fully balanced by
the "red terror" of the revolutionists. The enthusiasm,
courage and ingenuity displayed by the Russian socialists,
men and women, during that period, defy comparison.
The annals of these few years of the movement are the
most romantic in the history of international socialism,
and are characterized by numerous political assassinations,
and by the imprisonment and execution of the most gifted
leaders of Russian socialism. The movement culminated
in the assassination of Czar Alexander II, and this triumph
of the first period of revolutionary terrorism in Russia
was also its end. The Russian revolutionists had expected
that the killing of the czar would be the signal for a general
revolt, but in this expectation they found themselves sorely
disappointed. The population of Russia was not ready
for a revolution at that time, and had but little sympathy
or understanding for the youthful socialists.

The Will of the People, the famous fighting organization of the revolutionary terrorists, survived the assassination of Alexander II only a few years.

In the meanwhile, modern industrial conditions rapidly

developed in Russia, and with them developed a new social power, the class of factory workers.

Thus was prepared in Russia the soil for a socialist movement after the pattern of Western Europe, and the soil rapidly produced a plentiful harvest. Already in the days of revolutionary terrorism a small group of Russian socialists, headed by George Plekhanoff, Paul Axelrod and Vera Sassulich, had based their hopes for the future of Russian socialism in the nascent class of industrial workers, and their propaganda kept pace with the growth and spread of that class. In the early nineties of the last century, official Russia, greatly to its surprise and dismay, found itself confronted in all industrial centers by a well-organized and radical labor movement, which refused to yield to persecution or to be side tracked by governmental ruses. The organized labor movement gave a new impetus to the political socialist movement. The Social Democratic Party, originally organized by Russian political exiles in Switzerland, soon had a number of local committees in various parts of Russia, and was reënforced by the organizations of the Jewish, Polish, Lettish and Armenian social democrats. At the beginning of the present century, the Social Democratic Party, secret and persecuted as it was, had developed into a power of no mean proportions, and during the most agitated days of the overt outbreak of the Russian revolution, towards the end of 1905 and the beginning of 1906, it was this party that led the movement.

With the revival of the socialist movement in Russia, revolutionary terrorism, the natural child of unbridled autocracy, gradually reappeared. This movement was at first represented by a number of scattered groups, but in 1901 the large majority of them combined their forces and created the party of Socialist Revolutionists, which is responsible for the numerous political assassinations preceding and accompanying the present war between the government and the people of Russia. It is impossible at this time to estimate the number of Russian subjects enlisted in the ranks of socialism of one shade or another, but the fact that the second Duma, elected on a restricted suffrage and under government surveillance, had about one hundred socialist members (social democrats, socialist revolutionists and representatives of the Group of Toil), is eloquent testimony to the immense spread and power of socialism in Russia.

Austria

The socialist movement in Austria is closely linked with that of Germany, so much so that in their earlier stages the two movements are hardly differentiated. In the famous convention of Eisenach, held in 1868, the Austrian socialists were represented as well as their German comrades. But notwithstanding the common beginnings and intellectual identity of socialism in the two countries, the movement in Austria soon fell behind that of Germany. There were many reasons for this phenomenon, chief among them being the industrial backwardness of Austria, and the difficulty of carrying on a systematic and uniform propaganda of socialism among the many heterogeneous nationalities constituting the Austrian Empire.

The beginnings of the socialist movement in Austria appear in 1867, when the Imperial Council granted a partial right of assembly and association to the people of Austria. Two years later the movement was strong enough to force the government to revoke its ban against socialist propaganda by a most remarkable and unexpected demonstration on the streets of Vienna (December 13, 1869). The succeeding period (1870–1888) is principally noteworthy for the dissensions within the movement. The practical disfranchisement of the working class and the brutal government persecution had bred among the more radical workingmen a spirit of embittered pessimism which made them unusually susceptible to the propaganda of anarchism, then in its prime all over Europe, and the main work of Austrian social democracy during that period was to combat the anarchist movement. The turning point of the socialist movement in Austria may be considered the Hainsfeld Congress (1888), which marked the final victory of social democracy over anarchism in the Austrian labor movement, and created a unified and well-organized party which has since been making rapid and steady progress. In the parliamentary elections of 1907, for the first time held on the basis of universal suffrage, the Social Democratic Party polled over 1,000,000 votes, electing no less than 87 deputies to the Reichsrat.

England

Notwithstanding the fact that England is the most industrial country of Europe, its socialist movement was rather tardy in appearing and in its growth.

The organized socialist movement of England may be dated from the formation of the Democratic Federation in 1881. The Federation, called into life by H. M. Hyndman, Herbert Burrows and a few other well-known socialists, was originally not of outspoken socialist views, but became so in 1883, when it was reorganized under the name of Social Democratic Federation. The Federation has ever since continued a somewhat uneventful existence, and is to-day the orthodox representative of Marxian socialism in England.

In 1893 another political party of socialism was founded, principally through the efforts of Keir Hardie. The organization assumed the name of Independent Labor Party, adopted a somewhat broader platform than that of the Social Democratic Federation, and laid more stress on the political side of the movement. But contrary to the expectations of its founders, it did not acquire a much larger following among the working classes of England than the older organization.

Besides these two parties, the socialist movement of England is also represented by the well-known Fabian Society, founded in 1883, principally for the purpose of educational propaganda along socialist lines. The society has published a number of popular tracts on the main aspects of theoretical socialism and has achieved considerable success in the field of municipal reform. The outspoken socialist organizations in England are not a factor of great importance in the political life of the country, but it would be a mistake to measure the strength of the socialist movement in England only by its organized portions.

The socialist sentiment in England largely expresses itself in the radical or "new" trade unions. These trade unions together with the Independent Labor Party and the Fabian Society constitute the Labor Party, which has 32 representatives in the House of Commons. The Labor Party has recently adopted a very radical declaration of principles, and it is the masses behind that party which to-day must be considered as the main factor making for socialism in England.

Italy

The socialist movement in Italy antedates the International. When the latter split between the adherents of Karl Marx and Michael Bakounin, the socialists of Italy, like those of almost all southern and economically backward countries, sided with Bakounin.

The first manifestation of socialist political activity occurred in 1882, when several scattered socialist groups united for the ensuing parliamentary elections and nominated candidates. The elections gave to the socialist candidates about 50,000 votes, 4 per cent of the total vote cast, and secured the return of two of them to parliament. Encouraged by this success, the socialists of Italy organized a national Socialist Party in 1885, but the party made little progress, and between government persecutions and internal dissensions, it led a very precarious existence.

It was only in 1892 that a socialist party, after the general European model, was organized in Italy, and since that time the socialist movement in Italy has made large and steady gains. In 1907 the party consisted of more than 1200 local groups with a total dues-paying membership of over 38,000; it had 25 representatives in the Chamber of Deputies, and had control of about 100 municipalities, besides having representatives in almost all other of the most important cities and towns of the kingdom. In 1904 the party polled 320,000 votes, about one fifth of the total number of votes cast in the country.

One of the most remarkable features of the socialist movement in Italy is its strength among the rural population of the country, principally the farm laborers; the membership of the Socialist Party is largely made up of them. The Socialist Party also took the initiative in organizing these laborers into an independent national organization. In 1900 that organization numbered over 200,000 members. The organized socialist movement of Italy is divided into several camps on questions of policy and methods, but that does not seem to interfere with its work or progress.

Belgium and Holland

The history of socialism in Belgium and in Holland is so much alike in many respects, that it may well be reviewed together. In both countries the movement had its inception during the last years of the International; in both countries the split of the International in 1872 divided the local movement into two hostile camps — the Marxists and Bakuninists, or Social Democrats and Anarchists — and in both the former finally prevailed.

Belgium possesses the stronger movement. The first distinctly socialist political organization was founded in 1885 under the name of Socialist Labor Party of Belgium. Notwithstanding the frequent dissensions and heated disputes among the Belgian socialists, the movement has made rapid progress. It has a large and influential press, and a strong organization. In 1908 the party polled about half a million votes and had 33 out of the 166 members of the Belgian Parliament.

The activity of the Belgian socialists is principally

marked by their repeated and embittered struggles for universal suffrage, and by their successful organization of coöperative enterprises.

The first political organization of socialism in Holland was the Social Democratic Union, founded in 1878; but it made but little progress until 1893, when the anarchistic elements under the leadership of the eloquent Domela Nieuvenhuis withdrew from it. The party is represented in parliament by seven deputies, and its methods and activity are practically those of the socialist movement of Belgium, though on a smaller scale.

The Scandinavian Countries

Another group of countries whose socialist history may be reviewed together, is that of Denmark, Sweden and Norway. Of these, the movement of Denmark is the oldest. It dates back to the days of the International, but the present socialist organization of the country, the Social Democratic Union, was founded in 1878. In 1889 the Danish socialists elected one deputy to the Folkething (parliament), out of a total of 114, and in 1907 the number of their representatives rose to 28. In that year the party had over 35,000 dues-paying members and no less than 25 daily papers; it was also very successful in local politics, having elected over 850 councilors in different towns and villages.

The movement in Sweden was initiated under Danish influence, and grouped itself around three socialist papers, the *Social Democrat*, published in Stockholm since 1885, the *Arbetet* (Worker), established in Malmö in 1887, and the *Ny Tid* (New Times), founded in Gotheburg in

389. As in the case of Belgium and Holland, the main activity of the Socialist Party was for years directed towards the conquest of universal suffrage, and its campaign in that behalf was as picturesque as it was energetic and effective. The party has 15 representatives in Parliament.

The socialist organization of Norway, the Norwegian Labor Party, was organized in 1887, but it constituted itself as a socialist political party only two years later. In the elections to the Storthing in 1906, the party polled about 45,000 votes and elected ten deputies; it also has several hundred representatives in the various municipal councils, a number of them being women.

The distinguishing feature of the socialist movement in the three Scandinavian countries is its complete fusion and unity with the trade-union organizations. In fact, the organized workingmen of each of these countries up to a very few years ago constituted but one party, operating simultaneously or alternately on the economic and political fields. The types and methods of the socialist movement in the three countries are similar to such a point that joint conferences or conventions of the socialists of Denmark, Sweden and Norway are quite frequent.

United States

In the early part of the last century, the United States was the chief theater of communistic experiments. The disciples of Owen, Fourier, Weitling and Cabet alike sought the realization of their utopian ideals on American soil, and during the decade 1840–1850, Fourierism in America developed great strength, both as an intellectual movement and as a practical experiment. Among its adherents were many persons of national reputation, such as Horace Greeley, Nathaniel Hawthorne, Charles A. Dana, Albert Brisbane, Margaret Fuller, George Ripley, John S. Dwight and William E. Channing. Among its experiments the famous Brook Farm and the North American Phalanx each lasted a number of years.

But modern political socialism made its first appearance in the United States years after the Fourierist and other utopian socialist movements had died out, and there seems to be no direct connection between that movement and its early utopian precursors. The present socialist movement in America may be dated from 1868, when the Social Party of New York and Vicinity was organized. That party immediately after its formation nominated an independent ticket, but its vote was very insignificant, and the organization collapsed with its failure at the polls. The Social Party of New York and Vicinity was succeeded by the General German Labor Association, which in 1869 became the first local organization or section of the International Workingmen's Association. Between 1869 and 1872, additional "sections" of the International were organized in almost all the principal industrial centers of the United States from New York to San Francisco. The socialist movement thus organized by the International at the time seemed so promising, that the latter transferred its general council to the United States, but after a few years, and especially during the industrial crisis inaugurated by the collapse of the Northern Pacific in 1873, the organization rapidly disintegrated.

The first socialist political party on a national scope

organized on American soil, was the Social Democratic Workingmen's Party, called into life on the 4th day of July, 1874. This party, together with several other then existing socialist organizations, merged into the Workingmen's Party of the United States in 1876. It was this party, which had in the meanwhile changed its name to Socialist Labor Party of North America, which maintained the undisputed hegemony in the socialist movement during twenty-three years, and was largely instrumental in laying the foundation of the present socialist movement in this country. In 1892 the socialists of the United States for the first time nominated a presidential ticket, and they have since that time invariably adhered to the policy of independent politics, steadfastly refusing to ally themselves with any other political parties.

But notwithstanding the untiring efforts and persistent propaganda of the Socialist Labor Party, the growth of the socialist movement in the United States was exceedingly slow and entirely out of keeping with that of the movement in other countries. As a matter of fact, the movement was largely borne by foreign workingmen, principally Germans, and until the end of the last century it did not succeed in acquiring a foothold in the broad masses of the native population; but during the last decade a number of circumstances have combined to insure a more favorable reception to the gospel of socialism in the United States. The rapid industrial development of the country, accompanied by the growth of gigantic trusts and powerful labor unions, the growing intensity of the overt struggles between capital and labor, and the collapse of the populist and other reform movements, all served to prepare the soil for the socialist seed. Alongside of the

2 A

Socialist Labor Party, largely built on the narrow lines of a mere propaganda club, a new party, the Socialist Party, sprang up, absorbing the greater part of the members of the Socialist Labor Party, and attracting large numbers of new converts, Americans of all parts of the country, recruited principally from among the working class. The Socialist Party has at this time (1909) about 3200 local organizations in the different states and territories of the Union, with a dues-paying membership of about 50,000. It polled a vote of 423,969 in the presidential election of 1908. Its press consists of more than fifty periodical publications in almost all languages spoken in America. The socialists have no representation in the United States Congress, but they have lately conquered a number of seats in several state legislatures and municipal councils.

The New International

When the International Workingmen's Association was formally dissolved at Philadelphia on July 15, 1876, the last members of the expiring organization issued a proclamation of which the following is a part: —

"'The International is dead!' the bourgeoisie of all countries will again exclaim, and with ridicule and joy it will point to the proceedings of this convention as documentary proof of the defeat of the labor movement of the world. Let us not be influenced by the cry of our enemies! We have abandoned the organization of the International for reasons arising from the present political situation of Europe, but as a compensation for it we see the principles of the organization recognized and defended by the progressive workingmen of the entire civilized

world. Let us give our fellow-workers in Europe a little
time to strengthen their national affairs, and they will
surely soon be in a position to remove the barriers between
themselves and the workingmen of other parts of the
world."

The statement was prophetic. Only thirteen years later
the first of the new series of international socialist and
labor congresses was held in Paris, and it was followed by
six more as follows: Brussels, 1891; Zurich, 1893; London, 1896; Paris, 1900; Amsterdam, 1904, and Stuttgart,
1907. And as the socialist movement grew and extended
steadily during that period, so did each succeeding congress
excel its predecessors in point of representation and general strength. The first Paris congress was attended by
391 delegates (221 of them Frenchmen), representing 17
countries of Europe and the United States; the Stuttgart
congress was attended by about 1000 delegates, representing 25 distinct countries of all parts of the world.

At the London congress of 1896, it was resolved to try
the experiment of establishing a permanent International
Socialist Bureau with a responsible secretary, but the
practical realization of the plan was left to the succeeding
congress of 1900, which definitely created the Bureau and
prescribed its functions.

The International Socialist Bureau is now composed of
two representatives of the organized socialist movement in
each affiliated country. Its headquarters are located in
Brussels, Belgium, and are in charge of a permanent secretary. The Bureau is the executive committee of the international congresses, and meets at such times as its
business requires. In the intervals between its sessions it
transacts its business by correspondence.

During the experimental period of its existence the International Socialist Bureau seemed to hold out but scant promise of accomplishing practical results for the socialist movement. But within the last few years, the International Socialist Bureau has rapidly adapted itself to the needs of the movement, and to-day it is a useful and important factor in the socialist movement of the world. It obtains and publishes from time to time valuable information on the progress and conditions of the socialist and labor movements of all countries; it advises on matters of socialist legislative activity, and it organizes the international congresses. The Bureau has established an archive of the socialist movement and has collected a library of socialist works, both of which are of the utmost importance to the students of socialism; and finally the Bureau has often served as a medium for mutual assistance between the socialist and labor movements of the different countries.

INDEX

CPSIA information can be obtained
at www.ICGtesting.com
Printed in the USA
LVOW06*1259231017
553442LV00007B/44/P